TRAVELS IN TAIWAN

EXPLORING ILHA FORMOSA

GARY HEATH

Caoshan Press

CONTENTS

Travels in Taiwan: Exploring Ilha Formosa

by Gary Heath

Text and map © 2009 Gary Heath

Third Edition, 2020, published by the Caoshan Press of Birchington, Kent, England
www.caoshanpress.com

First published 2009 by Ozaru Books, Second Edition 2011 by Ozaru Books.

Cover Design and Interior Formatting by *Hannah Linder Designs*
www.hannahlinderdesigns.com

Chinese personal and place names have been romanized using the Tongyong system, which was invented in Taiwan, although some names may be otherwise transliterated depending on local convention or the personal preference of a named individual.

ISBN: 978-1-8381577-0-8

FOREWORD

For many Westerners, Taiwan is either a source of cheap electronics or an ongoing political problem. It is seldom highlighted as a tourist destination, and even those that do visit rarely venture far beyond the well-trod paths of the major cities and resorts.

Yet true to its 16th century Portuguese name, the 'beautiful island' has some of the highest mountains in East Asia, many unique species of flora and fauna, and several distinct indigenous peoples (fourteen at the last count).

On six separate and arduous trips, Gary Heath deliberately headed for the areas neglected by other travel journalists, armed with several notebooks… and a copy of War and Peace for the days when typhoons confined him to his tent. The fascinating land he discovered is revealed here.

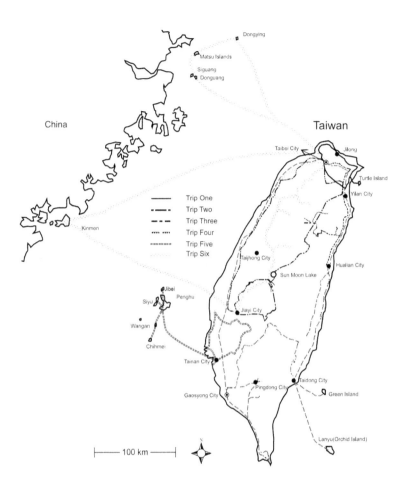

China

Taiwan

Dongying

Matsu Islands
Siguang
Donguang

Taibei City

Jilong

Turtle Island

Yilan City

Kinmen

Trip One
Trip Two
Trip Three
Trip Four
Trip Five
Trip Six

Taijhong City

Sun Moon Lake

Hualian City

Jibei

Siyu

Penghu

Wangan

Jiayi City

Chihmei

Tainan City

Taidong City

Pingdong City

Green Island

Gaosyong City

Lanyu(Orchid Island)

100 km

N

TAIBEI CITY

THE SOUND OF A POLICE CAR SIREN KEENING ON SELF Strengthening Street soon fades and gives way to a steady stream of scooter vrooms, the rasp of a mechanical circular saw, assorted voices, doors banging, dogs barking and tinny radio music echoing in the bowels of a motorbike repair shop. A bit groggy, I crawl out of bed, splash some water on my face, get dressed and head out of my third-floor bed-sitter apartment. The sidewalk on the street outside is barely passable because of piles of joss money lying about, crumpled ghost cash that will later be burnt in temple furnaces as an offering to the next world's corrupt officials. The fake money isn't made locally, but is repackaged downstairs by a small bevy of female workers in a shop factory. Finding a passage through the assorted paper parcels, I squeeze past the carpenter's workshop, taking care not to get too close to the circular saw, and dart along past the hole-in-the-wall Taoist Northern Dragon Temple, holding my breath to avoid inhaling incense smoke. In the clear, I then cross the street, take a second or two to let my internal barometer assess the atmospheric pressure, and head into a corner convenience store.

In addition to items such as milk, junk food, newspapers, cigarettes, beer and soft drinks, which one might expect to find in a convenience store anywhere, this store also hosts a photo-copier / fax machine, an ATM machine, a small selection of imported red wines, a judicious selection of imported Scotch whisky and — just in case you needed to pick one up — copies of bang up-to-date computer-operating-system software. A carton of milk and a bread roll is my usual. A man jumps in front of me at the cashier's desk apparently eager to get his daily supply of cigarettes. Unfazed by the queue jumper, I suddenly remember to check the magazine rack for maps. There are some maps there on the shelf, but not the type of detailed maps I am looking for. The road atlases on sale, which are reasonably detailed, would be too cumbersome to carry around. It then occurs to me to buy an umbrella and a cheap plastic raincoat to protect me from afternoon showers. It has not rained in a while, but it could start up any day now. After making my purchases, I slide out the door and turn right walking in the direction of the market.

"Six for 99 dollars only", shouts one man, pitching apples. He inflects the last word *only* for effect. The open, or "wet" market, operates every day; and there is a wide variety of fruit and vegetables available all year round. Today in the middle of February, piles of wax apples, baby tomatoes, sweet potatoes (along with sweet-potato leaves), cabbages (including Chinese cabbage), onions, spinach, kale, mustard greens and white radishes lie all about in bamboo baskets. At one neat mobile stall, a hawker is selling dried mushrooms, ginger, garlic and sumptuous red chillies. At another stall, pig's blood cake, braised pork knuckle, barbecued pork strips and steamed chicken lie steaming in their own aromatic juices. Tofu, processed fish products, fresh fish, oysters and birds' eggs together with many kinds of fresh leafy greens are also on offer to the mid-morning shoppers. I glance at the nice, firm custard apples, bulging papaya, imported apples, kiwis, melons, cher-ries, bananas and a number of local fruits, including limes, late season oranges and early season strawberries — it is all very tempting. Pots of ginseng soup, cups of freshly squeezed sugar-cane juice and bottles of fresh orange juice are being sold hand over fist. I wander around the stalls and finally buy some carrots, a couple of potatoes and a bag of cheap oranges before returning to my apartment. Alex is coming over for lunch; she's usually late so there's no rush to start cooking but I prepare the vegetables in advance when I get back.

––––––––––

WHAT IS it exactly that Westerners think of when the place name *Taiwan* crops up? People of my generation may think of plastic-handle screwdrivers, cheap household appliances, or fake consumer goods. My grandfather spoke of Chiang Kai-Shek and the Chinese nationalists, Formosa, Formosan tea, sugar and tinned pineapples. North Americans generally have a closer relationship to Taiwan than West Europeans; and some informed Americans and overseas Chinese in the States will have a bit more insight, appreciating, for instance, something of Taiwan's complex modern history, hybridized culture, ongoing democratization and developing post-industrial economy. Japanese people certainly have some knowledge of Taiwan, Japan having been the most recent colonial power to have ruled this singular territory. But how many people worldwide know, for example, that Taiwan has some of the most fabulous green mountain ranges in the world, is host to many wonderful endemic species of animals and plants, and is home to a strong and varied group of indigenous cultures? Taiwan, only about half the size of Ireland in area — an island that would fit into Madagascar 16 times! — is in fact a land of almost endless travel possibilities.

Working as an English teacher and sometimes editor, I lived and travelled in Taiwan for well over a decade and have never got bored of the place. What I found in Taiwan was a beautifully complex reality. At first I explored the cities I lived in — principally the parks, temples and rivers of Tainan City, Taibei City and Taibei County. I went through a phase of making bicycle trips in the countryside, mostly in and around Taibei County.

Later I made longer trips on a motorbike and also joined weekend hiking expeditions into the mountainous interior of the island. Sometimes I would travel with friends, but more often would venture out alone. I wrote occasional travel pieces about these trips for newspapers and magazines, which were well received but hardly did justice to the subject. Interestingly, Taiwan does not really exist in English travel literature outside of a couple of guide books and self-published titles. Over the years I thus gradually conceived of making a journey or series of trips in Taiwan that had not been done before, at least not in the aggregate, with the intention of turning this experience into some kind of literary production. Having finally achieved my master's degree the chance to travel for an extended period became a possibility.

For this "Taiwan grand tour", as I came to call it, my plotting and planning led me to adopt, and then drop, several travel concepts — it was hard to think of one single way of approaching the subject or to plot one satisfactory see-it-all single route through the island. At first, I considered making a journey through Taiwan's mountains travelling from north to south along the Central Mountain Range, but upon later reflection I realized this was overambitious: it was impractical and a bit too Crusoe-like. Personal circumstances then led me to entertain the idea of making a somewhat limited non-stop, ten-week tour of Taiwan's principal scenic attractions during the cool autumn months. This quickie tour idea had many merits, not the least being the likelihood of relatively dry weather and overall reduced costs. However, my ultimate goal of writing a *full* travel account of Taiwan presupposed travelling for longer than ten weeks: I wanted to go into the mountains, down to the south, and out to all the outlying islands. Covering this amount of ground properly would take some time, and an allocation of only ten weeks would have meant rushing it, if not missing out many places entirely. The nature of Taiwan's geography, I came to realize, suggested a series of separate trips, rather than one long journey — a spiral approach rather than a linear approach

— and I would need at least six months to do these multiple journeys: the basic idea of making six trips in six months finally emerged. *That* was the plan, a simple one, and without the need to plot out detailed routes in advance: improvisation would be the name of the game.

In terms of kit, a 20 year-old indestructible, British-made rucksack held my clothes, a two-person tent, a bedroll, a sleeping bag, a camping stove and some lightweight cooking utensils. The tent and cooking gear were, of course, essential for mountain trips, but also an economy measure. Travelling in the mountains, I had to be prepared for both rain and cold: I packed warm clothing, a motorcycle cape, waterproof trousers, gaiters and rubber boots, which added considerable bulk to the kit. A smaller backpack contained a large notebook, a copy of Tolstoy's *War and Peace* — which I had never read before — camera accessories and other assorted bits and pieces. When I came to try on these two backpacks, the entire ensemble made me look like some kind of specialized infantry soldier, my walking pole a rifle. But there was no way of reducing the bulk and weight of my gear without losing my independence. The bags felt surprisingly comfortable despite their bulk; at least they did during my first test walk in the hills surrounding Taibei.

———

THE POTATOES and carrots are boiling away in a pan that sits atop a small but highly efficient electric inverter on the floor in front of my bed. I had meant to juice the oranges, but the thought of the work involved makes me put this task off for the time being. Suddenly I hear a fumbling sound in the keyhole. This is Alex trying to open the door: she still gets confused about which way to turn the key, which is understandable given that it's a triple lock. Alex barges into the room. "Mind the wire, darling", I remind her: the main lead of the inverter lies across the entrance of the room like a tripwire.

Whilst I do the cooking, Alex changes and then tries to find a space to sit on the bed. But the bed is occupied by my two back-packs and assorted unpacked items lying about. Alex surveys the scene but makes no comment, and then, like a cat, she somehow manages to find a space to snuggle into. I juice the oranges and carve the Spam. Over lunch, Alex becomes cheerful and talkative. "When are you leaving?" she asks me, putting a slice of the pink processed meat between her red-lipsticked lips. "Tomorrow, I reckon: it's time to get moving", I glance at the bed and notice there are still some odds and ends to pack — packing was a more stressful experience than I had bargained for; one has to constantly rearrange things to fit everything in. Alex chips in, "Wow, you have such a lot of things. Better you don't take so many things; just one bag is enough". I sigh. Alex doesn't under-stand that I need everything in both packs, and that I have already got it down to the minimum, as I try to explain for the umpteenth time. "But why don't you stay in a hotel?" she then argues. Because hotels and guesthouses in Taiwan are now expensive, and I will be travelling for many weeks and there may not be any hotels or guesthouses in the mountains: Alex is supportive of my travel project, but she cannot comprehend what it means to travel independently for an extended period. After lunch, she tries lifting my main backpack, but can't get it off the ground. This prompts me to demonstrate putting on the backpacks, whereupon she comments that I look like a camel. I carefully lower the heavier backpack down upon the bed using my leg muscles to take the weight. During the rest of the after-noon, Alex and I chat about my first trip. I explain to her that for this first journey I will make a modest circuit around the north coast of Taiwan, and that this trip would be relatively short in terms of distance, and I would never be that far away from Taibei in the event of a mission-critical equipment failure.

A steady increase in noise from the street below, which had gone quiet during the afternoon, marks the beginning of the end of another working day in Taibei City. Alex has to get up early the next day, and so she dresses for outdoors and leaves to return home. She knows that I am a night owl, and she generally prefers to spend the night in her own abode. I accompany her to a nearby bus stop and then wave goodbye as she gets on the number 61 that will take her up to one of Taibei's burgeoning hillside suburbs.

The next day — "D-Day" — I rise early, eat an apple, stretch my lumbar spine and leave the apartment, taking care to triple-lock the door. I swiftly make my way to Wunlin Road, the main road nearest my apartment to the west. I do not exactly feel like a person who is about to begin a "journey of a thousand *li*", however such a person might feel. Rather, I feel a little like a burglar on the run with a bag of loot. I almost expect to hear the police siren again. Breakfast and a cup of tea at the nearby franchise burger outlet give me the opportunity to collect myself for this first trip and to make the opening entry in my travel journal. Ominously, the air pressure outside has dropped and it starts to drizzle as I munch away on a sausage burger. Perhaps I had timed the start of this grand tour poorly? A short while after leaving the restaurant, I find myself standing on the opposite side of the road moving into an area where the city ends and rural allotments begin. The temperature has dropped dramatically to about five degrees Celsius. I stop to dig a sweater out of my backpack, put it on, and then put a plastic disposable raincoat on top for good measure before heading off down the road past blooming magenta azaleas and red hibiscus. I then loop through some rice fields that take me down to the Jilong River, a tributary of the Danshuei River. And that is where the Taiwan grand tour would begin.

2

TRIP ONE: THE NORTH AND NORTHEAST COAST

THERE WERE SOME STEPS LEADING DOWN FROM THE HUGE NEW LEVEE that I stood on, symbolically the starting point of Trip One. Overhead stretched a major new expressway of steel and asphalt suspended from massive supporting pillars. The river levee and expressway in the air impressed me — modern engineering worthy of the ancients. The rice fields and horticulture on the unpredictable flood plain beneath the expressway marked a kind of boundary between the city and the countryside proper, and also between industrialism and traditional sedentary cultivation. But a long history was also evident. What is now called Taibei used to be covered by a lake that was enclosed by volcanic mountains. These volcanoes erupted five million years ago, uplifting sedimentary formations in the south. Over millennia, a northflowing river gradually — quickly, in geological terms — cut a path to the ocean; and most of the captured water in the Taibei basin drained away. Once forested, this basin now contains a bustling city of several million people. The Danshuei River provides a release from the tension of city life and plunges a giant ventilation shaft into the heart of a densely built-up mini-metropolis. It was via this river that I planned to reach the north coast.

Standing on the river levee I observed a small white launch

plough up the silky waterway of the main Danshuei River, but there was no obvious access path in sight. I tumbled down the already weedy levee steps, balancing my backpacks and watching my step. I still felt like an impostor of some kind, an interloper in a subtropical Nile Valley. And it required an effort to make the mental adjustments necessary to accept that this was it: the grand tour was underway, and there was no turning back now. I followed a smooth concrete bicycle track that led towards the confluence of the Jilong and Danshuei Rivers. No one was about. The light rain had stopped, but dark clouds were gathering in the sky, adding a touch of gloom to my rapidly altering mood. Within 30 minutes I had walked from a crowded, overdeveloped city into a kind of no-person's land. A lone cyclist on a new and shiny Taiwanese-made bike shimmered past like a ghost. I walked along the track tentatively, half expecting to be run over by some kind of rogue vehicle; the security of my modest apartment started to feel far away. Along the track under the expressway some voices finally interrupted my anxious reverie.

A small group of construction workers stood milling around an open fire in front of a cargo container that served as a makeshift office. They were obviously part of the team that had recently built the bicycle track and strengthened the river levee. Empty polystyrene boxes and beer cans strewn about told me that lunch had just ended. As I approached them, one of the men uttered a word that announced me again and again on my travels: "*Meiguoren*" — Mandarin Chinese for "American". I seldom bothered to correct people if they called me American — I was just too lazy to do so; and in a sense we are all Americans anyway. The same affable man asked me where I was going, apparently confident that I would comprehend his spoken Chinese, which I did. "To Danshuei", I said, asking for directions down to the riverside. "Oh, Danshuei — that is a long way. You should go back over there and catch a bus", the worker suggested, pointing his finger back the way I had just come. He did not understand that I was an interloper resolved to poke my

9

nose where it did not belong. Thanking the man for his proffered information, I walked away from the worker's encampment and headed in the direction of the riverside.

The Jilong River was about 80 metres across where I joined it; not exactly huge, but the speed of its eddying water indicated a powerful current. Spears of Kandelia candel, a mangrove species found widely on the west coast of Taiwan, grew thickly on the muddy banks of the river. On the right of the levee there was more of the semi-countryside horticulture typical of the Beitou area. The walk turned out to be pleasant enough, even if carrying 20-odd kilograms of kit was starting to strain a few muscles: it would take a while to get used to the weight. I followed the path through the mangrove and past a splendid metal sign that read *The right bank of the Jilong River* in English and Chinese, adding *23 KM*. The sign oddly seemed to assume that everyone was following a predetermined route from a common starting point. On the far side of the river I noticed a group of neglected concrete buildings, which apparently consti- tuted National China Marine University. Standing in isolation on a narrow spit of land between the Jilong and Danshuei Rivers, the university looked vaguely like a weapons-research centre of some kind. "Keep your English teaching job", I muttered on sight of the campus.

After walking for a total of two and a half hours along the riverside, a large temple came into view to the right of the path under some hills; this was the Guandu Temple. It stood there like all Chinese temples do: facing south like an emperor sitting on his throne with mountains behind, and the floors of the structure were stacked up in that inimitable pile-like way. A jogger wearing a bright yellow vest and white cotton gloves powered past as I hiked slowly in the direction of the temple's flower-pot red buildings. The temple adjoined the main road into Taibei City. I crossed a bridge and walked along this road a short distance. At a roadside food stall I bought an oyster omelette and a cold beer for refreshment. It had turned chilly and I put my jacket on to stay warm before tucking into the chilli-sauce-smothered omelette, a snack that has as many memories and associations for me as fish and chips; but this one was disappointing, confirming the fact that Taibei cuisine was a poor imitation of southern Taiwanese fare.

This was not my first time in Guandu, a town built next to the confluence of the Danshuei and Jilong rivers, but I had never walked the stretch from Guandu to Chuwei; and the path along this section of the Danshuei River proper afforded a full-blown view of the Danshuei waterway — here more than 500 metres across — and the impressive Guandu span bridge that crossed it. I moved out along an elevated wooden walkway towards the bridge. Just above the walkway, trains and cars screamed past, hurrying to get to and from Taibei City. A few small boats leisurely crossed the river. I continued on past the solid arching bridge into Chuwei, a clump of gothic, concrete high-rises that had already taken firm root next to the river halfway between Taibei and Danshuei. Near the local mass-transit railway station at Chuwei, a tidy new park was being constructed along the riverside, another bit of nature reclaimed for the human race. Fearing a turn in the weather, I terminated my riverside walk at this park and bought a ticket to Danshuei at Chuwei's neat redbrick and chrome station.

A surprisingly large crowd of people tumbled out of the mass-transit train's shiny carriages at Danshuei twenty minutes later; the town had effectively become a dormitory extension of Taibei City. I left the busy station and directly crossed the road facing the Danshuei terminus, not an easy task on a road that had been completely surrendered to private-car and bus use. Having found a place to get across, I dived into the nearest American fast-food outlet, just like the American I was always mistaken for. In the restaurant I ate another meal under fluorescent lights in the gathering gloom before catching a bus out to the outskirts of town. It was getting dark and the black clouds that had been forming all day over the river started to disgorge their load. I put on my raincoat and changed into gumboots before getting off the bus at the "Fisherman's Wharf", a marina and tourist park located on the Danshuei estuary, alone and slightly bemused by the oddness of the situation.

After vainly hunting around in the rain for a cheap hotel, I finally opted to pitch my tent on a grassy verge next to a car park. It did not take me long to get the tent up, despite a howling wind that had joined the bad-weather party. Once my shelter was up, I felt surprisingly happy and cosy despite the slightly unpromising start to my travels. After a little rest under the waterproof, nylon sheeting I went off to do some nocturnal sightseeing. In almost total blackness I walked around the deserted 15-hectare riverside park, staring at empty white yachts moored in the inky marina and crossing the 162-metre-long Lover's Bridge across the harbour. The harbour and the inclement weather reminded me of the English Channel in mid-winter, and I quite enjoyed the night prowl, even if I did almost get blown into the harbour from the suspension bridge. It was not cold at all. But nothing was actually going on in the harbour; and with the wind not relenting, it made sense to return to the bosky verge where I had set up camp.

The next morning I awoke to find the storm had not abated; in fact it was raining with almost the same intensity as the night before. After stewing in the tent for a while, I breakfasted and then kicked back to read *War and Peace*. I was at the point in the narrative where Pierre and Dolokhov have their pointless duel. Tolstoy portrays this duel with great verisimilitude and telling comic-tragic effect; it somehow unfolds in slow motion, and we are as surprised as Pierre is at the outcome. Including the novel in my kit was a wise move, I thought, even if it added yet more weight to an already heavy load. The pleasant literary diversion notwithstanding, I started to resent the holdup handed to me by the atrocious weather; by midday I simply had to go somewhere. In an inspirational moment I decided to abort the trip temporarily and return to Taibei to spend the weekend with Alex, and thus broke muddy camp happily.

DURING TAIWAN'S Japanese colonial period (1895–1945), Danshuei was known as the "Venice of the East". This is one of those comparisons that people dream up using the first famous name that comes into their head as a reference point. To my mind, Danshuei more closely resembled a Southend-on-Sea or a Coney Island than the drowned world of the Italian Renaissance. I liked Danshuei's workingclass holiday feel, its historical associations and, most of all, the fresh air and open views of its estuarine landscape. The artists and students knocking about Danshuei also added a dash of glamour to a postmodern tourist and university town that has almost imperceptibly been absorbed into Taibei's gravitational pull. Previously, it had been the town's ongoing helter-skelter development that dissuaded me from spending more time exploring its environs; I was determined to see a bit more of the place this time around.

But the weather was not cooperating. In Taibei the rain came down in light, but incessant, drenching sheets typical of the northeast monsoon, which usually visits Taiwan in February. This monsoon is an off-and-on affair, but sometimes it can rain for weeks on end, sending one completely troppo. Back in my bed-sit I tried to, well, sit it out. A story in one of the local English-language daily newspapers during this rainy spell caught my attention. The article concerned the settlement of Guinsaugon, located in southern Leyte Island, the Philippines. The story coolly reported that the total population of 1,800 people in a small farming village had perished in a sudden and catastrophic mudslide. Persistent rain and logging had apparently caused the calamity, a repeat of similar mudslides in 2003 and 2004. The disaster had an awful poignancy because of the almost 100% fatality rate — it was a truly horrifying event, but one forgotten the next day as the restless media immediately moved on to other news.

On the heels of the Guinsaugon tragedy and happy to be alive, Alex and I decided to try to walk from Chuwei to Danshuei again. But no sooner had we got out the door than it started to rain. Alex complained bitterly about her clothes getting wet, but I unsympathetically told her to stop whining; she should have prepared properly for the wet weather. Dark clouds once again hung over Guanyin Mountain on the far side of the river near Chuwei as we got off the train and made our way to the riverside. The misty scene was reminiscent of a Chinese water-andmountain ink painting. Braving the rain on the elevated walkway near the river, a local man and his three children fished under a multicoloured golfing umbrella, a family stoically determined to have fun together, come what may. "Let's go home; I'm soaking!" Alex demanded, interrupting the assembly of a scene I was sketching in my head. We stopped briefly to observe the new Mackay Hospital being built at Chuwei. Danshuei will forever be associated, in the minds of Taiwanese, with a Canadian Presbyterian missionary, the Reverend George Leslie Mackay — known simply as Dr Mackay. By the end of the 19th century, Danshuei had become the biggest international commercial harbour in Taiwan and was the place where most resident foreign nationals lived at the time. After arriving in Danshuei on 9 March 1872, the energetic Mackay learned to speak Taiwanese and went on to establish numerous congregations and chapels during the next 30 years. He also founded a modern hospital and a girl's school, which set a prece-dent for female education in Taiwan. Mackay would have been stunned by the new hospital, a worthy memorial to his good works — almost an airport terminal in size and conception, as it was gradually taking shape in the rain. Walking via a path through the mangrove, Alex and I then pushed on but only got as far as the Hongshulin Station before calling it a day. From the train window on the way back to Taibei I tried to spot the umbrella family, but the heavy rain had reduced visibility to less than the distance between the railway line and the river.

Temporarily putting my tour of the north coast on hold — there had in fact always been the possibility of turning back — I subsequently visited Danshuei during a break in the weather. Renting a bicycle after arriving by train, I made Mackay's Danshuei Junior High School for Girls the first stop on a brief tour of the town. The girls' school, located just off a small road on a hill overlooking the Danshuei River, looked neat and tidy if slightly paranoid with its outer walls, gatehouse and closed-circuit television cameras. I parked the bicycle just inside the gate, signed the visitors' book at the gatehouse and entered the school. In the rain, which had now become an intermittent drizzle, I stomped about the campus hoping to find someone to talk to, but all the kids were dutifully in class. Between the junior high and a nearby co-ed high school sat a rugby pitch, a throwback to the school's neocolonialist origins. I wandered through the Dr George William Mackay Memorial Garden. The tightly landscaped garden gushed with small camphor trees, Formosan sweetgum, a Taiwan cycas, sweet olive bushes, cane palms, bamboo and some other rare specimens of flora. The oleanders were a bit of an odd choice, I thought, as these flowers are highly poisonous.

I discovered the so-called "foreigners' cemetery", a small cemetery where about 80 foreign nationals were laid to rest, behind a block of school classrooms. The known history of the graveyard dates back to 1867. In 1891, the nearby British Consulate cleaned the place up, a job now done annually by the Canadian Society of Taiwan. The graveyard was in good condition considering there was so much potential for vandalism — not that Taiwanese teenagers go in for that sort of thing in a big way. One typical tombstone inscription read "Sacred to The Memory of C.D. Brown, Apprentice U.S. Navy, Age 22 Years, Who Was Drowned At Tamsui on March 20, 1903". Most of the deceased in the cemetery lived longer than C.D. Brown, but a surprising number died relatively young and probably never intended to be buried overseas. Dr George Mackay did choose to be buried here; his wife, children and several students followed suit in later years. By the time I had finished my stroll around the tombstones, it was break time and blue-uniformed high-school kids weaved in and out of the nearby classrooms in the vivacious manner of youth. No one seemed to think my interest in the cemetery anything unusual; they were clearly used to visitors. Suddenly a bell rang and the youngsters all obediently filed off into the classrooms. I heard English-speaking voices, and then saw a posse of Caucasian females heading for the classrooms. They were English-language teachers most likely, perhaps missionaries; but they had no time to stop and talk.

Athenia University, a short bicycle ride down from the girls' high school, is a private Christian school that started life as "Oxford College" — another of George Mackay's educational projects, the first buildings of which were completed in 1882. The school was dedicated to higher learning, and the original charming red-brick quadrangle house still stands on the grounds of the campus today. Around it, a plethora of modern, utilitarian concrete high-rise buildings have been erected. I wanted to visit the school because over the years I had met a lot of people who had studied there, and I was curious to see what Jhenli — "Truth" — University was like. The school, tucked onto the lower slopes of Datun Mountain, turned out to be an unremarkable place, a fact no amount of flower beds could successfully camouflage. The crown-of-thorns, found in several soil troughs, sort of summed the place up: hardy and worthy, but not exactly a stunner. A university professor once told me that the best way to feel the pulse of a country was to go to a local university and talk to the students there. But what if they did not want to talk to you — what does that tell you about the country? Full of self-absorbed kids, Athenia University seemed more like a high school that refused to grow up. The students buzzed about intent on attending apparently pressing appointments — the intense individuation of modern Western-style university education together with the clannish nature of Taiwanese culture had left everyone striving to perfect themselves but unable to socialize with strangers, or at least just slow down a bit. *Shy* is the misnomer usually used to label this disposition. Giving up on the idea of talking to someone, I took some photos of the river from the top floor of one of the school buildings before quietly disappearing.

In the afternoon I went to Danshuei's golf course and hiked

around it, not intending to spoil the walk by madly knocking balls everywhere. The green expanse of the fairways, nicely landscaped with ferns and other evergreen trees, made for a pleasant diversion after all the concrete of the morning; the two schools I had visited left me needing a breath of fresh air. Some golfers were out and about on the fairways, but no one paid any attention to me, a wandering lark. Yet I had company. By one unattended green a couple of magpies were striding about, also making the most of a lull in the rain. My invasion of the golf course presently over, I watched some players putting at the final hole as I quaffed a beer. The golfers looked charming, retro-dressed in plus fours; and one or two of them could actually play very well. Cycling back into town later I turned and glanced over my shoulder and saw the massive hulk of a container ship gliding out to sea, its silhouette telescoped against the red traffic light of an as-yetundeveloped new street. Danshuei was expanding in all directions.

On another day I visited Dankang, or "Tamkang", University — Alex's alma mater — also located on the slopes of Datun Mountain. First impressions were positive: the campus was neat, clean and tidy; at the entrance, a clear, colour-coded map of the large but compact site resembled a modernist art work. I entered the college, young again. Some students were playing basketball and other sports on an allweather sports ground just inside the gate. Further inside the campus old and new buildings seemed to blend quite well; and the geomancy of the place, with hills behind and the Danshuei estuary below, was excellent. I wandered around a landscaped garden near some old preserved, but still-in-use, classrooms. The garden had been planted with a range of tropical and subtropical plants that one finds in many Taiwanese parks. The trees included Cuban royal palms, Australian beefwoods and Japanese black pines. Surrounding these trees, bamboos, purple cordyline and palm lilies filled stuffed borders. A lot can actually be gleaned about Taiwan by looking at its agriculture and flora: one can clearly discern the ability of Taiwan to take something foreign and incorporate it

17

into the local culture so that it becomes apparently naturally Taiwanese. In other words, Taiwanese culture represents a complex hybrid of influences. But this garden was also a tad overcrowded and eager to please, which perhaps reflects other aspects of the Taiwan experience.

So far, I had not talked to any students. There were plenty of them about at smart Dankang, a decent private university, but alas our eyes and hearts never seemed to meet. I decided to have a look around the library; maybe it would have something to say to me? The large multistorey building was busy enough. I made a beeline for the English-language collection. I discovered the library had one abridged volume of Karl Marx's *Capital* in it, and judged that this book was probably the only item worth reading on the whole of one floor devoted to the social sciences. Returning to the lobby of the library, I noticed an attractive young lady who was wearing pink plimsolls, tight-fitting jeans and a brown denim jacket, lingering in an open space letting people admire her. Could this be the interlocutor I needed to unlock the secrets of Taiwan? I looked at her; she looked back straight through me. Obviously there was no hope of me having a deep and meaningful discussion with this particular student. Shrugging off the lack of social interaction, I continued on with my discreet investigation of the library. The reference section on the first floor, I noted, contained no fewer than 20 metres of journals dedicated to literary criticism, a subject surely destined for the dustbin of academia.

I was about to leave the library building when I came across some English-language texts displayed in the foyer. The first text formed part of a small exhibit dedicated to the history of the University. Part of it read as follows:

Tamkang University is situated on top of the "Five-tiger Hill" in the town of Tamsui, near Taipei, overlooking the Tamsui River, Kuan-yin shan (Goddess of Mercy Mountain) and the Taiwan Straits. As a comprehensive university based on Chinese culture and orientated towards Western technology,

Tamkang University is a higher institution without walls devoted to fostering advanced cultural and technological professionals in addition to laying emphasis on research and public service".

Like all texts, this particular text contains within it the echo of many discourses. The attempt to separate culture and technology, for example, harks back to the 19th-century Self-Strengthening Movement in China, after which the street I lived on was named. The implicit meaning of *self-strengthening* was that Chinese people could remain Chinese culturally whilst adopting Western technology and capitalist economic practices to strengthen the country militarily and economically. By and large this strategy failed in 19th-century China, but was more or less realized in twentieth-century Taiwan. The observation is a bit of an oversimplification, but one could say that Taiwan is highly modernized without being deeply westernized.

Another text belonged to a splashy multimedia exhibit on global warming that took up a fair bit of space next to the revolving glass doors of the library's entrance. The text was part of a transcript highlighting a discussion between one Professor Hall and a questioner, "Q".

PH: The concentration of these natural gases in the ice core indicates that runaway warming pushed Earth into an ice age which lasted two centuries.

Q: I'm confused. I thought you were talking about global warming, not an ice age.

PH: Yes, it is a paradox, but global warming can trigger a cooling trend. Let me explain. The Northern Hemisphere owes its climate to the North Atlantic Current. Heat from the sun arrives at the equator and is carried north by the ocean. But global warming is melting the polar ice caps and disrupting this

flow. Eventually it will shut down... there goes our warm
climate.

Q: Excuse me. When do you think this could happen, professor?
When?

PH: I don't know. Maybe in 100 years, maybe in 1000. But
what I do know is that if we do not act soon, our children and
grandchildren will pay the price.

The discourse of apocalyptic disaster is now penetrating
many academic disciplines through the subject of climate change
and its related themes. I wondered how many students visiting
the library read this text and understood its implications. It
occurred to me that Dankang was just a bit too good to be true;
the well-groomed appearance of the university was actually part
of the way the school was being sold to the consumer-students,
many of whom aspire to the very middle-class consumption
patterns that have contributed to the runaway global-warming
crisis we now face. Maybe I should have talked to some of the
students to get their take on global warming, but no one else was
taking any interest in the exhibit, which said it all really.

Before leaving Dankang I dropped by the on-campus
maritime museum. The museum, which was very quiet when I
popped in, consisted of three floors displaying scale models of
famous ships, plus some other bits and pieces of maritime
memorabilia. The museum had the great virtue of being modest
and informative. The painstakingly constructed models were
actually a fascinating anachronism. For an hour or so I became
the captain of ships such as *The Victory, The Endeavour,* the *Queen*
Mary, the *Missouri* and the *Bismarck,* etc. There were also scale
models of impossibly large container ships belonging to
Taiwan's largest shipping line, which happens to be one of the
world's leading sea-cargo carriers, but these blocky ships had
zero romance about them — and even a model of a latter-day
aircraft carrier seemed like some kind of aberration of science.

No sightseeing tour of Dankang would have been complete without a visit to the former British Consulate, known as the "Red-Haired Fort" to locals — a reference to the Dutch. The old consulate, a red-brick Victorian colonial house, stood next to a Dutch fort that overlooked the Danshuei River. Getting to the consulate by taxi only took five minutes, and soon I was walking around the gardens and admiring the open views of the river and of the ocean beyond. I had been out here before in the mid-nineties and the consulate was in essence the same, but with an added layer of commercialization in the form of a garden restaurant and a new gift shop. The aspect of the site was superb and it was strange to wander around the rooms of the British consul of 100 years ago. He — it would definitely have been a he — had a wonderful view of the river, his own supply of clean drinking water, generous living quarters, and servants. Back in the 19th century a few tourists would no doubt have come up here to take a look at the dumpy Dutch fort. "No photos please", suddenly barked an attendant as I took some photographs inside this fort. No photos? Why not? As though taking a few photos out of the windows could do any harm… Later I checked out the VR Garden Café next to the consulate, which was busy serving afternoon teas. As I rested at one of the café's tables sipping a soda and nibbling on a tasteless sandwich, I observed a couple of Canadians sitting nearby, one of whom was taking pictures with a sophisticated, but compact, digital camera. What impressed me was the way he professionally used a small tripod to steady the camera, and a cable release to avoid camera shake, as he took a photo of his friend. "No photos, please", I almost uttered, authoritarianism being contagious, but then remembered myself and shot a video of the café.

Late in the afternoon I wandered on foot down to the Fisherman's Wharf to witness the evening life on the embankment. A number of day trippers were out taking a promenade, and these were later joined by numerous commuters returning to Danshuei from their sweatshop offices in town. Along the harbour wall, throngs of visitors, including a Taiwanese tour group from southern Taiwan and some Japanese tourists, gathered for the sundowner. The Canadians turned up, the photographer snapping away freestyle with great panache. The early evening sunset did not disappoint — a bright orange globe that faded mysteriously from sight like a magician's vanishing trick, while a small silhouette of a boat in the foreground paddled across the last light. After the "ooh, aah" sunset I walked back to the mass-transit railway station, passing the grassy verge where I had camped on my first night in Danshuei, and took a train back to base.

AFTER BRIEFLY REGROUPING IN TAIBEI, I got back on the road and for the last time took the train up to Danshuei. The bus heading north out of town was surprisingly crowded on a midweek day. The vehicle's suspension was completely shot and the continuous shocks to my spine left me wincing as we left the railway station and travelled through the densely built-up town. There were many old people on the bus, probably returning to their rural homes after visiting children in Danshuei and Taibei over the weekend, but with Confucian restraint and Buddhist repose they just blanked out the shock problem. The outskirts of Danshuei, with its new high-rise suburban residential districts plonked in the middle of open fields, slipped by — passengers disembarking from the bus in ones and twos along the way. I grinned and held on for dear life.

From the rather poor map of Taibei County that I had in my possession I could at least make out the main rivers running down from the volcanic peaks of Yangming National Park into the ocean. The first of these blue lines was marked the Datun River, which cuts across Route 2 near the boundary of Danshuei Town and Sanjhih District. This was also more or less the starting point of the North Coast Scenic Area. The scenic area arches around the coast for about 50 kilometres, inclusive of a very beautiful rocky coastline, a number of small capes and a swathe of countryside stretching inland five kilometres or so. I wondered how much of this scenic coastline I would be able to walk. At the Datun Bridge bus stop I got off the now-almost-empty bus and meandered into Datun Village on a cooling afternoon. In stark contrast to Taibei City and Danshuei, there were not many people about in the settlement. In front of a closed shop front opposite the bus stop, a somewhat distressed-looking dog sat chained, howling terribly. When I approached the animal, intending to soothe and pet it, she pissed on the ground out of fright. This was the Taiwan countryside. Leaving the dog to its fate I moved away from the road, crossed the tiny Datun Bridge, and hiked down a lane that I presumed led to the coast. Following the lane at Datun, I walked straight through a line of dunes down into a tiny harbour. To my amazement, about 15 teenagers on their winter school break were sea-angling off the small harbour wall, not an alcoholic drink in sight. In the harbour sat a dozen idle skiffs waiting for the professionals to arrive. The well-adjusted kids started to mount their scooters as I entered the harbour area. I then noticed a small café by the harbour side. There were people in it, so I decided to introduce myself.

The café was actually being renovated, and the owner was obviously preoccupied. I shouted hello and ended up chatting with a pleasant woman. She immediately tried to establish my nationality and marital status in the way that many Taiwanese women do when they meet a "foreigner". I gave evasive answers to her questions, which mildly frustrated her. "Are you someone's son-in-law?" she asked, trying a more indirect way of getting the information she wanted. In the end I told her I was single, whereupon she started talking about her three unmarried daughters, who were away in Danshuei studying. I was more interested in the old stone weir next to the harbour. The chatty woman told me that this was used for fishing when she was a child, but it was no longer in use. When I asked about accommodations, thinking she might offer me the floor of the café for the night, this daughter of a once-poor fishing family directed me to a hotel located back the way I had just come. Our minds thus not quite having met, I filled my water bottle, said goodbye and headed onto the sandy beach north of the harbour. The café owner waved me off frowning slightly but not warning me away from the beach.

Hopping on stones, I crossed a rivulet and carried on walking along a wild and isolated coastline. The brown-grey sand of the wet beach was strewn with driftwood and rounded stones of various sizes darkening in colour nearer the water line. The waters of the Taiwan Strait lapped the stony beach fairly gently despite a wintry turn in the weather; it had been spitting with rain since I had got off the bus, and now it rained harder necessitating the donning of waterproofs and gumboots. For the first time since getting properly underway I felt perfectly happy because I had escaped the global-consumer society, at least temporarily. Under palls of drizzle the daylight started to bleed away and I wondered where I might camp the night. Atop a sand dune I surveyed the unused agricultural fields landward, but none of them looked promising from a camper's point of view. After walking another two kilometres, I came across a small, unoccupied military observation post on the beach coded AF300071. The post's camouflage netting blew in the wind; on the inside walls, posters illustrated People's Republic of China's navy ships, military uniforms, military insignia, tanks and aircraft. A path led away from this observation post, over the sand dunes, and into some bushes and trees. I followed the path, relieved to get out of the full force of the wind and rain, and soon found a suitable place to camp within a thicket of trees. I was a little worried about the possibility of spooking a patrol of soldiers during the night, but in the end no one came by. Another north-easterly gale blew in off the ocean bringing plenty of pelting rain with it, a kind of storm lite. The wind gusted fiercely, but the trees, enmeshed in screw pine, acted as a natural harbour for my tent. A little cramped but snug inside the shelter I thought of all the nights ahead that I would be on the road, and realized how useful this splendid tent was going to be.

In the morning I rejoined the beach and carried on walking along it some distance eventually stumbling across a substantial walled military base. The presence of closed-circuit television cameras and sentries indicated this large outpost was both occupied and operational. I walked by the camp's outer perimeter, but it was pretty quiet and inactive inside and there was nothing to see. Radar of some kind twirled out of sight within a large bubble; the base may have been an ultramodern missile battery for all I knew. I hurried on not wanting to attract attention. A little ahead stood a settlement of some kind. On the way to this seaside village I bumped into a man who was picking herbs from the side of the path. I asked him where I was and he replied "Cianshueiwan". I chatted with the man for a minute or so, our life trajectories intersecting for one fleeting moment, before heading over to the village by the sea.

At Cianshueiwan, or Shallow Water Bay, the gravitational pull of the Taibei-Danshuei conurbation finally seemed to wane. The rain also started to ease off, and by the time I reached the first houses of the bay area, it stopped completely. The settlement, like many others along the north coast, proved to be a collection of fishers' residences, some of which had been converted into restaurants and guesthouses. Beyond Danshuei, this kind of development was very much a patchwork quilt: as many houses stood disused as were gentrified. One restaurant was open and I popped in for some lunch, an eager consumer once more. The boondocks restaurant was decorated in an ersatz manner with bricà-brac stuffed into every available corner. The restaurant dished up a crappy rice risotto smothered in mozzarella cheese. But it was worth buying a lunch to get the chance to watch a soon-to-be-married couple having their photograph taken on location in full marriage regalia. Using the restaurant as a backdrop, the pretty bride sat smiling for the photographer in a tightly cut white dress, rouged cheeks puffing. An assistant held a dedicated flashgun as the youngish photographer danced about his subject. The ignored groom fiddled with his hair distractedly. It was a slightly bizarre spectacle to behold on a winter's lunchtime in the middle of nowhere.

Provincial Route 2, which follows the shoreline of Cianshueiwan Bay northward, passed by just outside. After settling my bill, I left the restaurant and hiked up the road a good few kilometres, occasionally dipping down onto the shoreline for variety. There was an odd assortment of dwellings by the roadside, some of them kept in good repair but others tatty and neglected. Storms had obviously done damage to many structures. On the shore the detritus of civilization in the form of tangled fishing lines, fragments of empty plastic bottles, and at one point a 22-kilogram container of refrigerant, lay washed up on the wet sands. Black all-purpose close-mesh netting had been deployed as makeshift windbreaks higher up on rapidly shifting dunes. Further up the road a large apartment block lay abandoned by the roadside, its concrete sides greening in the humid climate. Joining the apartments in decay, a complex of derelict, multicoloured, circular, fibreglass beach chalets stood out against the horizon like an ancient monument. I explored the chalet complex for an hour or so; but tiring of the potentially dangerous escapade, I left the site and then hailed a bus back on the road.

There was not much to do in Sanjhih, the next major settlement along the highway, and so I continued my journey by immediately getting on another northward-heading bus. The faster mode of travel provided me with a rest and the chance to cover some distance quickly. The weather remained wet and gusty. Glancing out of the window of the bus, I saw a container ship of considerable size beached on the shoreline, a victim of the recent north-easterly gales. No sooner had I taken my camera out to snap it than the bus had already driven past, the great hulk of the ship disappearing out of sight behind rainstreaked windows. The creaky coach bus continued to drive steadily around the northern tip of Taiwan. We passed various small harbours and promontories, including the scenic Fuguei Cape, which was dotted with an unusual amount of military radar.

Here the coast directly faced the Pacific Ocean and the sea churned a bit harder as the coastline gradually became more indented and rocky. Having reached the far northern tip of Taiwan, I thought about stopping in Shihmen, but in the end sat it out all the way to Cinshan located on the eastern coast. After arriving at this small town I checked into the nearest cheap hotel, took a hot bath, and fell into a deep sleep.

Leaving my heavy backpack at the hotel the next day, I took a walk around a small peninsula park that jutted out into the Pacific Ocean near Cinshan. On the way to this park, I came across a visitor centre where I was able to acquire my first reasonably detailed maps of the north coast — better late than never. In fact, I was able to collect a lot of useful maps there. The centre was run by the Tourism Bureau of Taiwan; and if it was oversized and overstaffed, then at least they had some helpful printed materials to give away. Eager members of staff at the centre fawned on me assuming that I was an overseas visitor. Finally escaping them I walked down the asphalt path that followed the ridge of the peninsula. From the path one could see a harbour to the north and the beach resort of Cinshan, a popular spot with locals in the hot summer months. On the other side of the peninsula, a river crawled parallel to the coast before empting into the ocean. I walked to the end of the path and descended onto a promontory that overlooked boxwork rocks below. A middle-aged couple were just walking back up the cliff. The woman asked me, "Are you alone?" This question, part query and part accusation, irritated me. "No: you are here", I replied somewhat facetiously but not inaccurately. They gave up on me after that and we went our separate ways. At the edge of the promontory near an old pillbox, one could make out the uplifted rock plane of Yehlyu in the distance. In the sea two enormous twin rocks projected out of the water, Poseidon's sentinels guarding the otherwise unguarded peninsula.

Since it was nearby, I also visited the Juming Museum, an arts centre dedicated to displaying the works of one of Taiwan's foremost sculptors, Chu Chuan, a.k.a. "Juming". I took a taxi up to the sculpture park located amongst the hills and trees above the north coast, arriving mid-afternoon, just as a thick spring sea fog was rolling in. The museum was mostly dedicated to the outdoor display of sculpture, notably the artist's monumental Taichih series — gigantic figures of individuals, cut from stone, engaged in Chinese shadow-boxing. These figures and other quirky works, such as those of parachutists and tubular steel figures, greeted me through the thick mist as I strolled around the museum, which was almost completely deserted. Juming, the people's artist, had been busy since my last visit: in addition to the familiar Taichih works, a whole host of new sculptures had been added to the collection, filling out previously empty spaces in the park. Most of these sculptures reflected military themes: lines of life-size soldiers stood at attention, marched, sat in jeeps, and inspected weapons; a full complement of sailors stood arrayed on a ship made out of scaffolding; feisty women walked in air-combat overalls; and so on. Indoors, the museum contained yet more sculptures by the prolific artist, these ones sculpted from wood and therefore in need of protection from the elements. The indoor figures represented assorted ordinary people of varying occupations engaged in miscellaneous activities, or just sitting. Meanwhile, an annex building by the main entrance to the park held Juming's small but very tasteful private art gallery. The collection included original works by artists such as Henry Moore, Andy Warhol, Pablo Picasso and Bernard Buffet as well as a number of drawings and paintings by several notable Taiwanese artists. It had been well worth the taxi fare to catch this amazing display of art off-peak, and I returned to Cinshan in a suitably uplifted mood, feeling as though I had stolen the visit.

Spring sunshine warmed the coast on the following morning, and this naturally put me in a good mood for a walk along the Yehlyu peninsula. The main attraction at Yehlyu is a series of surrealist, winderoded rock formations found on a small peninsula that is of great geological interest — emerging out of the ocean at a sharp angle as it does. But US$5 for a park ticket did rather put the dampers on things. I resentfully paid for the ticket and dived into the park a little ahead of an arriving group of overseas tourists. Among the tourists one pallid-faced American teenager was having problems coping with the sudden blast of heat and humidity. "It's hot; I'm so tired", he opined out loud, trudging up the short flight of steps leading into the park. Poor guy... the pace of a Taiwanese group tour is rather intense, so he would probably need a second holiday to get over it. Ambling along the paths inside the coastal park, I stared at the wind-sculpted sandstone heads, nipple-like intrusions, and wave-cut platforms and caves. This was all very fine and dandy, as was the charming presence of a number of unidentified wild birds. But then two Taiwanese amateur ornithologists passed by me, busy making professional observations; they made me feel very amateurish. I made a mental note to buy a pair of binoculars for myself sometime and then, for the sake of form, I followed the path that ran up along Yehlyu's ridgeline. Below the path and crouched on some rocks, a man fished in the eternal sea. From his distant outline I traced the patterning of the rocks and watched the waves as they broke over them with tireless energy. The horizon was hazy, as is often the case in Taiwan, but I could spot my next destination along the coast in the distance. Finally, I walked back to the park entrance, tired but happy to have got my quota of sightseeing in for the day. The sun suddenly disappeared, but at least it did not rain.

"HELLO EVERYBODY, WHO AM I?" went a strained American-accented male voice that sounded like Captain Nemo castrated. The voice continued, "I'm your receptionist. Whoops, where am I? Let me say hello to you again..." It was not an encouraging start. "...How are you!" This rhetorical question was uttered with unexpected venom, for which the "receptionist" promptly apologized: "I'm sorry, I must have scared you. I'm going to explain what a nuclear reactor is... Now let's talk about the structure of a nuclear reactor". The recorded voice then slipped into a scientific discussion that was Greek to me. Diagrams of neutrons, chain reactions, fission and the like popped up on the suspended television. The recorded voice ended smoothly enough with a clear ideological message: "Nuclear energy is clean and cheap, and due to replace petroleum. It will be the main energy source in the future". On that note, the animated cartoon face of the receptionist on the screen suddenly disappeared into a dot, and one was left to marvel at the mysterious power of a silent model reactor that looked like a church organ.

My next planned stop had actually been the port city of Jilong on Taiwan's northeast coast, the outlying suburbs of which I had just about been able to see from the end of the Yehlyu peninsula. But en route I dropped by Taiwan's Number Two Nuclear Power Plant, constructed 1974–83. The plant was not marked on any tourist maps, but the two encased reactors sitting near the coast road were impossible to miss, and there was in fact a visitor centre there. This facility was conveniently located just inside the plant's entrance and walking into it, I found a surprising number of people there all taking a keen interest in the scientific displays, models and diagrams affixed to the walls of the centre. Rubrics on these displays included "Environment Monitoring", "Radioactivity and Radiation", "Nature of Alpha, Beta and Gamma Rays", "Radiation in Daily Life", and such like. An odd multimedia display featuring a miniature replica of a reactor together with some talking robots and a television screen stood in the middle of the centre's hall. After placing my bags at the front desk of the hall, I strode up to this display and hit a button marked *English* on a control panel in front of me, intrigued to see what would happen, only to hear the confused presentation of the self-styled "receptionist".

I liked the visitor centre at Taiwan's Number Two Nuclear Power Plant, as I was supposed to. Even if one was scientifically dyslexic like me, there were still plenty of interesting models and photographs to look at. One such model showed the power plant in relation to the ocean, the former's cooling waters warming the ocean by about five degrees Celsius at the point of discharge. The atomic girls employed by the plant to keep an eye on things at the centre were happy to answer basic questions, like DIY store assistants. They were not scientists either, but one of them told me when I asked her that this plant produced some 300 barrels of radiation-contaminated waste per year. A little arithmetic is within my ability: 300 barrels times 23 years equals around 6,900 barrels of contaminated waste produced since 1983. My next question to the girl concerned where all this waste ended up; her answer was to a purpose-built storage facility on Orchid Island, one of Taiwan's offshore islands in the Pacific Ocean. I noted these answers, and then took another quick look around the centre. Conspicuous by its absence was any mention of previous nuclear power plant accidents or unfortunate leaks of high-level radiation that might suggest that the use of nuclear energy was not entirely risk-free. The story of how high-level radiation entered Taiwan's housing stock is one that is not very well known compared to the sensational accident narratives of Windscale (1957), Three Mile Island (1979) and, most spectacular of all, Chernobyl (1986). But in its own way, the Taiwan incident is disturbing.

In 1985, a Taibei dentist using an X-ray machine detected dangerous amounts of radiation emanating from the wall of his home clinic. When he notified Taiwan's Atomic Energy Council (AEC) about the radiation, their response was to cover up the facts and to suggest that the dentist had been using the X-ray machine improperly. Incredibly, the dentist was subsequently banned from operating the Xray machine. Not until 1992 did the truth about the contamination and their cover-up emerge, when a whistle-blower at the AEC informed the press. With the facts out in the open, the AEC was now obliged to do what it should have done in the first place, and carried out a check on all buildings suspected of having high levels of radiation. The radiation in the dentist's clinic walls had originated from rebar contaminated with cobalt 60: re-cycled, irradiated steel had found its way into the rebar, and this rebar then found its way into the housing stock. The company responsible for the smelting of the rebar was no longer in existence by 1992, and detailed information about where the rebar ended up was difficult to obtain. The AEC checked thousands of buildings in Taibei City built between 1982 and 1984, the ones thought to be most at risk. More than 100 buildings including offices, schools and kindergartens in the city were confirmed to be contaminated. Some of these buildings were immediately evacuated — the abandoned apartment block I came across on the north coast of Taiwan could well be one of these for all I know — and in others, steps were taken to reduce radiation to acceptable levels. According to information available in the public domain, Taibei City Government went on to list 7,800 residents as victims of radiation contamination. But this was just in Taibei. When the AEC survey was extended nationally, a total of 1,648 housing units were identified as radioactively contaminated, 263 of which had radiation levels beyond annual exposure safety limits. After the implementation of remedial measures, many of these buildings are now more or less safe. But how many residents were exposed to the low-level radiation, for how long, and with what long-term effects on their health is not really clear. About 7,000 tonnes of the rebar used in 2,000 homes and 30 schools, affecting more than 10,000 residents, has been accounted for. The 1980s ironworks responsible for producing the radioactive rebar, however, actually produced an estimated 20,000 tonnes of the contaminated construction material, which means undiscovered radiation-contaminated buildings are almost certainly out there in Taiwan. Again, it is hard to say how dangerous the contamination is now, but the health risk increases with long-term exposure and if you have never known about the contamination, you are obviously at risk from this kind of exposure. In 1993, three AEC officials were mildly censured for neglect of duty. In 1994, lawsuits for state compensation were filed at the Taibei District by a group of housing residents. But it was not until 1997 that 46 of the plaintiffs received compensation amounting to an average of approximately US$40,000 each. These are the only people who have successfully claimed damages from the AEC. But here is the kicker: many residents have continued to live in radiation-contaminated buildings because they cannot sell their apartments on the open market, and because the AEC will only offer to buy the contaminated apartments at a high discount. Between 1995 and 2000 a high incidence of cancer was found in a sample group of 4,100 people that once lived in these contaminated buildings. The victims of this serious and ongoing radiation-poisoning incident were conveniently forgotten by nuclear power lobbyists — "Yes! Nuclear energy is cheap and clean..." — but a newly-elected government went on to halt the construction of a fourth nuclear plant in 2000, and that project was still in limbo at the time of my visit to Number Two Plant.

Exiting the power plant's enclosure, I crossed the coast road to view the water-discharge area next to the ocean. The two windowless reactor buildings of the plant stood powerfully in the misty background on the gentle slope land opposite. In front of me massive amounts of warm water gushed into the ocean with great force from pipes laid underground. I strolled out to the edge of the concrete discharge channel and then walked slowly back to the road. By the roadside a man had set up a stall and was selling toys and hot dogs to families who stopped at the lay-by to stretch their legs. Colourful kites fluttered in the afternoon wind above his stall, the very picture of innocence, as a stiff north-easterly wind brought cooler, damper air to the north coast again.

HEMMED in on all sides by hills and mountains, downtown Jilong — with its five-storey concrete-tenement block buildings, old but soulful railway station and numerous cheap hotels — was redolent of a previous era, the 1960s perhaps. Some modern high-rise buildings can be found along the edges of Jilong Harbour, a huge rectangle of water facing the old streets, but a chronic land shortage has prevented the kind of extensive development associated with major ports elsewhere. Jilong used to be a centre of the once-important mining industry of northern Taiwan and remains a key transportation hub for the east coast. The city thus retains a very provincial feel to it, even though it is located only half an hour from the Taibei metropolis. Jilong also has some of the highest average rainfall in Taiwan, and I just had a feeling it was going rain when the Cinshan-to-Jilong bus deposited me at the harbour waterfront.

Would the weather ever improve? That was the question on my mind in the morning as rain banged down on the plastic sheet covering the air-conditioning unit outside my hotel-room window. I switched on the television in the room just to cover the noise of the rain. Thinking to do a little sightseeing, I had procured a Jilong tourist map from the railway station, but there had been no let-up in the downpour; it had been raining for two days non-stop, and I had hardly been able to make a move since arriving in town. I laid in bed half watching a weird programme on cable television about independent realty agents in the United States who sold expensive properties for and to rich people and made hefty commissions in the process. The arrogance of the realtors in this programme, who were totally dependent on their wealthy clients, was just astounding. Who cares about all that shit anyway, I wondered. Stuck in a small hotel room in a rainy port city on the edge of Asia, I was still managing to have more fun than all those one-dimensional realty agents and rich people put together, for one simple reason: I was not burdened by wealth.

To my relief, Alex came to rainy Jilong, making the half-hour journey from Taibei by train on the weekend. We walked around the harbour and window-shopped together like two out of town country bumpkins. We visited the Jilong Cultural Centre, located in an old 1930s hotel, on our perambulations; but beside some ink-wash paintings hung up on its drab walls, there wasn't much of note to view. Around the corner from the cultural centre we found a cinema that was playing Sam Mendes's film, *Jarhead*. I was curious to see this movie, and so we bought tickets and went in to watch the matinée showing. Given the wet weather, this was a good move, and the movie turned out to be an extraordinary tour de force. Clearly influenced by Stanley Kubrick's *Full Metal Jacket* but employing the voiceover narrative technique of *American Beauty*, Mendes I thought brilliantly succeeded in translating to celluloid Anthony Swofford's account of his experiences in the US Marines during the first Iraq War. If the soundtrack was a little intrusive in places — a common fault with many contemporary films — this was more than made up for by the stunning visuals and skilful storytelling. Jake Gyllenhaal's stellar performance as Swofford carried the narrative forward seamlessly as the tension of real combat started to take its toll on his character. The madness of the burning of the Kuwaiti oil wells was particularly well portrayed, an Arabian horse covered in oil symbolizing both the cause and result of this war in the desert. After watching the movie, Alex and I dragged our stiff bodies out onto the streets of Jilong and joined the crowds at the nearby night market, where we ate fish soup and pork dumplings for supper. Not unexpectedly it started to rain as we sat at a stall, but the downpour did not deter the many visitors who were intent on enjoying the evening. Raindrops flashed in the glare of street lights like fireflies.

Alex took the bus back to Taibei the next day. Determined to come to grips with Jilong, I eventually hired a scooter from a rental outlet down by the harbour, put on my wet gear, and made a sally. Not really thought of as a tour destination in general, Jilong apparently had a good smattering of tourist sites within its hinterland, including various temples, some caves, parks and a couple of historical monuments. Any place of the remotest interest, any place in fact that was not a built-up residential area, seemed to get a mention on the back of the official Jilong tourist map — an impressive propaganda document. I took one quick look at this map and then dumped it before heading off into the pouring rain. As soon as I got on the bike, it rained harder as though out of spite.

On the zippy 125cc Taiwanese-made bike I cruised out of town and up into the hills overlooking Jilong Harbour. Undaunted by the inclement weather, I drove slowly around the winding roads taking care not to slip on the tarmac. Willing a positive frame of mind, I ignored my misting spectacles and cold hands and drove on steadily, finally stopping at Battle Park. A young couple — a family — and I made quick work of photographing an M40 battle tank, an LVR vehicle, a navy battle-ship turret with 5-inch guns, and an old navy seasearch and surveillance jet. This military hardware had been placed on some grass by the roadside in honour of Taiwan's defence forces, but a nearby indoor museum was closed for renovations. Wiping my glasses, I turned and headed back to the parked scooter, remounted, and made another thrust up the road.

The late 19th-century cannon forts of Taiwan, built during China's Self-Strengthening Era, are all located at strategic points along Taiwan's 15,000 kilometre-long coastline. Low earthen battlements with strong points at the corners, the forts have been fairly durable. Ershawan Fort, which I stumbled upon next, had seen some action. During the Opium War of 1840 the British apparently made several attempts to gain a foothold in Taiwan — its invasion force directed in the first instance towards the port of Jilong. They picked the wrong port. With hills all around the harbour, it was easily defensible and the strategically placed cannons did a pretty good job of picking off British vessels, several of which were sunk. The fort played a significant role in beating off the invaders three years running; many British soldiers were captured in the repeatedly failed attempts to seize Jilong. There were enough of the battlements left at Ershawan to make it still feel like a fort, and the replica cannons added a touch of realism. But it seemed amazing to me that these crude guns could have hit anything in the water a kilometre or so away let alone sink a ship, but that they did. The larger cannons were supplemented with smaller pieces that were once used to defend the entrances to the fort. Looking like harmless antiques today, such weaponry and the forts built to hold them once constituted a state-of-the-art military-defence capability, much like the batteries of American-made missiles now emplaced around Taiwan's coast at discreet bases. Walking to the edge of the battlements and wiping my glasses off every few minutes, I tried to sight the approach to Jilong below. Trees obscured the view of the harbour in most places, but I caught glimpses of the ocean. The more I walked around the place the more I realized how substantial and imposing this fortification would have been 150 years ago. But Ershawan was captured by the French in 1884 before falling into disuse soon thereafter.

Later that evening after driving back to Jilong, I observed a large cruise liner berthed in the harbour's black water. The ship had evidently arrived whilst I had been away sightseeing. The big vessel added a mysterious chutzpah to this workaday port, and I was intrigued by it. On the street ahead of me I saw two Westerners darting about like lost exotic birds, no doubt passengers from the ship on a shopping jaunt. An odd assortment of shops can be found in the back streets of Jilong, selling everything from military surplus bags and boots to fake brand-name jeans; one store catering to sailors and harbour workers sold Soviet-style watches and US-brand toiletries, a kind of superpower pick 'n' mix. I sauntered over to the cruise liner, subconsciously hoping to be spotted by someone and invited to dine at the captain's table. But no sooner did I get within a stone's throw of the great leviathan than it upped anchor and left port with what seemed like indecent haste, exit stage left. It was a sign. Blooming azaleas, dotted about Jilong's thoroughfares, defied the pouring rain and I took heart from them — time to move on.

An arm covered in a see-through plastic raincoat wriggled about inside the reinforced glass display case. Eventually the hand of the arm managed to get several extended fingers underneath the 220.3kilogram block of pure gold that glinted under a spotlight like a huge Christmas chocolate ingot. The woman wanted to touch it for good luck no doubt, but she would have struggled to take the bar away by herself unaided, even if limited security measures had failed to prevent her from doing so; the valuable bullion just sat there like a Buddhist trinket. If Taiwan lacks a royal family and a set of glimmering crown jewels to show off to the world, then this single gold bar, which required 40 million tons of ore to make, was rather an eloquent way of saying that social prestige counts for less than money in the modern world. The mercantile philosophy perfectly epitomizes Taiwan, the world's 16th-largest trading nation, host to the 17th-largest economy, and proud owner of the largest pure gold bar in existence plus ten million troy ounces or so of gold reserves in the bank. The woman's empty hand withdrew from the transparent case, and then her friend had a go. I was rather mesmerized by the sight of this huge gold bar sitting in the Museum of Gold in the Gold Ecological Park, Jinguashih, hands of the common people mauling it. What struck me was just how low key everything was — the Taiwanese like money, but they don't worship it.

The last time I had visited Jinguashih, a 45-minute bus ride from Jilong, this museum and the nearby reconstructed Benshan Fifth Tunnel had yet to be opened. The first time I visited the area, almost 15 years ago, Jinguashih was not even on the tourist map, though neighbouring Cioufen's revival had been underway since 1989 thanks to its inclusion as a location backdrop in Hou Hsiao-Hsien's awardwinning film, *City of Sadness*. Jinguashih and Cioufen lie on two sides of one mountain that was once mined for its treasure of metal ores. The rush started in 1890 when gold was accidentally discovered by road builders in nearby Taibei County. The deposits were traced back to the Cioufen area; a small enclave bordering the Pacific Ocean surrounded by mountains over 500 metres in height. In the late 1890s the Japanese colonial authorities took over mining rights and brought the first heavy mining machinery into the area, but it was not until the 1930s that Jinguashih was fully expanded to its optimum potential with modernized shafts dug into the mountainsides and new factories for the separation of minerals set up on the grassy hillsides. At this time, the Cioufen-Jinguashih area became known as "Little Hong Kong", an epithet used by Chinese people to describe any small boomtown bursting with economic activity. The production of gold, copper and other minerals in this area were of real importance to the Japanese. Expecting a visit from the Crown Prince of Japan during the war, they built a swank Japanese-style chalet in the heart of Cioufen, but the next-in-line to the Chrysanthemum Throne never made it. Instead, prisoners of war came to Jinguashih.

During the Second World War, more than 1,000 Allied prisoners of war were held in what was known as the Kinkaseki Prisoner-of-War Camp, one of some 15 similar POW camps spread out around Taiwan. At Kinkaseki the prisoners were forced to work in the nearby tunnels of a copper mine. The working conditions in this mine were appalling; temperatures of around 40 degrees Celsius and poor air quality were the norm. The men were driven to work extremely hard and brutally beaten by their Japanese captors if they did not reach their work quota for the day. Early departure from the mine was forbidden no matter the reason, and proper food and medical treatment was not available. It is a miracle that any of the POWs survived this traumatic forced labour, but it is a testament to their resilience that many did. Inevitably, others fell under this regime, and in all about 4,300 allied prisoners of war died of starvation, beatings and disease in Taiwan during the threeyear period 1942–45. A memorial park was set up on the grounds of the former Kinkaseki Camp in 1997, the outcome of a sustained effort by former camp inmate Jack Edwards, author of *Banzai You Bastards*, and Canadian Michael Hurst, later MBE, director of the Taiwan POW Camps Memorial Society. I went looking for this park once in the late 1990s and met Michael, who was at that time on site putting the final touches to the memorial plans. He told me that only about 110 of the former inmates of the camp had actually been traced, and it is amazing to think that there may be surviving former inmates of Kinkaseki out there who don't know about the memorial park built to honour them and their sacrifice.

After arriving in Cioufen from Jilong I booked into a guest-house and spent two nights there, delayed by yet more heavy rain. The grassy, fog-swept steep hills of the Jinguashih area with its abandoned buildings and rusted machinery retain a ghost-like aura that new tourism has not diminished in any way. Indeed, some parts of Jinguashih — the derelict "Thirteen Levels" factory, for instance — have remained untouched since 1970, when gold mining in the area became uneconomic and the Taiyang Mining Corporation closed for good. I enjoyed my walks around the area during breaks in the rain, a time traveller in a corner of the world where a proud self-contained mining community once flourished. The guesthouse was located in Cioufen at the far end of a narrow street popular with day-trip-pers. Many of these visitors never make it over Jinguashih, or even to the far end of the street where one can enjoy impressive views over the Rueifang District that stretches down to the ocean. With cafés overlooking the distant sea, and small winding streets criss-crossing the mountain in all directions, Cioufen had something of a Mediterranean feel to it, except for the persistent rain, which was unmistakably Taiwan.

Apart from the gold bar at the new gold museum, miners' artefacts from the gold-boom period had been put on display. Mining is dangerous, toilsome work — I know this because my father was a coal miner, and I have been down a mine myself — but the work brings miners together and gives them a special kind of solidarity, the kind of nobility expressed in the 1954 black-ink painting of miners by Hung Rui-Lin that I had seen in Juming's private art gallery. I liked the inclusion at the gold museum of some video interviews with aging miners talking about the old days in Cioufen, even if the presentation was a bit overproduced. The nearby Benshan Tunnel had been recon-structed to feel like an operational mine shaft, and I enjoyed the short trip through this "interactive" tunnel exhibit, which was a bit like a ride through a haunted house. The few visiting children loved it. In the tunnel recorded voices of miners spoke Mandarin Chinese with a peculiar local lilt, an accent unique to Cioufen but very natural sounding in the manner of all regional dialects.

By accident, I had found myself in one of the wettest parts of Taiwan on some of the wettest days of the year. There was nothing to do but hole up in the guesthouse and mark time. A break in the weather on the third day gave me the opportunity to break out. I headed out of town along a mountain road that passed by the base of Jilong Mountain, a local landmark that can be clearly seen from many points along Taiwan's northeast coast. On the spur of the moment I decided to hike up to the top of its angulated form. I left my heavy backpack at a store next to the road and got going. The hike was very straightforward and in less than an hour I was at the top of the hill enjoying great if slightly hazy views up and down the coastline and inland towards the Central Mountain Range. The sides of the gentler slopes in the mountain's saddle below me were encrusted with three- and four-storey residential and administrative buildings, graveyards, and abandoned mining buildings. Random small pavilions and viewing platforms on distant mountainsides revealed other vantage points in and among the hills. From the top of Jilong Mountain, the outline of one nearby peak seemed to justify its "Teapot Mountain" moniker. Ironically, the place where so many POWs and other generations of miners had literally sweated their guts out was stunningly beautiful on the surface. As I walked back down the mountain path, a military helicopter whizzed by the ridge I had just climbed up. Its low-level flight path looked slightly reckless, almost as if the pilot was doing a stunt; but that impression may have been an optical illusion generated by my position above the helicopter. A real bird — an eagle — flew more effortlessly and languidly in the skies over me, one of many eagles and buzzards I would spot in the weeks to come along the east coast of Taiwan. Although the familiar magenta azaleas bloomed cheerfully beside the path, a cold north-easterly breeze chilled my bones as I descended. Back at the road, the mercury in the thermometer hung up on a nail outside the store where I had left my backpack read ten degrees Celsius — not especially cold until you factor in the wind and high humidity. Shuangsi, which lay about 15 kilometres south-west of Cioufen along County Highway 102, was not far away, but the small mountain road was extremely quiet, and there were no connecting buses. I decided I would hike as far as I could along the mountain road in the remaining daylight and camp out wherever I ended up by nightfall.

After walking three or four kilometres away from Cioufen on an ascending mountain road, my legs started to tire and I thought about hitchhiking for the first time. Just as I was despairing at the lack of traffic, a saloon vehicle came along, screeched to a halt and offered me a ride. The driver, a doctor out hunting for medicinal herbs, wasn't actually going to Shuangsi, but planned to pass nearby and so readily volunteered to make the small detour necessary to drop me off at my target destination. The journey took about 40 minutes by car; it would have taken all night to walk. Upon dropping me off at Shuangsi, the doctor told me to stick my tongue out; when I did so, he examined it and then said, "Get more sleep and don't drink so much". I smiled, took the small bottle of herbal medicine proffered me, and waved goodbye to the good doctor as he drove off in his dust covered car.

SHUANGSI, MEANING "TWO RIVERS", is a common place name in Taiwan — rather confusingly, there are two settlements named *Shuangsi* in Shuangsi District alone. At Shuangsi-on-the-railway-line, I called old friends who lived in the area. They said they would be along in a while, so I sat down inside the small, sleepy, but proud little station and waited for them to turn up. Whilst waiting, I glanced up at some yellowing maps and tourist information on the walls of the waiting room. Taibei County — a county slightly bigger in area than Kent County in Texas, USA, but only two thirds the size of my home county of Kent in England — is divided into 29 townships, of which Shuangsi is but one. Looking at the map, I ascertained that Shuangsi itself was divided into twelve village areas, each an administrative sub district. The rest of the tourist information on the station wall consisted of fading, but quite tasteful, enlarged photographs. They had captions under them reading "Temple of Peaceful Longevity (Tai-Ping-Shou) Mountain", "Ancient Foot Path of Ci-Zhi Ridge", "Lake of Tiger Pond", "Orchid Stream for Summer Cooling", "Bat Mountain", "Ridge on County Road 102-A", "Mountain Retreat Ma-na" and similar grandiose names. Just as I was admiring the pictures of the district's undeniably attractive temples and mountains, my friend Apollo Lin turned up. "Hey Gary!" he yelled.

I had first met Apollo on Fulong Beach in the neighbouring Gongliao District. He was a life guard at the beach, and a single parent to a bright Eurasian boy. The likeable youngster would attach himself to me whenever I visited Fulong, which was quite often during the 1990s, and we would sketch together. His mother, an American woman, had left Apollo when Steven was very young. The boy remained in the father's house, as is the custom in Taiwan. There are kids like Steve all over Asia, and many of them are normal, if not above average in intelligence, happy kids. It was our habit to meet up once or twice a year, but I had not seen Apollo and his son for some time before rudely turning up out of the blue. Like any real friends they thought nothing of the suddenness of my visit and soon we were chatting away as if no time had elapsed since our last meeting. Apollo looked tanned and unperturbed, as always. We walked back to his home by the Shuangsi River. He asked me how long I would be staying. I told him just the night.

We arrived at Apollo's ancestral home, a simple two-storey concrete building located right next to a pretty tributary of the river. The house was so close to the tumbling shallow waters that you could almost cast a fishing line into it from the second-floor window. Nestled in among dirt and plants the house felt like a quiet retreat and I always enjoyed going there. Once indoors we talked more as friends do and later I played ball with Steve who told me about his plans for the future. Steve had become quite adult since I last saw him: he could now outjump me on the basketball court, and he was less clingy than before; he kept his room neat and tidy. To my relief, relations between him and his aging paternal grandmother, whom he previously would not talk to, had much improved. This was another sign of the young man's growing self-confidence, and he was not in the slightest bit selfconscious of his biracial background. Why should he be? Having seen him in such good form on this occasion, I would not worry about him again, and felt the poignancy of watching a youngster cross over into adulthood. Apollo was also in good spirits, as always, and he cooked us a meal of chicken, vegetables, rice and fish-ball soup — standard Taiwanese rural fare. "Eat! Eat!" he would order, even after I had eaten my fill. Apollo's mother, elderly and badly arthritic, warmed to me on this occasion, finally coming to trust me after a ten-year acquaintance. But the time went by quickly and I knew it would be a while before I would see these friends again, and felt sorry for it. I respected Apollo who did all he could for his son, and I felt sad to leave their subtropical oasis. With its deep green foliage, fertile soil, snakes and glorious Formosan blue magpies, the house and its environs must have made as perfect a place to grow up as anywhere in the world; no wonder Steve wanted to buy a place of his own in Shuangsi one day.

FROM SHUANGSI STATION, I took the next electric commuter train east towards Fulong late the following morning. Throwing most of a greasy pork-rice lunch box away at Fulong, I sat back to enjoy the view out of the window as we travelled towards the coast. Miraculously, solar energy had returned after being totally blotted out by the monsoon for days, and the temperature had suddenly risen above ten degrees Celsius. The train hurtled through many short, and one or two long, tunnels before emerging onto the Yilan Plain. The wild coastline along the way was quite beautiful in a dramatic sort of way: anglers stood on distant outcrops of uplifted rock, silhouetted in the bright sun, white breakers crashing onto the solid-rock seashore below them. I got off the train at Toucheng, formerly a major fishing harbour and the first major railway station in Yilan, as it was my ambition to go to Turtle Island, a dormant volcano sitting a couple of nautical miles off the coast in the Pacific. I had booked a visit to Turtle Island with a tour group but the scheduled trip was still a couple of days away. With the nice weather and open spaces, camping was definitely on the cards and so I walked from the railway station through the spread-out town and on to a beach. I found a spot to camp on the grey volcanic sands that were dotted with large quartz-streaked stones. Ahead, my objective, Turtle Island, could be clearly seen in the ocean. From the clean and refreshing spot on the sands, I also had a pretty good view of Yilan's backdrop Snow Mountain Range landward.

At night it became hot and humid in the tent as another sea fog dusted the shoreline, and in this incubator of bad dreams I had a nightmare about tsunamis. It is a recurring dream I first had after walking along a similar stretch of coastline in Japan many years ago. In the dream, as I had in real life, I come across a sign that warns people to run for high ground in the event of an earthquake. As I glance out to sea I see a huge wave rapidly approaching me and start to run up a cliff path away from the shoreline. The dream is open-ended and has variations, but it always includes this moment of panic. By an incredible coincidence I read in the paper the next day that a couple of people had been killed by a small tsunami that occurred along the southern coast of Taiwan on the day of my arrival in Toucheng. My position on the beach was only 100 metres from, and about two metres above, the waterline — not a safe place to camp considering that a highly active tectonic subduction zone lay just opposite in the sea.

During this time on the shore I met a bunch of students at a beachside park not far from where I was camped. I was looking for some showers when I came across their little soirée under the palm trees. At last, I thought to myself, some students to talk to: a chance to feel the pulse of the nation! We got chatting easily enough after I introduced myself. It materialized that they were all studying for business master's degrees at a local private institute of technology. Their goal of attaining master's degrees seemed ambitious enough, though the students held their school in low regard. I learned that the fees for the five-year business course were US$2000 per year. Our conversation meandered about. One of students had spent some time in the US and spoke English quite fluently, and he liked to poke fun at his friends' relatively poor English: "His English sucks!" The other five boys and two girls looked up to this individual who handed out the beers and cigarettes. The boys did not know what they were going to do after they left school. They all dreaded the 16 months' military service they would have to do after completing their degrees: "waste of time" was a comment repeated several times. The girls sat and demurred in the diffident way Taiwanese girls do when outnumbered by males in public but did not drink or smoke, showing they possessed sufficient self-esteem to resist peer pressure. They probably had clear ideas what they wanted out of life, but wisely kept their own counsel. I accepted a beer, declined a cigarette, and continued to talk with the students, who were amazed I had decided to take at least half a year off to travel around "their" country — an almost inconceivable selfindulgence according to "their" value system; but as I pointed out to them, I was really just skipping class, just like they were. Later in the afternoon, and getting bored with the scatty social chat, I left the group to enjoy the remains of the day by myself. They looked a bit crestfallen as I left, perhaps assuming I would join them at the local karaoke, but I read Tolstoy instead.

DAPHNE TSAI SHELTERED under my diminutive UV screen-lined umbrella as we walked slowly around the small lake on Turtle Island. She had seemed pleased to welcome a large crowd of visitors to this isolated double-peaked island that arose sharply out of the sea. After hooking up with me, the lone ranger, she asked me the usual things like "How often do you go home?" not realizing this question could be construed as hostile. Daphne, a pretty 32 year-old Taiwanese woman, had an interesting ancestry and background: her mother was one third each Japanese, French and Ketagalan; her father was Hoklo Chinese. She was born and raised in Taibei City and later studied drama at Taibei Arts University in Beitou. She had lived for seven years in Vancouver, Canada, with her brother, and now lived in Yilan working as a personal assistant to the general manager of a five-star hotel. She regularly guided hotel VIPs on small tours around Yilan and the Taroko Gorge and occasionally volunteered to act as a guide on Turtle Island. Was she interested in becoming an actress? "Oh yes, but I have no talent", was Daphne's modest but untruthful reply.

I had come over to the island on a large and powerful tour boat that had departed from Toucheng at midday together with a work group from southern Taiwan. The pleasant ride over to the island took about half an hour and was doubly enjoyable after the days of anticipation I had spent on the beach. On the fast approach, the island's twin peaks and the ridge between them reared up and looked more like the profile of a water buffalo's head than the outline of a turtle — the name of the island is derived from its silhouette seen at distance, not because turtles visit it — but each to their own imagination. After arriving on the precipitous outcrop, we all got off the boat and immediately set off on the prescribed hike around the nearby lake. We went our own way for a while and then found that the tour group had crowded around some blooming St John's Wort flowers where Daphne and I bumped into them. Engrossed in our conversation, we ignored the running commentary coming from the tiresome megaphone-wielding tour guide who thought it was his duty to eradicate every silence. The megaphone was totally unnecessary anyway, and definitely not a good idea with rare birds nesting around the lake. Daphne explained to me that the ecology of the island was quite delicate, and hence the restrictions on the number of visitors allowed per day — though groups of 50 and megaphones were evidently not a problem. Our tour of the lake over, we soon found ourselves at the entrance to an 800metre long tunnel chiselled into the rock, site of a former battery of anti-aircraft guns.

By the time we got to the tunnel, Daphne had left me to pay some attention to other members of the tour group. Entering into the smoothly cut 3.5-by-3-metre tunnel a little behind the group, I made my observations. According to the tour guide, to whom I tuned in now and then, the gun emplacements were once an important part of the defensive lines shielding Yilan and its beaches from an invading force. From the 1950s onwards, eight M1A1 90-millimetre US-made guns, capable of firing 22 rounds of explosive shells per minute, lay in these well-protected gun emplacements, ever ready for action. With a range of over 1.5 kilometres and barrels 50 times the length of their calibre, these guns could have hurled some murderous and accurate crossfire into any boats approaching the beaches of northern Yilan. Before more sophisticated jets were developed, they would also have been useful functioning in their original capacity as anti-aircraft guns. We walked into one emplacement where the tour guide pointed to a map and explained in great detail the guns' role. In this emplacement a welloiled and freshly painted M1A1 gun sat on its original guiding rails; the positioning wheel still worked.

After our little exploration through these military tunnels, it only remained to complete the circuit around the lakeside area. On the way, we passed an old elementary school, set up for the kids of local fisherpeople back in the 1950s, but now occupied by the Taiwan Coast Guard. Disappointingly there was no sugges-tion of climbing either of the steep peaks of the island. In fact the power boat moored at the island's little jetty was itching to leave, and people were already walking back to the boat. I saw Daphne standing by the inspection office on the jetty as I boarded the power yacht, preparing to give me one of those understated but somehow still entirely melodramatic Japanese goodbyes. She pulled it off perfectly, not budging from the jetty until we were well out of sight.

The captain of the hired yacht took us once around the island so we could all have a good look at it before returning to Toucheng. Formed out of jointed andesitic rock, the island's shoreline was steep, crumbing and unapproachable. Made up of two treeless, grassy peaks, the tiny interior of the island was useful only to birds and, at one time, military observers. The boat stopped near a hydrothermal vent indicated by a steaming and whirling turquoise sea near a cliff on the far side of the island. One last view of the gun emplacements from the sea, and our skipper then pointed the vessel in the direction of Toucheng Harbour, opening up the powerful engines of the yacht to full throttle. On the way back to harbour I watched the captain in action. He chain-smoked whilst chatting with all hands that joined him at the helm. Casual to a fault, I noticed he yet kept one beady eye on a sonar screen, perhaps alert to the dangers of bumping into a pod of whales, or a sneaky submarine.

The visit to Turtle Island effectively marked the end of my circuit around the north-northeast coast of Taiwan. Although I was eager to continue travelling, I needed to go back to my start point for the beginning of Trip Two. I therefore took the train from Toucheng down to the hot spring resort of Jiaosi, a little further south into Yilan County. From Jiaosi, it was a simple matter to get on a bus that crossed the mountains directly back to Taibei, a trip I made at night in the company of some local revellers headed to the big city.

3

TRIP TWO: JOURNEY TO THE CENTRE
OF TAIWAN

THE TRIP OUT TO SINDIAN, OR "XINDIAN", AS THE STREAMING LED
inside the mass-transit railway carriage alternatively spelt it,
took about 40 minutes. In one fell swoop I had cut right across
the splurging cement of Taibei City, travelled under the
Danshuei River that marks the southern boundary of the city
proper, and arrived on the banks of the Sindian River. The
waterway was difficult to spot — so built up had the area
become since my last visit here, the city's suburbs endlessly
growing and expanding all over the place like a dominant weed.
But the river was still there, running behind the main station exit
underneath another new elevated expressway. In front of the
station, a small queue of people waited for the Wulai bus. Within
a short time I was on that bus headed out to the mountain hot-
spring resort.

Under yet more rain the insides of the bus's windows
steamed up and I had to wipe them constantly to see anything.
But the dampness of the mountains supported a marvellous
subtropical flora that made the countryside about Wulai and its
neighbouring districts a wonderland of misty peaks, deep-cut
gorges, waterfalls and evergreen forest. I was about to see it all
again and, in a sense, for the first time because on this occasion, I
planned to walk the old Tonghou trail from Wulai into Yilan.

With no particular schedule, I thought I would hang out near the village of Wulai for a day or two and wait for the weather to improve before attempting the mountain crossing. The Wulai bus gradually wound its way up a wet, green river valley, the views mostly hemmed in by thick foliage. We finally arrived at the terminal station and stopped at a car park by a gushing river.

I got off the venerable bus together with a handful of tourists and ambled through the recently expanded car park towards the village. The village high street, packed with stalls and restaurants catering to day trippers, was subdued in the rain. Crossing a short bridge I glanced down and noticed an alluvial sand bank down by a small tributary of the full flowing Nanshih River. This tributary, low and behold, was the Tonghou Creek — the watercourse I planned to follow all the way back to its source high in the mountains. The creek, only a few metres across at its widest point, was nonetheless a considerable force of nature. Turning off the main village street, I walked down a lane past hot-spring spas and restaurants, and then scrambled down a path to the creek below. On the concave sand bank next to the creek and within sight of the bridge I had just crossed, I set up camp.

The drizzle continued to fall and I sat a while in my tent viewing the riverside. The rest of the creek was made up entirely of smoothed rocks and boulders, some of them quite massive, and there was hardly a sliver of flat ground anywhere. The erosive powers of this small creek were evidently very strong, even if its width at this time was modest. Ahead, the alluvial bed gave way to shingle and the odd large stone sitting in a sea of stone fragments. Large stones sat in the centre of the creek further away up near the bridge, loosened and moved by the effects of gravity and rain, a phenomenon to be seen in all midreach and upper-reach river-valley systems. Next to the bridge, a summer pavilion tottered on the edge of some rocks, apparently disturbed by a land movement and liable to fall into the river at any time. Nearer to my tent white Chinese hydrangeas bloomed next to vermillion busy lizzies on the banks of the creek. White angels' trumpets, a Brazilian species, hung down rather ostentatiously amongst them. The predominant colours though were greens and sandstone greys. The forest stretched up the steep slopes on the opposite side of the creek, a place of mystery one could not enter. This creek was a magic universe unto itself, and it was a while before I shook myself out of a long reverie and got on with camp chores.

WULAI IS one of the main cultural centres of the Atayal people, an indigenous nation that inhabit a large area of northern Taiwan. With a population of around 90,000, the Atayal are officially the secondlargest indigenous ethnic group on the island today. The origins of Taiwan's indigenous cultures are somewhat obscure, but the ancestors of today's Atayal population in Wulai migrated into the area along river valleys from central Taiwan two to three hundred years ago. All of Taiwan's indigenous cultures are by definition hunting cultures. The Atayal, who in some ways may be likened to the Apache of North America, were once a proud and aggressive warrior nation fond of raiding. Almost all of the indigenous cultures of Taiwan and of the wider Malayo-Polynesian indigenous grouping were also previously keen on fighting and headhunting. In the case of the Atayal, for a male to come of age — signified by a chin tattoo — he had to decapitate an enemy. Thus the Atayal's reputation for aggressiveness was due to their sometimes violent nature and predilection for severing human heads — though like the Apache, the beauty and sophistication of their culture has never been foregrounded, for political reasons. As soon as the Atayal started to interact with ethnic Chinese traders and farmers, however, their culture began to change, or change far more rapidly — a process that was greatly accelerated by Japanese colonial policies.

The Japanese insisted the Atayal assimilate to modern ways, outlawing headhunting in 1913 and concentrating the indigenous population into accessible villages where the children could be schooled and the people policed. This pacification process had its antecedents in colonial history elsewhere, and is being repeated at this very moment in places like Tibet and Burma. Although the Atayal heroically — as one might expect from a warrior nation — resisted pacification, penetration and progress in the form of camphor logging, commercial hunting, tourism and related economic development was unstoppable. After World War Two, the Chinese nationalist political and education system helped to incorporate the traditional indigenous culture into the modern economic system more fully; and the adoption of Christianity dealt the final death blow, as it were, to headhunting. After all this change and modernization it is amazing that any authentic Atayal indigenous culture survived at all, but survive it did because the mountain valleys of Taiwan are sufficiently isolated, and left a space for Atayal culture and language to thrive in a recognizable form down to the present day.

Some curious Westerners visited Wulai in the past, one of them leaving an interesting account of his experiences, which offers an insight into this process of acculturation. In 1885, William A. Hancock of the Chinese Customs Service made an intrepid journey up the Danshuei River, and then along the Sindian River to Urai, as Wulai is known in the Atayal language. His report of this journey survives as an extant text. At that time, the Atayal people lived in dispersed villages on the mountains in the traditional manner; their preference was to live in settlements lying between 500 metres and 1,500 metres in altitude on easily defended steep slopes. Hancock was determined to meet some of the "savages" he had heard so much about, and whom he likened to Mohicans. Through intermediaries in Wulai, he got to know some Atayal folk by sharing a feast with them. After this initial meeting Hancock walked out to an Atayal village with his new friends acting as guides, which was quite a brave thing to do; not that his Atayal companions would have behaved treacherously, but other Atayals sitting in the bushes might have included young braves eager to acquire a head — and Hancock, a stranger, would have made the ideal target: ambush was the Atayal way. Hancock reflected on "the wild and wary nature of this people", and was warned not to stray away from the group lest he be killed. He eloquently describes the forest he walked through: "Conspicuous before all, magnificent camphor-trees reared their shapely branches, clothed with glistening green leaves. I saw clean-stemmed liquidambars and a host of other trees unknown to me; and under their shadow, in dark interstices, raised like feathery palms, tree-ferns 20 to 30 feet high, whilst close beside were dense clumps of smooth-bladed bananas". Hancock finally arrived at an Atayal village, untouched by modern civilization, and finds that the feared "savages" were just normal people, if anything rather innocent and naïve. He notes that the children are "bright" and "intelligent", and the women "fearless". In the village, human skulls were laid out on a scaffold of camphor branches, part of the normal trophy collection of any Atayal settlement. Hancock did not stay long in the village. He was escorted back to Wulai via a different route so that he would not become familiar with any one access path to the village. The Chinese customs official sensitively ended his report by remarking on the emerging exploitative relationship between the Atayal and the new dominant culture: "ignorance and simplicity permit them to barter their noble forests for a mess of pottage". But in time the Atayal became less naïve and held some ground. Of course, modern norms meant the skull racks had to go, but many Wulai residents are direct descendents of the headhunting folk that Hancock met on his trip.

"YAROII!" The non-Chinese language and loud growl of a scooter up on the creek road prompted me to go and explore more of the village. The afternoon was damp and cool, but the rain had eased off sufficiently to allow a short walkabout. The first street of the village was almost completely given over to tourist outlets of one kind or another, most of them owned by Hoklo Chinese immigrants. Business was slow on this wet and overcast day. After reaching the end of the street I crossed the Tongshih Bridge, which spanned the Nanshih River. Land on the other side of the river had been reserved for the local Atayal people, though there was substantial tourist development there too. Looking down from the bridge as I walked across to the reservation I noticed the river had swelled with runoff water and one could see how heavy boulders eventually got transported down the valley. On the east bank some locals bathed in the alfresco public hot springs built right next to the river. I turned left at these springs and followed a road upstream through a small tourist area of modest hotels and restaurants, which were nice but overpriced establishments. Further along the narrow road I passed an old-style Japanese guesthouse, tucked away with typical Japanese discretion into the side of a slope, and then followed the road up the side of the misty, lush valley. The dampness of the day seemed to agree with the mangle of broad-leafed plants, ferns and tall evergreens, all of which glistened with the same vitality observed by William Hancock. The low hum of insects, which I noticed for the first time this year, added to the sensual luxuriance of the forest. A group of gang-like black bulbuls out on some kind of determined mission hovered about on some trees nearby. They flitted about nervously as if wary of ambush; the Atayal believe the bird to be extremely unlucky, a representative of evil spirits. Under a traditional Atayal village watchtower built at the side of the road, one Taiwanese family were doing their best to enjoy a picnic. I walked on up past the picnickers and some crude, but quite effective, relief carvings of indigenous people chiselled onto the roadside concrete railings. On the other side of the river the valley side rose steeply from the creek, becoming a sheer vertical rock face in places. The Wulai waterfall then came into view; once more I found myself in a tourist zone.

A cable car enabled me to quite literally make a flying visit to the cliff top above the waterfall. I assumed the park above the cliff was some kind of tourist trap, but Taiwan constantly throws up surprises and even the tackiest tourist venue was likely to have some redeeming feature. Sure enough, after getting into the cable car, I was pleasantly surprised. The ride up to the park was really quite fantastic; the car with about 20 people in it ascended at a rapid rate. As our car zoomed up, another car sped down, giving passengers that momentary collision-averted frisson. The view below of the river and the road I had just walked up and of the Taibei basin beyond was superb, even on a wet day, and one could see for several kilometres into the distance. Exiting the car after the short ride I found myself in a pleasant enough little park, nicely landscaped and containing a few dilapidated children's rides. I took a quick walk around, passing a couple of peacocks that had spread their wings in front of the new arrivals. The park was fairly small, a kind of lost world of childhood, and evidently not easily accessible on foot. Wanting to fit something else in before the end of the day, I took a last look at the valley beyond Wulai, and then returned to the tourist settlement below to catch a dance show.

In traditional Atayal culture, singing and dancing is a group activity. Every time I had seen Atayal people dancing and singing before, I had been impressed by the easy and relaxed harmony of the group, the atavistic rhythms and the beautiful melodies of the singing. How would a show especially laid on for tourists at the Wulai Cultural Village Centre compare? I walked into the first floor of the dance centre, not far from the cable-car housing, and bought a ticket in the souvenir shop. I was told to wait a while before going up to the second floor, where the show would take place. This was apparently a delaying tactic to give some girls who worked in the store a chance to sell something to the tourists. I never buy souvenirs, but a young woman sitting down weaving did attract my attention. The girl, perhaps half-Chinese, was exceptionally pretty and shyly aware of her beauty. She had the good bone structure, upright posture and healthy look of all young indigenous people — the result of a healthy gene pool and all the exercise they got

56

walking up and down mountains. By way of a conversational gambit I asked the girl, who was genuinely shy, what she was doing — the answer being quite obvious. I then asked her how long it took her to weave a shoulder bag; and she told me two hours, which seemed extraordinarily quick to me. Oppressed by the watchful eyes of older women around her, the young girl was not exactly talkative, but giggled delightedly when I complimented her on her excellent weaving. The compliment was almost tantamount to a marriage proposal, as I was about to discover.

The second floor of the centre held a small auditorium with seats for maybe 30 people. Although small, the polished wooden floorboards and stage lighting added a professional touch to proceedings. Several paintings of traditional hunting scenes on the walls provided an indigenous cultural atmosphere — one of the paintings, done in the style of a Japanese woodcut, depicted an Atayal man making a fire with a stick and a woman crouched nearby smoking a pipe; both wore the traditional colourful woven panel clothing of the Atayal. A few overseas tourists entered the auditorium after me, and the small audience settled down for the afternoon's performance. The lights then dimmed and the public address system started to hiss. All of a sudden the music started up, a pop version of traditional indigenous music, and in burst the vivacious dancers. A dozen girls, including the princess I had spoken to downstairs, and a token male swirled into the dance area with great panache. In its own way this youthful flourish was quite breathtaking. The smiling dancers did two or three routines, each one involving a costume change. Their clothes were a hybrid of traditional indigenous, Western and Chinese designs; their headdresses sported a profusion of garish multicoloured feathers, a kind of pastiche of indigenous styles. The dancing was cleverly choreographed to impress and to show the girls' legs off. In a dance that dramatized a couple getting married, I was chosen to participate playing the part of groom opposite the Atayal princess. A woven garment was thrown around me, and my partner laced me up as if she were dressing a child. I submitted passively to the mothering. We then had to kneel and pretend to drink something from a common vessel. This was followed, curiously enough, by a fairly rough flagellation. The play beating, perhaps symbolizing the need for obedience, obviously had sexual connotations, and was mildly exciting when it was not painful. One of the older women brought the brushwood down on my butt with all her might and I almost withdrew from the play, but did not want everyone to lose face and so kept with it. In the final segment of this wedding drama I had to carry the princess in a basket hung from my back, not at all easy considering the girl must have weighed at least 50 kilograms, a lot of weight to carry let alone dance with. After the pretty girl had been loaded up I got up and swayed around in a circle for a minute or so. Mercifully, the married-couple dance routine then came to end and some other people in the audience — who had been having a good laugh at all this — were invited to participate in the grand finale, which involved some simple hokey-pokey type moves that anyone could manage. As the show ended the male dancer came over with an instant-photo camera, took a picture of me and the Tayal beauty in our garb, and then presented me with the photo framed for twice the admission ticket price: a neat consumer ambush. I paid for the framed photograph, but somehow my budding romantic relationship with my dance partner had been irrevocably broken by this modest but ruthless bit of exploitation, and I left the centre feeling a bit stupid.

Outside in the street, the afternoon was getting on and the skies had darkened. It was still raining. The wet and gloomy scene brought me back to reality. I decided to look up some old contacts in the Atayal Village on the east side of the river. The riverside road from Wulai waterfall switches back along the mountainside and leads to the main Atayal residential village that is located well away from all the tourist activity. I managed to hitch a ride there in a van. The village had not changed much since my last visit, when I had interviewed the local Presbyterian pastor, an Atayal elder, for a magazine. My article had been about Atayal cosmogony, and as we got talking about the subject it became apparent to me that the pastor did not really know that much about the Atayal creation myth, which involved a man and a woman born to a giant stone that cracked open and split into two halves. The location of the stone was in Pinsbkan, Nantou County, in central Taiwan. At the time I thought it was interesting that this legend made no reference to an earlier migration from outside Taiwan. For the Atayal, the beginning was in Taiwan, and indeed this squares with recent DNA evidence, which suggests that the Malayo-Polynesian expansion may have originated in Taiwan. Alas, after asking around in the village on this occasion, I discovered that the pastor and his family had moved on. But a version of the Atayal creation myth had been inscribed on the sides of a wall near the pastor's former home, as if to memorialize our creative conversation held years before, a rare example of a journalist leaving a lasting cultural impact at the local level.

Just as I was about to leave the village I heard some lively voices emanating from a small restaurant. I went over to investigate and to get something to eat. The owner of the small eatery, a structure cobbled together out of corrugated iron and bricks, welcomed me in a friendly enough way. She was obviously Atayal, a plump middle-aged mama. I ordered some food. One of the men sitting inside the restaurant hailed me in Japanese, and then tried English: "Hey you halloo! American!" Well, whatever. A strong and confident Taiwan hunting dog started barking at me, but I quickly subdued it with a perfectly weighted tap on its nose. This impressed the burly man who spoke again. "Do you like Taiwan?" This was a compliment-fishing question often asked of foreigners: I assured him that I did. A woman sitting next to him looked a bit nervous, as if her boss had caught her loafing, and soon disappeared to join big mama in the kitchen. Billy the kid, a local young gun, then piped up. "Are you married?" he asked me, in Chinese. Once it had been established that I was not married, Billy considered himself my social equal and insisted I join him for a drink. I liked Billy, but I noticed the others were afraid of him. Over a bowl of noodles, I chatted with the scarred local tough and gradually eased him onto the topic of hunting. Yes, he hunted frequently and knew where to find animals. He told me he once killed a bear, which was surprising because killing bears is taboo among the Atayal. Billy seemed guilty and regretful about killing the bear. "I only took its paw, and then left it there where I killed it", he said, stating the facts plainly. He invited me on a hunting trip. "Okay, okay we hunt!" he said. We shook hands on it, but sadly we would both end up missing the appointment.

It rained steadily during the night. My tent was only inches above the waterline of the creek, but by the time I got up in the morning the creek's water level had barely budged. Not yet ready to risk a mountain crossing, I decided to head over to the new Atayal Museum erected along Wulai's main street. This museum, built on ground that once belonged to a logging concern, turned out to be a gold mine of information on traditional Atayal culture. On presentation of my old press card I got free admission and was promptly introduced to an Atayal woman who spoke impeccable English and acted as my guide. The woman went by her clan name, Talanan. She was married with two children and was extremely attractive by any reckoning. I let her read her script as we wandered about the museum, in fact more charmed by her than any of the exhibits. Facing a distribution map of indigenous peoples in Taiwan I asked her what she thought of the Bunun, an indigenous nation that inhabits territory to the south of the Atayals in central Taiwan. She hedged for a while, and then said "they were traditional enemies, but we indigenous people basically get on fine today", which I knew to be true. I shot a short video clip of Talanan speaking Atayal in front of a map illustrating the Atayal's population distribution in northern Taiwan, but though she could communicate in English and Chinese perfectly, she struggled to speak more than a few pat phrases in Atayal. On one wall, blow-up photos of old Atayal folk with facial tattoos stared down at us. One man had a boyish face but his eyes had seen violence, and a chin tattoo confirmed he had taken a head. I broached the topic of headhunting with Talanan. How did headhunting become a widespread social practice in the first place? What was its real function? What were the rules? She was not able to give me precise answers to these questions, but she felt no shame at all about this former aspect of her culture. She remarked: "It's hard to understand why you might kill a stranger who has done nothing wrong to you for their head, but that was what happened. It was no worse than modern war". Conflicts and feuding were carried on between distant villages and sometimes large attacks would take place, hence the need for watchtowers. Clearly the violence of indigenous culture was something the Atayal just took for granted, a sudden violent death being an existential hazard. We finally took a look around the third floor of the museum, which was dedicated to traditional Atayal textiles and weaving. The clothes and textiles were really beautiful, and the process of weaving as it was described quite elaborate. In traditional Atayal culture, a woman competent in weaving would also have her face tattooed, in a band from ears to mouth. Looking at the photographs I felt these female facial tattoos actually looked rather becoming, and it is well-known they served as a sexual come-on. Talanan took me outside onto a balcony and we stood there a while as stray tourists flowed around the museum like water around a stone in a creek. "You are a beautiful woman", I told her. "No I'm not", she replied modestly, but actually pleased with the compliment. Talanan, with her complex identity and beliefs was herself an important representative of modern Atayal culture. She told me her children were learning Chinese and English at school, but not much Atayal language; and we agreed this was a matter of concern. What was she doing later? She was busy and had things to do, and so we said our goodbyes.

On the far bank of the river across the Tongshih Bridge I found an old hotel where it was possible to take a bath privately for a couple of bucks. Wulai was named after its old name of *Urai*, derived from "uraikirofu". *Urai* means "hot springs", and *kirofu* means "heat" in Atayal. In the Spartan hotel room I enjoyed a soak in the naturally hot clear healing waters that emerged directly from the river. The bath helped me get rid of some aches and pains accrued from sleeping on the sand bank. I reflected on my encounters and experiences of the last couple of days and of similar ones from previous visits. A late spring cool breeze flowed around outside the window, the fresh air clearing my mind and cooling my upper body as I sat propped up on my elbows listening to the river flowing over rocks outside. Everything was dynamic and in motion, and everything will end, I philosophized. Perhaps this was the end of my relationship with Wulai, though I barely knew the place. It was a fine locale, and indeed why would anyone want to live anywhere else? But tourism had brought profound changes to Wulai, and if it was still a little Shangri-la in the mountains, everyone now knew about it. Not for long would a cheap hot-spring bath be available in these parts and, in that sense, at least, things had already come to an end.

On the way back to the creek after bathing I stopped in for a coffee at a new outdoor café that overlooked the bridge and the river. At an empty table I sat down to write some notes in my journal over a beverage, but ended up gazing up and down the valley, awed by the steepness of its sides. The rain had stopped, but the mists lingered over the peaks, giving them a fantasy-like quality. Below me in the street some kids were returning home from school and opened umbrellas on the bridge in the distance started to crowd. On the street next to the café a young Atayal man drove by on a scooter, a girl riding pillion. The girl glanced back in my direction, and I recognized the princess from the Atayal dance troupe, but she did not acknowledge me. I decided then and there to leave Wulai.

THE TONGHOU CREEK TRAIL, an old Atayal path, followed the creek back to its source in the Snow Mountain Range and then dropped down to Jiaosi in Yilan — the town where I had ended Trip One. It was not easy to get any reliable information about this trail from the residents of Wulai. The general consensus put its length at 15 kilometres, but where that distance began and ended no one really knew for sure. How long would the hike take? By way of an answer most people agreed I would have to camp out at least one night. My biggest concern was to try to find out the condition of the trail. From experience I knew that trails at lower elevations in Taiwan were not necessarily a cakewalk; sometimes one had to scramble over obstacles and up steep slopes, and muddy paths could be really hard going. If it was a tough trail or a damaged trail, I wanted to be forewarned. But no one could help me with my inquiries regarding the condition of the trail because almost no one used it these days. Basically, I went into the hike blind.

Early the next day I got up onto the creek road and started walking in the direction of the interior towards the trailhead. It felt good if a bit strange to be moving again. The morning was very mild and a little damp; the air was fresh and invigorating. But the backpacks felt awkward — I would never get completely used to them. To ease the discomfort, I adjusted the straps of the packs to reduce movement, flung a small towel around my neck, put my head up, and then started walking steadily. Past the last traces of the Wulai settlement the road narrowed. This road was in marvellous condition all things considered: landslides had been swept aside and broken parts of the highway perfectly repaired — not for the last time I admired the handiwork of Taiwan's brilliant road-repair crews. About a kilometre or so from Wulai, a police vehicle came down the valley road. It slowed and stopped beside me. I remembered the Tayal police officer from Wulai's police station where I had made inquiries the day before. "Are you going to Yilan?" he asked me politely, for he knew my plans. I said I was. He seemed to think this was a great undertaking and told me it would take about four days to walk there. Hang on, four days to walk 15 kilometres? This did not quite make sense, but I did not contradict him — and I had prepared for four days out in any case. "You are one person — be careful", he warned me, fulfilling some kind of official obligation before saying goodbye and driving off. I continued up the road after making another adjustment to the backpack straps.

The Tonghou Creek valley was very inspiring. The densely foliated, precipitous sides of the valley soared several hundred metres into the sky. The trees on these slopes reflected a full spectrum of greens — dark and light juxtaposed in an attractive patchwork. By the road, tree ferns were just erupting as if coming alive after a long sleep, their arms springing out like octopus tentacles. Below me the creek twisted around sharpened valley spurs, small streams entering the creek from no less dramatic side valleys. Birds sat on overhead phone lines twittering and allowing me to see them, the whole beauty of walking being that I had the time to look. Further up the road the vista became even more impressive, the high peaks of the Snow Mountain Range serving as a fitting backdrop to this misty, pristine landscape. Five kilometres in and I passed over a couple of bridges, which had been almost completely engulfed with floss flowers and busy lizzies. One or two isolated farmsteads existed, where a determined farmer had cleared a couple of hectares of land for planting cash crops; but mostly the mixed forest of the valley was impenetrable. Eventually I arrived at a small police post. The road beyond fell under Taiwan Forest Bureau protection, and one was supposed to sign in before entering the area. There was no about when I arrived, however, and so I just slipped by the barrier and continued my walk. By now I was about halfway along the road to the trailhead, but there was still a long way to go. Very few cars had passed by me during the morning and early afternoon, and nothing had gone by since the police station. Then my saviours, Vivian Lin and her husband Paul, came by in their small car.

Vivian and Paul did not know what to make of a Chinese-speaking foreigner, much less one walking alone along an isolated mountain road carrying a load of kit. I sat silent in the back of their car, exhausted and thankful for the ride. After a few minutes I decided to break the ice by asking the couple where they lived. They were from Taibei and were taking this weekday off together. They knew the trail I planned to walk along and were going to walk a part of it themselves that very afternoon. According to Vivian and contrary to what I had been told, the trail could be walked in a day and there was no need to camp out. We soon came to the end of the creek road where there was a small dam and some off-road parking space. Getting out of the car, I noticed the forest was as dense and impenetrable here as at any point along the valley. One naturally had to follow the creek to get anywhere. We duly hit the trail, forded a stream, and entered a path that was passable only on foot. Not far into the walk, Vivian drew my attention to a rare, wild orchid flower. A bit further on and switching into English, Vivian became loquacious and communicative. She wanted to tell me all about Taiwan's mountains and she enjoyed having an attentive listener. Vivian set the scene for me: "Yes, you know Taiwan's mountains are so beautiful. I went to the Swiss Alps and Nepal, but Taiwan is best. I am so proud of Taiwan". It was nice to hear a Taiwanese person say that. She went on to tell me about several trips she had made in Taiwan's high mountains. One of her comments: "Last year I went to Jade Mountain and we went for five days, and it was so wonderful. You know on the mountain, everybody just helped each other — it doesn't matter you knew them or not". Vivian had obviously enjoyed the camaraderie of an ad-hoc hiking group. Walking slowly up the path deeper into the forest, our conversation got onto the topic of hiking equipment and clothing. Vivian told me that mountain guides in Taiwan were expected to be able to carry 30 kilograms of kit, but that most of them had busted knees by the time they reached middle age. She then recounted an odd story about a young male student who had joined a hiking trip organized by Taiwan University. Out on the mountains, and apparently bursting with health, he had been the first in the group to reach a high mountain lake, whereupon he rather foolishly stripped off and dived into the lake. The shock of jumping into the cold water killed him outright. After having walked and talked together for an hour or so Vivian and Paul stopped and turned around. Vivian wished me luck on the trail and assured me I would be in Yilan before the end of the day.

The Tonghou Creek Trail turned out to be a much easier walk than I had imagined: it ascended at a gentle angle with no serious obstacles or vertical slopes to negotiate — a very pleasant walk in the woods, almost a Sunday afternoon stroll in the park. I stopped here and there to listen to the birds, observe some plants, or to wipe the sweat off my brow. The day remained cool, fortunately, for the hike did involve some physical effort even if the path was not particularly steep. The creek became a shallow stream that danced over rocks. Sunlight reflected up from small pools formed by the irregular placing of the stones, illuminating the dark path ahead. Ironically, just as I was thinking that this hike was indeed a cakewalk, I slipped on some wet rocks in the middle of the creek. I was trying to reach the middle of the stream, where I planned to cook a meal, but lost my balance and fell into the stream. Faced with the choice of sustaining some kind of legmuscle injury or getting wet, my brain had decided to let me fall. This small accident meant the inconvenience of returning to Taibei to repair my camera which got soaked in the water. I had some dry trousers, boots and a spare shirt to change into, but I cursed my bad luck and the possible ruination of the camera. After putting the dry clothes on, I continued along the trail in an altered frame of mind, and resolved to make it to Yilan the same day.

Climbing higher up the trail in the late afternoon, the air became noticeably cooler as mountain fog started to creep in around the trees. Replaced by grass, the forest eventually thinned — a sure sign that an exposed ridge was not far away. Meanwhile, the source of the creek petered out. This fog-shrouded area marked the extremity of Wulai District. At the end of the dried-up creek bed, the path began to gently descend what was obviously the other side of the ridge. A campsite marked on the map amounted to little more than a tiny patch of trashed ground. At this "campsite" a dirt road joined the path, and I presumed it led into Yilan County. But somehow that seemed to be too easy, and so I took a turning off of this dirt and ended up getting lost. Plastic hikers' tags hanging from bushes near an isolated farmstead looked promising, and I followed these tags. No doubt this was one way to get to Yilan, perhaps the four-day option? After 40 minutes of stumbling around in brush and woodland I realized that taking the fork off the track had been a mistake and I started to backtrack and got almost completely lost in the dark which made me panic a little. I eventually made it back to the deserted farmstead, where I was obliged to camp the night. Never did I appreciate having the tent more than on that cold, wet and foggy night in the depopulated hills above Yilan.

Like a miracle, the sun shone the next day and all was well again. I felt blessed and in a good mood on my birthday. I knocked on the door of the farm for the second time, but it was definitely unoccupied. Taking some time to warm up in the sun, I slowly ate my standard noodle-and-vegetable breakfast and observed the farm in front of me, which consisted of a simple hectare of cleared forest planted with vegetables. Behind the small one-storey farm building, a slope fell down precipitously, showing that although the immediate vicinity was quite flat, the area in general was actually mountainous. In addition to various farming paraphernalia, there were a number of Buddhist items hanging down from racks and shelves in front of the farm, giving the place a cult-like air. Around midmorning, I broke camp and left the farm without looking back. A little way down the track, I met a farmer who was cutting grass by the roadside. He stopped his work to chat with me for a short while. He was impressed when I informed him that I had hiked over from Wulai, even though I assured him that it had been a relatively easy walk — he had probably never been along the trail in his life and so considered the journey from Wulai a mysterious and difficult passage. The farmer told me that the Yilan plain was just a couple of hours walk down the road. That was a relief to hear. I started down the road. The forest soon gave way to clearings in which labourers wearing banana-leaf conical hats toiled in the hot sun. I walked for an hour or two, sweating profusely. There were quite a few people about in the fields all busy doing something, but no one was going anywhere at that time of the morning, and so I kept on trudging along in my rubber boots. The hazy view of the plain in the distance was the reverse of the view from the beach I had enjoyed only a week before. I stopped to drink from a roadside stream, parched by the surprising heat of the day. The walk down the hillside had inevitably become tiring, and I was glad for the chance to hitch a ride when a truck appeared. I lifted my bags and myself into the back of the vehicle and sat mute as the driver sped down to Luodong, the biggest town in southern Yilan. At Luodong Railway Station, I thanked the driver for the ride, hopped off the truck, and bought a ticket for the next express train headed to Taibei, where I remained a couple of days, waiting for my camera to repair itself in the sun.

THE EXPRESS TRAIN arrived in Yilan City at 11.00. I had slept all the way and somewhat comfortably on a roomy seat in a clean, airconditioned carriage. The train from Taibei had zipped through Fulong, Toucheng and Jiaosi in less than two hours and for a ticket price of only US$7. This was a smooth start, but what was there to see in Yilan? How would I see it? These were the questions I mulled over whilst sipping a cup of tea in my Spartan, but perfectly adequate, hotel room in Yilan. (The fact that the hotel owner had tried to squeeze an extra couple of bucks out of me over and above the going rate seemed to be a sign of the times.) Meanwhile, in the exhausted-looking city, the sleazy bars and clubs of yesteryear had disappeared in favour of crummy video arcades and Internet cafes. Renting a scooter without proper papers also proved difficult because the local police had started to enforce the driving-licence laws. In other words, the whole town was completely dull. I eventually found a motorbike rental outlet that did things in the old way: no questions asked in return for a handful of cash. On a hired iron horse, I proceeded to scoot about here and there in search of some action. Deciding to ignore the city, I quickly made a plan to head up into the mountains of southern Yilan.

Over at the Yilan tourist information office near the railway station, I asked about Taiping Mountain, an old logging centre and latterly a tourist resort. Apparently the mountain road up to Taiping had been badly damaged by rain and was closed. Trying to get any more detailed information than that proved impossible. So I decided to drive out to the Fushan Botanical Gardens located in northwest Yilan County, one of the largest botanical parks of its kind in Asia. I had been up the 22-kilometre approach road before only to the find the gardens closed, as they were on this occasion too. When I got there, a park official at the gatehouse informed me that the place was shut for a "rest". A phone call would have saved me the unnecessary trip, but the ride along the mountain road made for a pleasant enough diversion, even if it rained on the way out. Back down on the triangular plain, I drove through the countryside more or less at random, but generally heading in a westerly direction through open paddy fields divided by a grid road system. On a back road I stumbled across a noisy religious procession, something like a carnival parade complete with a brass band, majorettes and some real soldiers — it could have been a wedding, or it could have been a funeral. I visited an orange-candy factory at another village that produced additive-free orange candies. Here I bought a couple of bags of sweets to send back to Alex. The general manager of the factory introduced himself to me in the factory shop, and we had a brief chat. He whined about business being bad just as about 50 people walked in from two tour buses. Giving up on the hopeless general manager, I left and then darted about here and there on the chessboard county roads. But the sky became overcast and the rain started to fall again, this time heavily. The National Centre for Traditional Arts, an enormous development that had been built near the old coast road, presented itself as a convenient rain shelter.

Not knowing what to expect, I parked the scooter and entered a slightly sinister-looking redbrick building. The modern and excessively large museum had ostensibly been created to showcase Taiwan's traditional arts and crafts. But the centre was overambitious: it tried to cover too much, and the exhibits were nothing really special in my view — some sad lifeless puppets, some "ancient" jumbled shop furniture, an array of tawdry costumes and a potpourri of traditional artefacts. Superficially impressive, the centre did not add up to very much on the inside, and a replica traditional street full of overpriced souvenir stores was to be expected, I suppose. The place was a bureaucrats' dream "community". After a furtive walkabout through the centre, I drove back to the city. Tired and dispirited by my lacklustre sightseeing in the rain and by my failure to gain admission to the botanical gardens, I returned to the hotel and watched television like a zombie. There was one consolation: my camera worked. Out of boredom I played with it, photographing parts of maps and hotel-room fittings before pulling the plug on the television and reading a few pages of *War and Peace* to calm my nerves.

Luodong, a couple of stops down the railway line and the end point of my hike from Wulai, was my next stop. I left Yilan City on a local train that crossed a long bridge that straddled the Lanyang River, Yilan's major waterway and the reason the plain existed. The Lanyang, like most of Taiwan's rivers, is not navigable — and for most of the year it is not even that wide. But every now and then, almost always in the summer months, the river turns into a raging torrent when Pacific typhoons dump enormous amounts of rain in the area. A parallel derelict railway bridge beside the one I travelled down proved just how destructive the Lanyang could be at times. But as I crossed it — and astonishingly so, given it had rained so much the previous day — the river below disappeared into a wide delta of sand bars, bushy plants and loose moraine. On both sides of the river, rice had grown to about three inches in height. The mineral-rich soils of the Yilan plain were evidently extremely fertile, and prosperous-looking three-story residential houses with well-kept gardens stood in the corners of many a neat paddy field.

Luodong exuded a warmth and enthusiasm missing in Yilan City: even the flowers and vegetation looked more cheerful. It was not, however, easy to find a cheap hotel. Leaving my backpack at the station I therefore wandered about, on the one hand speculatively looking for a place to stay, but also trying to figure out my next move. I dropped by a local post office and mailed the additive-free orange sweets to Alex. There was a local bus station next to the post office, and it occurred to me to check what buses were leaving town. There was no bus to Taiping — the road to there was indeed closed. On the spur of the moment, I decided to take a bus out to the Atayal settlement of Hanshih. From there it was theoretically possible to hike through the foothills to Taiping on foot. On the way back to the railway station, I visited the offices of the National Forest Bureau thinking they might be able to give me some detailed information about the trail. That was wishful thinking of course: the person I spoke to at the offices did not have a clue. Dissatisfied, I pushed the forestry official to pull out some maps so I could make some analysis by myself, but the bound forestry maps turned out to be pretty useless too. Even with a bit of educated guesswork, it was not easy to visualize the trail from these maps. I duly thanked the patient official for her time and left. On the way out of the offices, I passed a polished-up tree fragment. The cross section, 178 centimetres in diameter, was of a 1,000-year-old Taiwan hinoki falsecypress — the type of tree that once made Yilan's mountains profitable until commercial logging was banned in the 1970s.

THE RIDE OUT to Hanshih took about 45 minutes, the road gently ascending through green countryside during the last few kilometres of the journey. Most of the children who had got on the bus in Yilan got off again at stops along the plain, but a handful of Atayal children remained in their seats. They were talkative and quite friendly, asking me various questions about where I was from and so forth, which coming from them seemed like innocent questions. The bus eventually stopped outside the police station in Hanshih, a relatively isolated rural district, before turning around and leaving empty. The village itself was typical of Atayal settlements in northern Taiwan: it consisted of a few streets of modest one- and two-storey brick and concrete houses.

There was also a church, two or three stores and an elementary school. Walking around I dropped by the local police station to try to get more information on the Taiping Trail, but was told by a police officer that the mountains were dangerous to explore alone and that someone had recently gone missing trying to hike the trail solo, a scenario I had no trouble imagining.

Resolved to interrogate the local Atayals about the trail — they would be able to give me more reliable information — I went off and found a place to camp near the village elementary school next to a stone staircase that led up to a street of Atayal homes, effectively a small community unto itself. At around five in the afternoon, a time when villages in Taiwan's rural areas spring to life, I walked into this community to make myself known. In the middle of the street, two men sat drinking rice wine and upon seeing me, one of them invited me to partake. I cannot stomach rice wine of any kind and so declined the offer. We got talking anyhow. They asked me the usual questions, and I answered them patiently building up a relationship with them. Atayal men typically did a variety of odd jobs to make a living. Sometimes they worked on road repairs or in other construction on short-term contracts. The males of Taiwan's indigenous peoples are respected for being strong and able workers. But this respect has not prevented Taiwanese businesses from hiring cheap imported labour, which has undermined local wage levels in recent years, the men complained to me. Somehow, Atayal men — or at least the majority who do not become, say, professors, politicians, or professional athletes — get by. After chatting a while, I mentioned the mountain trail. The general consensus was that the trail, which started about 16 kilometres from a point north of Hanshih and led to the Taipingshan Mountain resort, was somewhat ragged, and it was best not to attempt walking it alone. One dissenting voice was the middle-aged man who had offered me a swig from his bottle. He looked me straight in the eye like a hardened pirate and said "Oh yeah, you can do it. The trail goes over there to Taiping", and as he said this, he waved his arm in the direction of the mountains behind. A young brawny man who had just returned from work on his motorcycle stood in a doorway listening to us; he interjected: "It is better you don't go alone. The trail is overgrown, and you could get lost. We set hunting traps in the mountains, and it's dangerous". Our conversation ended as it started to rain. I went back to my tent and ruminated on the conflicting advice. The second man had obviously pegged me as a city softie, and I decided I would need a third opinion on the trail. Later I returned to the street ostensibly to buy some provisions. I sat in the front yard of the street's tiny store and nursed a beer, waiting for people to appear. Some fearless women played a Chinese board game in the yard, and we made some desultory conversation, but no one mentioned hiking or the trail.

Nicely ensconced in the forest, like an outlaw, I bided my time. The hillside was quite damp and lushly foliated, so the potential problem of snakes came to mind for the first time. There was no real danger so long as the inside of my tent was zipped up, but one had to be careful stepping out at night. Many species of venomous snakes are found in Taiwan, several of which are quite famous for their ability to kill people. Green bamboo vipers, Taiwan branded kraits and Taiwan cobras are all ones to watch out for. I put getting lost, getting seriously injured, and snakebite all about equal, at number one on my grand-tour fear list. Though snakebite is a type of injury, it deserved a category by itself because self-treatment is not easy and in fact almost impossible without an anti-venom pack, and this left me feeling vulnerable. A full bite from a Taiwan branded kite, for example, would kill me within two hours unless I got immediate medical treatment. On the other hand, I knew these snakes were not aggressive, and so long as I remained alert, getting bitten by one of them was actually unlikely to happen. The easily irritated Russell's pit viper, or Chain snake, found all over Taiwan was more dangerous, and definitely not a snake I wanted to step on late at night.

By the next day the weather had cleared up. I got up early, and carefully and gingerly stepped around the tent before giving myself the snake-all-clear. I cooked breakfast over some rocks, all the time watching out for any stray serpents. Some kids ambled down the stairs on the way to school, stopping, talking and shouting in the way children do, but not noticing me at all in their rush to get to class, which somehow was charming and magical. Later I popped down to the local elementary school to wash up and collect some water — a perfectly acceptable thing to do in Taiwan. As I made my way out of the bathroom I bumped into the principal of the school and gave him a bright "good morning" in English. After this I felt obliged to show my face in one of the classrooms and say hello to the kids too. It was all part of my "hearts and minds" strategy, but the preoccupied children were blessedly not that interested in me, and so I managed to escape class before getting dragooned into giving an English lesson.

I spent the rest of a beautiful day exploring Hanshih's immediate environs. The village was quiet now that everyone had either gone to school or to work. Down by the river levee builders were busy reinforcing a wall of rocks held in place with thick steel wire. A long suspension footbridge looked inviting. The bridge, perhaps 200 metres long, had been decorated with a paint scheme that copied the abstract triangular patterns found on traditional Atayal woven cloth. I slowly strolled across the bridge over the mostly dry flood plain. On the far side of the bridge, baby orange fruit trees and beautiful subtropical trees of the beefwood type graced the riverbank. The village of Hanshih with the Republic of China flag flying over its dinky police station looked every inch a frontier settlement from this side of the river. I followed a country lane into a pretty landscape of orchards and small farms. Before long I arrived at another bridge, this one a proper road bridge. The river below, like the Hanshih I had just crossed, was just a trickle of water, the dry river bed thickly overgrown with grass and bushes. A mechanical digger lay to one side of the road ready to clear any debris from a landslide. It was a peaceful Constable painting of a scene to behold, but the digger hinted that a storm could radically alter the scene at any time and bring tons of rock and mud onto the road.

An Atayal village across from the bridge probably had a population of about 200 people. There are many such Atayal villages in northern Taiwan distributed over a wide territory in several counties. These Atayals would have originally lived dispersed in the foothills and mountains beyond the present-day villages. In the warm sunshine I felt motivated to walk through the village and go beyond it. The second settlement was simple, consisting of a main street, a side street and a few stand-alone houses. A small group of people were drinking and playing a board game of some kind at one of these houses as I passed by. Laundry had been hung out to dry on a fence surrounding a deserted basketball court. A small, dirty canal ran by the side of the court, carrying litter with it. As I walked up the village street, a young child followed me only to be quickly reined in by his mother. The group of people sitting in a huddle then acknowledged me and invited me over for a chat. I declined their invitation in favour of exploring behind the village and walked on. After passing another small farm, I hit a dirt track and followed this track a kilometre or two into the hills. Some of the forest beside the track had been cleared to plant betel-nut trees, rape greens and vegetables, but a lot of forest remained untouched. Mountain birds tittered on the branches of tall hardwood trees that towered over the cultivated fields. Reaching a high point I surveyed the foothills and mountains in the distance. Though at the time I did not realize it, this was as close as I was going to get to the Taiping Trail. The mountains positively glowed in the sun — an inviting cornucopia of life — and not for the first time did I dream of walking off into the forest and making a secret camp somewhere. But this was just a romantic fancy, and who knows how many pit vipers there might have been out there.

Erba — hand, gagai — arm, muhu — nose. A communicative young girl was teaching me some Atayal words. I had bumped into her and a bunch of other children down by the elementary school after arriving back in Hanshih. Out of the classroom, they were curious about me, and I chatted with them in Mandarin Chinese a while before getting into the Atayal language. I was curious to find out how much Atayal they knew. Baba — ear. I held my ear repeating the word *baba*, which means "dad" in Chinese. I then held my other ear and said "mama" — Chinese for *mum*. The children thought my joke was funny. The girl was about eleven years old, pretty and responsible; she was obviously an experienced child carer. I liked her positive learning attitude, and she evidently enjoyed teaching me some Atayal. They also knew a few Japanese words, which is apparently blended in with the Hanshih Atayal dialect. But the kids did not know the Atayal words for *mountain, river* and *tree*. And though it is quite possible that Atayal does not have such generic words as these, I came to the conclusion that the children did not know their native tongue very well. Despite the indigenous motifs displayed on the walls of the elementary school, Taiwanese Mandarin was the medium of schooling for the kids; sadly they were not learning nearly enough about their own language and culture. One of the girls asked me if I were gay, which was a bit of an odd question coming from an eight year-old. But to the villagers, a bachelor running around alone was very odd. I told the girl that everyone is gay, which is true in a sense. The boy asked me about my walking pole. He seemed to think it was some kind of hunting weapon. I pulled it out and let him try it out, explaining the function to him. After that I cooked a meal at my campsite and demonstrated camp cooking to the children, who inevitably became bored of watching me and finally disappeared into the forest to play their games of violence.

The thermometer hanging from a nail in the door frame read 22 degrees Celsius, but it felt cool. I was back in the small Atayal community, and by now everyone had heard about the strange foreigner camping in the woods. A steady stream of people popped into the store, some of them expressly to say hello to me. There were no board games that night. Instead an Atayal man named Sokal, evidently a senior figure in the village, was sitting wining and dining a Hoklo businessperson; they picked over a couple of tins of mackerel and jellied eels and drank beer. The two men were haggling over the price of a wild boar. They smoked up a storm and toasted each other, quaffing the local brew by the plastic cupful. During their prolonged negotiations I made some notes in my journal. Seeing this, a woman asked me if I was a university teacher of some kind; they had obviously had a few linguists and anthropologists out this way. I told her I just liked to keep a written record of my travels and that the business negotiations interested me insofar as it gave me an insight into the economy of the village. During the ongoing discussions a plump woman ran into the store's yard, fretting. She and a friend had been tasked with slaughtering the wild boar, but the animal was fighting back. "It's so fierce. It bites!" she exclaimed. "Shoot it", said Sokal, cool as a cucumber. A deal had been struck. The pig was worth 10,000 Taiwan dollars — about US$300 — and the Hoklo man handed over a wad of cash. The doughty pig was shot and dragged into the yard in a sack, which the businessperson then humped into the back of his car. After another quick toast to good health and good business, he speedily left the village, returning to the plains where he would sell the game meat for a profit. This kind of commercial exploitation of Taiwan's wildlife was not the traditional Atayal way, and the transaction I had witnessed was almost certainly illegal, but the villagers obviously needed the money.

The wheeling and dealing over, I sat down with Sokal to pick his brains over a beer or two. He had been informed of my intentions to hike up to Taiping. He offered to guide me up the mountain, but wanted top dollar for his services. I said I would think about it, but actually had no intention of paying for a guide. What could he tell me about the trail? Sokal, age about 50 but much younger looking, was sort of canny and sly and was not going to tell me too much. We sat and talked about hunting for a bit. He said he hunted occasionally — he had the level eyes of a hunter — but that mountain goats and deer were getting hard to find, and in any case hunting was tightly regulated these days. It seemed to me the villagers did not have a problem finding wild boar at any rate. We eventually got onto the topic of the Taiping Trail, and the seasoned hunter told me that the first 15 kilometres up to the Cueifei Lake was overgrown and one could easily get lost in the mountain fogs that commonly occurred at that time of the year. In addition, the trail was rugged and not easy to negotiate in the rain. He told me that hikers sometimes got lost and died in the mountains, something I knew well enough. So that was the end of it: I decided not to attempt to hike the trail alone.

A youngish woman came and sat with Sokal and me. Atayal girls are much more forward and natural with men than ethnic Chinese girls, and the girl introduced herself without ceremony. She had long hair, an attractive face, and dazzling hazel eyes. Her name was Pilak. She had been taking part in a karaoke party with some other young people in a room at the back of the store. She was evidently tipsy and lit a cigarette. Pilak talked to me about English, which we agreed was "important" but for all the wrong reasons, as I tried to explain. I liked Pilak's confidence and her unaffected manner, typical of the Atayals. She also had the intelligence to grasp the concept of neo-colonialism immediately. Pilak finished her cigarette and returned to her friends; she liked karaoke because, as she remarked, "everyone is equal". Meanwhile, Sokal and I finished off the crate of beers. He coyly said "You will sleep better", as he filled my cup for the umpteenth time.

On the way back to the tent, a natural-sounding voice called out: "Gary". It was Pilak, the attractive single mother of three children, and this was another one of those Atayal ambushes. She grabbed my arm and walked with me a while. She told me she had no home, by which she meant no husband. As much as I liked her, I wouldn't be coming back this way anytime soon and told her so. We spent a little time together anyway. But finally there was nothing for Pilak and me to talk about; only feelings remained. Eventually Pilak went back to the village, climbing up the staircase through the cool drizzle of the night. She briefly turned and waved, and that was the last we saw of each other.

THE HIGH MOUNTAIN ranges of Taiwan that stretch northwest and southwest greatly complicated my travel plans. They effectively made east-west and west-east travel very difficult and served to funnel me along one or two major north-south highways; only on the western plain was there relative freedom of movement in all directions. Travelling up and down the mountains one after another in a linear direction was not really possible: to move any distance, I was always obliged to get back to a road. Taiwan National Route 7, which begins in Yilan City and follows the Lanyang River valley all the way up to its source on the border between Yilan and Taijhong Counties, offered me a rare chance to cover some distance through the mountains. The road led up to Lishan, a small agricultural town located deep in the interior of Taijhong County. Originally I had planned to go up this road only as far as the turning for Taiping Mountain, but that plan was now in the bin. Instead I decided to travel down the full length of Route 7, which would take me, according to most maps, to the "Geographical Centre of Taiwan".

Chihlan seemed like a good place to aim for, and in the one hour available to me I dashed about Luodong, buying some provisions for the journey. The Chihlan bus was on time and it steadily wound its way up the road. The valley was really spectacular. Wide, strewn with sediment and rocks, and mostly dry because the river had been damned upstream, it had a neat symmetry to it. Enterprising farmers had cleared plots of ground and planted watermelon and greens in the river sediment by the steep valley sides — the best kind of soil to grow these crops in, apparently, but the downside was the risk of sudden flooding. A couple of road bridges, each more than 500 metres in length, spanned the flood plain, affording communication between neighbouring county districts. As the road gained elevation, the river valley narrowed becoming even more impressive. All the eroded material spread evenly over the valley floor made it look like a big, black glacier and the fast-flowing narrow river flowing down its middle resembled a melt-water stream. Diggers removed gravel from the valley floor for industrial use, a scene repeated in the upper reaches of rivers of all over Taiwan. After a steady hour's drive up this interesting valley we arrived at Chihlan where I jumped down onto the road.

Chihlan was once a flower nursery and, in the 1960s, location of the sometime country holiday villa of the late Chiang Kai-shek, the nationalist Generalissimo who ruled China in the 1930s and then Taiwan until his death in 1975. After losing the Chinese civil war in 1949, Chiang was obliged to retreat to the island, where he swore to regroup and "retake the mainland". This never happened — the tactical retreat had effectively become a permanent strategic withdrawal. Chiang was stuck in Taiwan, which became known as "Free China", and adopted the "Republic of China" as its official country designation. The Cold War gave Chiang a boost, and he was able to play on anticommunist sentiments to help legitimize his dictatorial rule on Taiwan, but as time went by, the strategic and diplomatic balance shifted in communist China's favour. By the 1980s and after the elder Chiang's death, the government of the Republic of China officially declared the civil war over and renounced any intention of retaking the mainland. The emphasis has now switched to China retaking Taiwan, the communist government of the People's Republic of China returning Chiang's uncompromising attitude in kind. The political stalemate continues to this day.

The Chiang country lodge at Chihlan was set in some lovely

gardens planted with imported fir trees and a broad range of subtropical plants. The lodge itself was unremarkable except for the connection to Chiang Kai-Shek, and it seemed that someone only fairly recently had come up with the idea of emphasizing that connection. The aging dictator stayed at the villa twice, in 1963 and 1966, both times in autumn. The dates, I think, are significant. The Chinese Cultural Revolution was at its height during those years and perhaps Chiang needed a quiet spot to get away to and ruminate over how he might retake China. Chihlan, with its commanding views over the Lanyang Valley, would have appealed to Chiang, the outsider in Taiwan and a natural introvert. I wandered about the grounds of the villa and then popped into the old holiday home, which was open to visitors. Inside the cabin an attempt had been made to recreate the atmosphere of the 1960s, and some Chiang family photos and memorabilia adorned the thin wooden walls. The most interesting thing about the restored Chihlan villa — a tiny minnow of pro-Chiang sentiment swimming against the modern tide of Taiwanization — was the bedroom. As I entered this room, an audio recording of Madame Chiang Kai-Shek's address to the American Senate in 1943 automatically started to play. Startled, I listened to the recording attentively, transported back in time by a crackly but discernibly charming voice.

Madame Chiang started, "I came to your country as a little girl. I know your people. I spent the formative years of my life amongst your people…" Having established her credentials in this way, she then made an effective, but typically indirect, appeal for help using the parable of a monk who sits all day waiting for grace, only to be told by his teacher that sitting all day doing nothing was an ineffective approach to life, much like trying to rub a brick was an ineffective way to make a mirror. After retelling the parable, Madam Chiang wrapped up by speaking the Americans' language: "So, my friends, I feel it is necessary for us for us not only to have ideals and to proclaim that we have them; it is necessary that we act to implement them [Applause]…" This successful appeal for American assistance by

Chiang's wife, Soong May-ling, is a famous bit of Sino history. May-ling spoke English in the manner of a native speaker and put her language skills to good use to garner support in the US Congress for China's antiJapanese struggle, and this contribution to the cause is well remembered by all Chinese people. But it was so odd to hear this speech in the bedroom of a country lodge in a remote mountain area of Taiwan — something completely unexpected. The homage paid to Chiang at Chihlan was completed by a standard replica, late-era Chiang statue, one that has the Generalissimo sitting, contemplating like the monk resolved to do nothing all day, in front of the villa. The irony of this pose would have been lost on those who had put the statue there, probably descendants of the late dictator's political associates.

The Northern Cross-Island Highway began not far from Chihlan. This road climbs high into the mountains, reaching a height of some 2,000 metres before dropping down into Taoyuan County. On a clear day, some spectacular views of the Snow Mountain Range may be enjoyed by anyone travelling over the pass road. I had done the trip once on a motorbike a few years back and remembered Mingcih, a collection of overpriced tourist cabins along the way. But after walking around the Chiang villa, I found myself heading there again with some of the Mingcih hotel and lodge staff, who had been down at Chihlan to attend a meeting. The gatekeeper at Chihlan had arranged the ride for me and promised a good deal on a room. Mingcih was 25 kilometres from the villa. The road there climbed steeply and heavy mountain rain started to pour down as soon as we got above 1,000 metres in elevation. We arrived at the fogged-in cabin-hotel complex in the woods about an hour later. I got my things out of the minibus, thanked the driver for the ride, and made my way to the reception. The lodge, similar in style to the villa at Chihlan, was unsurprisingly quiet. Negotiations with reception quickly led me to believe I had been conned. They had been expecting me and offered me what they thought was a reasonable deal on a room, but the price was still way over my budget.

Instead of taking a room — which would have been justified in the circumstances — I set up camp in a distant corner of the lodge's car park. Mingcih is actually the highest point on the Northern Cross-Island Highway, and it got very cold and stormy during the night. Hunched up in my tent, I felt as though I were somewhere in the Himalayas, the sudden change in weather and the vicious winds from nowhere so typical of high mountains. With nothing to do and nowhere to go, I went to bed early shivering and wondering why I had bothered to come back to this place.

"Did you sleep well?" This was the receptionist's sarcastic question to me the next day as I waltzed into the reception again, obviously looking a bit worse for wear. "Oh perfectly", I replied, lying. The rain had not stopped all night, and it remained cold after sunrise. At the reception I stowed my backpack before going outside to take a look around, since I was there. Rows of wooden cabins lined the hillside; the cabins were built within several hectares of carefully planted forest, which made Mingcih the ideal summer getaway resort. The specimen trees there included water fir, a large deciduous conifer and relic from the Mesozoic Era; ginkgo, a large deciduous tree native to China; and taiwania, a large evergreen conifer native to Taiwan. On a damp, foggy and cool morning, hardly anyone was in residence and the cabins looked forlorn. I tramped from one corner of the site to the other, lost in my own thoughts. At one point a young couple wandered out of a cabin and stared at me in amazement as if I were a visitor from another planet. The only other sign of life at Mingcih that morning came from some stray dogs that howled and barked in a disturbed manner. It was the rain that eventually did for it for me though, and I figured I needed to get back down the mountain.

Before long I cadged a ride down to the main road and resumed my journey up the Lanyang River valley. I settled in for the ride at a seat next to the window, the ever-changing landscape outside providing an absorbing distraction. The higher we climbed, the more dramatic the views became as the floor of the valley narrowed and the sides of the steep mountains drew in ever closer. At irregular intervals side valleys entered the main valley, their angular spurs sitting like cooled lava flows on the dry flood plain. Some of these side valleys looked about as pristine and mysterious as any landscape I had ever seen. The river bed of the Lanyang valley was highly eroded and produced abstract carved terraces here and there. Mud had fallen into the valley from the steep mountainsides in several places, a constant problem for the local Atayal population that lived in scattered villages along the valley. After journeying up the road for a couple of hours, we stopped at one of the villages for a break. At the local store a group of Atayal people sat around, some of them drinking rice wine, others just hanging out. One of the men offered me a drink, which I declined. I bought a soda at the store and then piled back on the bus which left presently. The other passengers were mostly high-school kids returning to Lishan for the weekend, the passing scenery not interesting them a jot. After leaving the village, the incline of the road started to get steeper, and the view from the bus closed in. It started to rain again, and fog further reduced visibility. We were approaching the Sihyuan Pass, the 1,948metre-high watershed along Route 7 that marks the boundary between Yilan and Taijhong Counties. I could not see a thing, but the bus just kept on going.

Just beyond the pass the fog miraculously cleared and the rain stopped. On the Taijhong side of the watershed, the weather was also noticeably less damp, and all this seemed to confirm Taijhong's sunshine-county status. As we descended down the other side of the pass, the landscape changed too and became more intensively cultivated. Pear trees were planted all over the place on every bit of available land, including right up to the roadside in many instances. The hillsides were dotted with innumerable huts and dwellings, some of them quite large and some of them in the most improbable of places. One farm stood proudly on the top of a very steep, isolated slope, like a Celtic hilltop fort. Fields of vegetables were being cultivated below it, a remarkable achievement given the terrain: the farm workers must have been wearing crampons when they planted them. Patches of tall trees, including Chinese hemlocks, which are found at high elevations on all of Taiwan's mountains, stood here and there in the farmland. The bus gradually eased its way into this fascinating agricultural wonderland, the area a kind of mini-Switzerland nestled between grand mountain ranges.

After a while the road dipped past the foot of the Snow Mountain Range. We had entered the Syueba National Park and passed by the Wuling Farm, a place I would return to on Trip Three. The bus then trundled along above the Atayal village of Huanshan, which sat at the foot of the gigantic 3,327-metre-high Jhihjiayangda Mountain, a peak I had hiked in 1999 on the way back from a trip to nearby Snow Mountain. Memories of that hike, during which I painfully injured my left knee, came flooding back as we passed by the behemoth mountain. Meanwhile, some of the kids got off the bus near Huanshan — which looked like a shanty town — and a few more at Songmao, another Atayal settlement a little further up the road. The highway narrowed in places where it was being repaired; the damage done to the road by landslides was quite considerable and clearly an ongoing problem in these parts. Finally, after a long drive, we arrived at Lishan. The bus stopped by a small circle opposite the now derelict Lishan Guesthouse. I alighted from the vehicle — the last passenger off — and happy to stretch my legs after the long journey, I breathed in deep draughts of the invigorating mountain air. It was damp and cool up in Lishan, not surprisingly given the 1,800-metre-high altitude, but the light had a wonderful clear quality to it, and visibility was excellent. I walked over to a viewing platform on the other side of the road from where one could survey a wide slope stretching down to a branch of the Dajia River. The over-3,000-metre peaks of the Snow Mountain Range stood opposite, and they felt close. The Central Mountain Range was out of sight from this vantage point, but could be seen a little further back down the road. The views were impressive and I felt like I had arrived somewhere.

In Lishan I made friends with the staff at the local tourist centre, which was devoid of tourists most times I visited. Until a major earthquake struck Taiwan on 21 September 1999, Lishan — the name literally means "Pear Mountain" — enjoyed a thriving tourist trade thanks to the Central Cross-Island Highway. The longest and most dramatic of Taiwan's west-east cross-island highways, this road ran directly up to Lishan from Taijhong City, Taiwan's third-largest metropolis. But the "921" quake damaged the famous scenic highway beyond repair and it may never be used again. The Grand Lishan Guesthouse closed down soon after the disaster. At the tourist centre, next to the defunct hotel, the staffers were always very hospitable to me, eager to supply me with every bit of information I might want, but I just went in to chat with Ms Wang, my main interlocutor there. She could not really comprehend my travel project — Western backpackers seldom made it to this part of the world — and was much more interested in life in America; even though I told her several times I was not an American, she seemed to think I could give her news of this wonderful other world she had seen so much of in the movies. Ms Wang did usefully help me to connect with a guesthouse in Huanshan, which I thought I should visit whilst in the neighbourhood.

Huanshan village was almost entirely ethnically Atayal. I stayed at a guesthouse owned by Aki Liu, a woman of part-Atayal and partJapanese descent. A former dancer and minor local celebrity, she was quite old but spry and enterprising enough to make some money off passers-by like me. Her guesthouse was divided into Japanese-style dormitories. On the third floor, the grand dame of Huanshan kept all her old photos, memorabilia and trophies from her dancing days, and also many other souvenirs from a long and cherished life. On another floor of the guesthouse, the old lady also kept a collection of traditional Atayal living and hunting artefacts. Aki was discreetly absent most of the time, however, and so we hardly met during my stay in her house.

Walking around the village it did not take me long for me to realize that Huanshan was a settlement divided in several ways.

There was the common social-class divide between those who owned property and those who rented. The property owners had prospered and had invested in their homes; they drove smart four-wheel-drive utility vehicles. Other people, including itinerant labourers, lived in very modest dwellings, some of them not much more than shacks. The village, with a population of about 200 people, hosted no fewer than four churches. Everyone seemed to be a Christian of one denomination or other and this concentration of sects in one village must also have been divisive. Another overlapping division was between the alcoholics and nonalcoholics. At night, small groups of people would gather in yards and sit by open fires to keep warm, as humans have done for millennia. Significantly, some groups drank and others did not.

On my second day in Huanshan I patronized a small restaurant owned by an Atayal man. He was a nice fellow if a bit reticent. After finishing my deep fried tofu and pickled cabbage, I helped myself to a beer from the drinks refrigerator and got talking to Pumak. I asked him about the itinerant labourers who came into the area, and he told me they were mostly indigenous Taiwanese; some Taroko Atayals, some Bunun, and many Amis from Hualian. As a conversational gambit, I asked him what the difference was between, for instance, the Atayal and the Amis nations. "We are completely different; we speak different languages", he told me. I pushed Pumak for a bit more. He said "Well, we Atayal are wild. The Atayals were the last nation to be pacified by the Japanese, and the Atayals of Huanshan were the last of the last. Here headhunting persisted into the 1930s". This was Pumak's introduction to Atayal culture in general. He continued, "Atayal people are lazy by nature; the Amis people are diligent. Atayal people are selfish; the Amis people are united", So far I felt Pumak, a 54 year-old man who had been educated within the Chinese nationalist education system, had repeated some half-truths that basically amounted to stereotyping. But on the matter of alcohol, he spoke with some authority from direct experience: "Huanshan used to have a lot more

87

people. All the Atayals from a wide area were concentrated here and at Songmao. From 1959, when the road came, there was an influx of outsiders into the area. Many Atayal people took to drink, and it has been very bad for our culture. Ten of my classmates have died of alcohol-related diseases, but between them they only fathered six children. That is why Huanshan is so quiet now". I waited for Pumak's words to sink in before downing the rest of my beer. Beer was not actually the problem — the Atayals who drank heavily favoured 18 percent proof rice wine and drank it almost like it was beer, a suicidal habit. After saying goodbye to Pumak and leaving the restaurant, I walked the short distance back to the guesthouse, passing a house party on the way. Music blared from an open window. Outside in the street a young man was kneeling down vomiting into a gutter whilst a girl, drunk and giddy, swooned about nearby. They made no attempt to hide their pain.

The unsettled weather worsened and heavy rain caused part of the Huanshan-to-Lishan road to collapse during my stay in the area. The response was rapid. Heroic road workers cleared a rough path through the obstructed highway with mountainside-hugging diggers. Steel girders were then rammed into the side of the landslip and metal sheets thrown down by way of a makeshift repair. Workers were doing some variation of this routine in at least three different places near Huanshan alone, and at many more places along the road further south. The mountain river below the road raged in a torrent, looping in semicircles around intrusions of hard rock. One night a veritable storm hit the mountain, and I could feel a pronounced seismic movement as I slept alone in the guesthouse dormitory. No wonder the roads got hammered by landslides: Lishan sat in the middle of one of the world's most dynamic centres of orogeny, and the awesome mountains of Taiwan were literally alive and kicking. As it was raining, I spent quite a lot of time hanging out in the guesthouse reading *War and Peace*. I had reached the point in the narrative where Nicholas Rostov, the bluff, aristocratic cavalry officer, finally proposes to Sonya during a romantic hunting trip. The description of the trip is vintage Tolstoy, and reading it, one feels almost as though one were in the sled with Nicholas and Sonya. But sometimes Tolstoy's famed psychological insight did not add up to much more than folk psychology, like where he writes, "This letter touched Nicholas. He had that common sense of a matter-of-fact man, which showed him what he ought to do". What constitutes "common sense" and a "matter-of-fact man" is very much determined by one's own socialization, and though this critical remark may seem niggardly, Tolstoy does tend to make these types of superficial descriptions quite often. On balance, of course, the novel is engrossing. Despite the welcome rest and the quality of the fiction, I inevitably got bored in Huanshan and slipped out of village one morning before dawn underneath the noses of dark, brooding mountains.

Over in Lishan I said goodbye to Ms Wang and I told her I would be back. But getting further south along Route 7 was doubtful. Yet more landslides had occurred and the road to Dayuling was temporarily closed. Apparently, the Taroko Gorge road had also been damaged by land movements. That left me with the option of returning to Yilan the way I had come, an option suggested to me by a stranded bus driver when I told him of my intention to travel south-westwards. But I had faith in Taiwan's road-repair crews and decided to wait it out. Sure enough, within an hour one of the waiting bus drivers received a message via his radio telling him that the road ahead was open again. I got into a small 15-seat bus and off we went, the pear trees and hillside farm buildings of Lishan disappearing behind us.

MOST OF THE damage to the high mountain road was evident on the hairpin bends. At some of these tight bends, water overflowed onto the road, and I thought the highway might collapse at any moment. Huge upended logs showed that the sudden collapse of tall tress was not an uncommon event on this high-elevation route. The bus driver knew the road well enough though and drove at a steady clip around the switchbacks and along other perfectly maintained sections of the road. To our left the valley side dropped off hundreds of metres down a steep slope. Hemlock, spruce and fir trees grew on the side of this slope, some of them towering up over the road. Herbaceous plants filled the gaps between the trees. The bus swerved left and right and I enjoyed this unique roller-coaster ride along the top of the Central Mountain Range, the magnificent views shooting past like the frames of a film. After an hour or so, the bus entered a long, narrow dripping tunnel on the far side of which was the 2,630-metre-high hamlet of Dayuling, no more than a couple of houses. There was a little more traffic on the far side of this settlement, and the bus joined part of a slow-moving convoy that edged its way up a steep road. The sudden disappearance of trees indicated the tree line above which the mountain transmogrified into an eerie landscape of fractured black slate. The bus nimbly swerved around the last few switchbacks up to the roof of Taiwan, where visibility dropped to only a few metres. We went up and over the highest highway in East Asia and then descended into a greener, warmer and wetter environment. At Hehuan Lodge, shrouded in mist, the bus driver gave me a friendly reminder, thinking I might want to get off the bus there; I decided that I did not and told him to carry on.

But I did get off the bus not far down the road at the Cingjing Farm, one of a number of state-owned farms set up after the war in Taiwan to absorb demobbed nationalist army soldiers. Such farms are nearly always located in scenic mountain areas and have latterly become tourist centres where people go for short holidays or just spend a few hours walking amongst grass and sheep, a novelty for Taiwan's urban dwellers. As soon as I got off the bus, I knew I had made a mistake. It was of course raining and misty; the farm was an obvious tourist trap full of day trippers, and there was nothing to do there except wander around damp fields full of similarly disappointed visitors. I therefore quickly gave up on it and got on a Nantou County bus at a stop just outside the farm. The decrepit bus, a museum piece, was at least headed in the right direction: down the mountain.

There were only two other passengers on the bus: myself and two young women who had just spent a couple of days at Cingjing. They were ordinary working-class girls from the city, and I sort of felt sorry for them when they told me how much they had spent on accommodation at the farm. They seemed to think the price was normal, which I suppose it is for those earning a middle-class income. In a case of false class consciousness, they adopted a superior attitude to me when I told them how I was roughing it by staying in cheap hotels and camping: it seemed like I was breaking some kind of unspoken code by travelling on a shoestring. The remaining drive to Puli, a journey of about 20 kilometres, was pleasant enough and the weather gradually improved as we descended from the high mountains. I once again observed the world going by from the bus window. We passed by tea farms, residential farmsteads and hot-spring spa hotels. The wide open vistas closed in and rocks and heavy foliage dominated the road as we entered the dynamic lower reaches of the Mei River system.

The bus stopped at Wushe, a town along Route 14 in the Renai District. The town is important in the history of Taiwan's indigenous peoples for an incident variously known as the "Wushe Uprising" and "Wushe Massacre", which occurred on 27 October 1930. On that day a large band of Atayal warriors, angry over increasingly oppressive antiindigenous policies, attacked a group of Japanese officials and civilians who had gathered for a sports event in Wushe, killing over 130 people. This unfortunate massacre led to predictably brutal reprisals by the Japanese authorities, which dragged on for two months. Using an old colonial tactic, the Japanese recruited other aboriginal scouts to hunt down those Atayals responsible for the massacre and their families, even paying a bounty to anyone who delivered a severed Atayal head to them. The aggressive and brave Atayal leader of the uprising, Mono Rudo, hung himself from a tree after he saw the level of violence enacted against his tribe. Sadly, this uprising followed the pattern of much heroic, but doomed, indigenous anti-colonial resistance in world history: outgunned and outnumbered, the Atayals never stood a chance. This particular burst of anti-colonial resistance has wrongly been portrayed by some as a patriotic nationalist rebellion in the Chinese mould. But in actual fact the uprising was triggered by outsiders running roughshod over indigenous land rights, and the struggle of Taiwan's indigenous peoples to reclaim those land rights continues to the present day. Wandering about Wushe, a fairly nondescript administrative centre, I thought about Mono Rudo and his fighters. Whatever were they thinking when they attacked the Japanese at that sports meet? Did they seriously think they were going to get away with doing something like that? To act in such a way just only goes to show how frustrated and desperate they must have become in their dealings with the Japanese. Like Pumak had told me, the Atayal were wild, by which I took him to mean proud, and I guess when the opportunity presented itself, the Atayal brave could not resist taking revenge on the colonialists who had bullied his people for years. With such thoughts in my head, I got back on the Nantou bus regretting the briefness of my stop at Wushe.

The bus finally arrived at Puli bus station in the centre of what was a surprisingly large town. I quickly checked into the nearest hotel before heading out in search of the Geographic Centre of Taiwan. A taxi driver knew exactly where I wanted to go and within ten minutes she dropped me off at the bottom of a staircase that led up to the Centre of Taiwan Monument on top of a 555-metre-high hill. I walked briskly up the steps into a small park area and soon found a circle with four pillars laid out cryptically on its circumference. It was an unremarkable monument, almost easily missed. As an Englishlanguage sign nearby explained, "A triangle point was established by the Japanese government on December 13, 1906 for the purpose of land survey around the island [...] After resurveying later, a correct centre stele was established on the top of Hutoushan in 1952 [...]

As it was not the real central point of Taiwan, a stainless steel long post was set up [here] in July 1979". Was this or was this not the geographical centre of Taiwan?! All centre points being relative, I thought this one would have to do, and that's the way most Taiwanese people obviously saw it too. From the top of the hill, I was able to get a splendid view of Puli — which spread out in a basin below — and of its rural hinterland, a blanket of subtropical rusticity. Back at the hotel that evening, I made a brief note in my journal: "Arrived in Puli. Found Geographical Centre of Taiwan. Nice view of town and mountains".

NANTOU IS the largest of Taiwan's 13 counties and the only one that is landlocked. The county has a reputation for bucolic prettiness and for a climate that is cool in the summer, thanks to its high elevation. I knew very little about the place. Most visitors to the county make a beeline for the Sun Moon Lake, a scenic area located in the middle of the county and a favourite spot for honeymooners. The lake area is also the home territory of Taiwan's Thao indigenous nation. Having considered my travel options, I decided to head out to the lake area and try to connect with the Thao — one of Taiwan's most critically endangered cultures — and so took the bus from Puli out to the Sun Moon Lake the next day. Although only a relatively short hop of five kilometres through hilly farmland covered in betel-nut trees, this gently ascending journey directly southwards took me away from the direct gravitational pull of Taijhong City, a force that had been acting on me since Lishan. The road was lined with cherry-blossom trees in bloom, but farmers here did not seem as prosperous as those in Yilan, no doubt because they had to plant their crops on marginal slope land. Betel nut was the main local cash crop and the planting of this palmlike tree had itself contributed to the degradation of the land through soil erosion. The latter problem had not stopped just about any farmer in the county from planting betel-nut trees everywhere; a veritable sea of them lay all around and on every hill.

Half an hour later the bus arrived at Shueishe, the main administrative and tourist centre at the lake. The Sun Moon Lake, apparently named after its shape, sits in middle of Nantou County at an elevation of around 750 metres. The lake looked small, but it had a circumference well over 35 kilometres in length. After spending an hour or two to get acquainted with Shueishe in the northwest corner of the lakeside, I proceeded to walk around the lake in an anticlockwise direction — on a sunny day walking naturally seemed like a good idea, though I did get one or two strange looks from people in the village that were obviously not used to seeing tourist infantry marching through. A few other tourists whirred past on electric scooters, but the lakeside road was mostly quiet on a midweek day, and the walking was superb, especially as the scenic high mountains that encircled the secluded lake provided a stunning backdrop.

At the Shueishe Dam a young couple were practising Chinese shadow-boxing — Taichih — when I came by an hour into my walk. Although moving in slow motion, they somehow looked tense as though they were expecting an ungainly foreigner to walk up to them and ask them a question in English. Another couple walked along the dam further ahead, only to get in a car and disappear up the road as soon as they spotted me. I got to the end of the dam — still friendless — where my walk became a little more adventurous: I skipped down onto a bike path that hugged the lake shoreline before tackling a footpath up a hill-side; taking a wrong turn, however, I ended up getting lost in some dense thickets of bamboo by the lakeside. In the bamboo forest I stumbled upon a fisherperson's shelter, complete with a table, plastic stools and cooking utensils — a kind of Taiwanese still life. Backtracking along the obscure trail, I eventually found my way back to the lakeside road. According to a sign, the Syuanzang Temple was six kilometres away.

In the afternoon the sun started to drop in the sky and a cooler temperature prevailed. I resumed my walk around the picturesque lake after a short picnic lunch, skipping past mid-elevation bamboo, banana trees and some planted dwarf evergreens. Occasionally I came across something odd, like an old washed-up lake boat, or some weird monument to hydroelectric engineering. Another lakeside bilingual sign read, among other things, *No sailing without license; No swimming; Camping prohibited*. The subtext of this message seemed to be something like "stay in a hotel and don't do anything independently". The sign was a perfect example of legalistic overkill — another cultural link to China and also to the emerging AngloAmerican world, strangely enough. I walked on and on and, after a tiring hike, finally made it to my goal, a modest and quiet temple overlooking the lake, where the bones of one of China's most famous historical figures lie buried. As I arrived, a small boatful of — appropriately enough — well-behaved Chinese tourists were just leaving to return back to their hotel across the lake in a chartered boat.

Syuanzang is the Saint Paul of Chinese Buddhism. A dedicated monk, he went on a 19-year-long scholastic journey / sojourn through India in the seventh century subsequently bringing many important Buddhist scriptures back to China. After spending some time in Japan in the mid-twentieth century, Syuanzang's remains were moved to the lakeside temple by the Chinese Nationalist government in 1952, where they currently rest. The dedicated temple was surrounded by some simple gardens in which stood a stone tablet with a map carved on it showing the incredible journey Syuanzang — variously romanized "Hsuan Kuang" and "Xuan Zang" — had made through China's western half and India. This true seeker travelled through deserts on foot in order to develop his knowledge of Buddhist religion and philosophy; there was no doubting the guy's sincerity and active learning attitude. Was I doing something similar? Was this what all my years in Taiwan and East Asia added up to, a spiritual journey? Well, maybe in some ways. I had not just flown in and out again anyway, but that is perhaps where the comparison ends. I had always regarded my time in the East as an important part of my ongoing social, political and cultural education, but I had never been a religious seeker; I was not looking for salvation.

Walking a little way along a forested path behind the temple, I found a wooden viewing platform above the lake, which made for an ideal campsite. That evening I had the temple together with its coinslot espresso-coffee machine to myself. But the place seemed to be infested with bull frogs that confidently jumped out all over the place, so I wasn't exactly alone. This worried me slightly: where there are frogs there are snakes, but no critters bothered me on the platform. Later on, a spectacular sunset lit up the lake, and I watched tourist motor boats traversing the calm water of the lake as I sipped a remarkably good coffee in the gathering dusk. During more than six months of travelling in Taiwan, I would never sleep so well in my tent as I did that night by the Sun Moon Lake. The temperature cooled to just about ideal; a steady breeze blew off the lake. The viewing platform itself, made of slatted wood, proved to be the perfect surface to sleep on. By now I had got my camp craft fine-tuned and had found a suitable place to put everything in the tent, thus maximizing space. If I had broken any rules by camping near the temple, no one would know — and Syuanzang was no doubt smiling down on me in Buddhist heaven.

The next day I continued my walk around the lake, two chirping black bulbuls and a stray dog seeing me off from the viewing platform. The forested path wound around the lakeside, sometimes rising to a height where one could view the farmland beyond the hills that circled the lake. The stepped trail eventually led back to the lakeside road, where I soon arrived at another temple dedicated to Syuanzang. This larger temple was evidently an active place of worship and study. When I wandered in, a group of women dressed in traditional Korean garb were preparing to do ritual obeisance over tea pots and other assorted items spread out on white sheets. Their blooming dresses looked very uncomfortable and cumbersome, like Elizabethan court wear. Across from the temple on the signboard of a souvenir shop, an aboriginal motif — a picture of two women pounding rice with a long wooden pestle — suddenly reminded me of why I had decided to visit Sun Moon Lake in the first place, and I moved on.

From the Guanghua Temple it was but a three-kilometre walk to the Dehua village, a place not marked on any standard handout map of the Sun Moon Lake area. On the way to the village, I dipped down onto a trail that led through the forest to the lakeside, a path known as the "Owl Trail" in honour of the Thao people's respect for the bird. A bilingual sign introducing the legend of the owl stood next to the entranceway to this short trail. The legend concerns a single woman who became pregnant, garnering the disapproval of the tribe. In order to escape her feelings of shame, she ran away to the forest. It isn't clear if the girl ever returned, but the Thao noticed an owl would linger near the pregnant women's former home, and henceforth the bird became a symbolic reminder to women to value their bodies — whatever that meant. To the Thao the owl was also thought of as a good-luck bird that helped lost hunters find their way home, and hunting it became taboo. After walking around the picturesque trail down by the lakeside, I hiked over to the Dehua Village; a finger sign marked *Thao Tribe* helpfully indicated the way.

ITA THAO, the term by which the Thao call themselves, literally means, "I am a person". The Thao part of Dehua, a lakeside village of private residences and tourist businesses, was positioned away from the main settlement on slope land like an apartheid township. The indigenous village, made up of a collection of simple one-storey wooden and bamboo dwellings, was quiet when I arrived: it was midday and most people were either at work or taking a siesta. I did, however, meet a man by the name of Talack outside his home. I introduced myself whereupon I was invited to take a seat on a tree stump. We proceeded to chat away in Mandarin, Taiwan's lingua franca. Talack, who was shelling baby bamboo, told me he worked locally on various odd jobs. He showed a polite interest in my travels and questioned me intelligently; he also kindly handed me a cold beer from the small refrigerator that stood in the yard. I asked him if he had a wife, and he did. It was while helping out on an archaeological dig on the small island in the centre of the Sun Moon Lake — sacred ground to the Thao — that he met his future wife, Sirulan, a university researcher hailing from Jilong City. Perhaps hearing her name being mentioned, the said lady emerged from the house cradling a threemonth-old baby boy. She invited me inside the house, and I accepted her cordial invitation.

Though they do not like to recognize the association, the Thao are actually a subgroup of the more numerous Tsou further south in Taiwan. But they have been geographically isolated for long enough to make their language, and therefore their identity, distinct. Thao tradition holds that their ancestors discovered the Sun Moon Lake after giving chase to a white stag; a moment of discovery often depicted on paintings and stencilled batik cloth found at souvenir shops in and around the lake resort. As the story goes, the hunting party was so taken with the abundance and beauty of the area that they led their whole clan there to live. The relatively accessible area also drew Chinese settlers, however, and the Thao population quickly dwindled in the twentieth century due to disease and out-migration. The remaining scattered villages were later concentrated into one settlement as part of the process of hydroelectric infrastructure development in and around lake. Officially, there are only 500 members of the Thao nation left — Talack was one, but his wife was actually a plains aborigine, who have no official recognition.

It was quite a privilege to be invited into a Thao home, not least because every Thao household keeps a "spirit basket" in which articles of clothing belonging to ancestors is kept and worshipped. When I sat down on the sofa in the small living room of Talack's home, my eyes drifted above the television set opposite. On a shelf a basket of neatly folded old clothes sat, flanked by two small red Buddhist lamps. I immediately realized the significance of the basket, and was quite touched to see it. Talack busied himself cooking the evening meal in the tiny kitchen whilst his wife nursed the baby and talked to me. Sirulan said that the Thao had basically lost their land rights when the Chinese nationalists took control of the lakeside area and made the land available for sale in the 1950s. After the big "921" earthquake, the lake's topography changed, which prompted the local authorities to further rezone the Dehua village, basically squeezing the remaining Thao population out of prime lakeside land and only leaving them a meagre site on which to build some new "temporary" homes. It was a sorry tale, but Sirulan said there had been an upside to the 921 earthquake, and that had been the re-forging of Thao solidarity.

I was curious to know how well the Thao language was holding up. Sirulan insisted that the language was regarded as important and was being taught again to children in the village. I asked what kind of teaching materials were available, and by way of an answer she played a video for me to watch. In the video an elderly, but very healthylooking, Thao man dressed in traditional Thao clothes recited Thao words apparently at random. He repeated each word twice, as though making sure he had got the words right by checking the second recitation against the first: "Farazay, farazay; ilalhumiz, ilalhumiz; papashzak, papashzak; kathna, kathna", and on he went like this. The vocabulary related to plants, flowers and small mammals; no mention of body parts at all. The Thao language was thus orientated to the outside world. (Though English is not naturally introverted, English-language learning materials typically start with an objectification of the self.) Could the Thao language survive though? The video seemed more like an ethno-linguistic record of a dying language than a pedagogic tool. The Thao were formally recognized as Taiwan's tenth official indigenous nation in 2001, and this recognition will help them get funding for a language programme — but will it be a case of too little too late? How many fluent speakers of Thao are left to work back from? These questions floated in my mind as I resumed my discussion with Sirulan, who seemed determined to teach her baby Thao. Later I duly said goodbye to my new friends. The Thao Seedling Festival was about to take place, and Sirulan invited me along. I promised to drop by.

Finding a discreet place to camp by the lakeside, I spent the next couple of days hanging out at Dehua. I observed the daily comings and goings of small groups of tourists. Up at Ita Thao, preparations for the Seedling Festival were, quite literally, in full swing. A group of about a dozen men prepared an area of flat ground on which a huge swing made out of 15-metre-long bamboo poles was built. I talked with a variety of onlookers at the village as the groundbreaking took place. Contrary to what I had imagined, the swing was only to be used by married adults and not by children. Flying high on the swing was supposed to bring good luck for the coming growing season. Such swings are also widely used in ceremonies by other indigenous nations in Taiwan, particularly in the south by the Rukai, Paiwan and Puyuma nations. Slowly the giant village swing took shape.

Renting a bicycle, I took some time out to ride around the lake and made a detour to visit the "Formosan Aboriginal Culture Village", a popular 62-hectare multifaceted theme park that opened in 1986. Entrance to the park — which included areas devoted to reconstructions of traditional aboriginal houses, a museum, and an amusement park with a cable car — cost 650 New Taiwan dollars, or about US$20. The park appeared to be exploitative of indigenous cultures; the considerable profits generated by its operation went to private investors and not to the local aboriginal people. The park evidently did provide employment to quite a few indigenous people though, several of whom expressed satisfaction with their work when I quizzed them about it. In addition, the replica indigenous dwellings were thoughtfully arranged, and one could pick up quite a lot of information about traditional indigenous cultures there. For example, wandering into a replica Puyuma village, I was quite taken by the lifesize models of traditional Puyuma warriors in training.

An information board beside the models noted that traditional Puyuma warriors used to be trained in a strict and regimented Spartan-like way from a young age, and that in their day the Puyuma were a "feared hegemonic power in south-eastern Taiwan".

The other part of the park I liked was the museum. Among the aboriginal artefacts on display were some arresting colour photographs of indigenous people blown up. One photograph of a group of Bunun men standing on a hilltop practising archery was amazing. The men stood perfectly erect and looked like medieval archers; the gathered assembly was purposeful but relaxed and exhibited no obvious signs of rank or hierarchy. Also in the photograph section of the museum was an interesting picture of an Atayal man sitting on the edge of the upraised platform on which his modest dwelling had been built. What interested me specifically about the scene were the large concave wooden plates under the platform's supports emplaced to prevent rodents and snakes from entering the house. Another group photograph, one that I had seen before reproduced in books, showed a group of young men — perhaps one should say boys — about to embark on a hunting trip. This photograph is a fascinating document. I am not sure which nation the boys belonged to, possibly Bunun, but the scene would have been a familiar one in Taiwan only a generation or two back. The four boys, one of them kneeling, are clearly posing for the camera, but their serious expressions betray experience of violence. Hunting in those days was an especially dangerous activity in Taiwan; not least because the hunter could quite literally become the hunted if warriors from another tribe came looking for a head. One boy kneeling seemed to be the eldest in the group and was carrying a home-made rifle. The two boys flanking the group, barely in their teens, were holding five Formosan hunting dogs between them on leashes. Most striking of all was the fact that all of the boys carried swords, which of course doubled as machetes.

On the day of the Seedling Festival, I watched a ceremony

performed by a group of female Thao shamans at Dehua. The five women, dressed in traditional Thao dress, sat and chanted a repetitive song somewhat like a Buddhist hymn. Observed by a small throng of interested onlookers wielding cameras and camcorders, the women sat in the doorway of a roadside residence, a spirit basket and jar of seeds placed on the road in front of them. A few cars passed by the gathering, but did not bother to stop. None of us understood what the shamans were singing, but it obviously was something related to communing with ancestors and praying for a good harvest. Watching this scene I became absorbed in my own thoughts. It struck me that the Sun Moon Lake may be considered the real centre of Taiwan, culturally speaking — a place where one culture was being actively subducted under another. What convinced me that the Thao culture would struggle to survive in its present form was not just the lack of Thao children observing these traditional ceremonies, but a conversation with a beautiful Thao girl I met at the big swing event, which followed the morning's ancestor worship. Siramowan, an attractive fine-boned young woman, was an architect by profession. She had also been busy recording events with her camera. "Can I look at your photographs" — these days the instant feedback of digital cameras affords, among other things, a very convenient conversational gambit. "Oh sure", she said, handing her camera over to me. Taking a minute to flick through her pictures, I saw she was a good photographer and that she had taken especial care to record small details, like the bird's nest ferns that had been lashed to the swing's bamboo poles. We later chatted about my trip, and she asked me questions of the usual kind I get asked in Taiwan. The conversation then got onto the subject of relationships. I asked her if she had a boyfriend: she did not. Pretty, intelligent, welleducated, in her late twenties, and without a boyfriend — it seemed absurd. Why not marry a Thao man? She hesitated to answer this question, and so I jumped in with a speculative answer: "Not enough choice". "Right", she agreed, pleased to have been second-guessed. That was indeed the problem: not enough choice of mates within the remaining Thao nation, at least not for this modern, educated girl. And if the boys and girls no longer fancy one another where does that lead a culture?

The Seedling Festival in Ita Thao was a pretty subdued affair. Had it been children playing on the swing instead of a gang of aging female shamans, I am sure the event would have been much livelier. I am sure there would have been fractured limbs, too. The swing, which had taken a dozen men two days to put up, really looked very impressive, but it was also rather dangerous. People who sat on the swing's seat were launched into the air by two people pulling on attached ropes, which afforded much more leverage than a simple push from behind. After some token swinging, the small crowd of guests and onlookers were invited to share some millet wine, a potent brew which tastes a bit like a sweet sherry but is about twice as strong. When she saw me quaff my drink right down, one of the grandma shamans quickly gave me a refill, and the second bowl of liquor instantly made me tipsy. Enjoying the effects of the wine, I thought about staying at Dehua a while longer, but in fact I left the village at lunchtime, taking some time to say farewell to Talack, Sirulan, Siramowan and some other people I had become acquainted with during my short stay in the village before departing. It seemed a shame to have to leave all of a sudden, but it was time to get back on the road. But before getting out of the area, however, I would have a little side adventure.

HITCHHIKING along the lakeside road back to Shueishe, I got a ride with a family who were out for a ride in their yellow van. The Bunun couple were travelling with one of their daughters and a young nephew. We had a pleasant chat before they dropped me off a few kilometres up the road. Maybe it was the booze I had drunk earlier in the day, or maybe it was the slightly distracting "Jesus loves you" farewell that the man gave me, but I forgot to pick up my camera when getting out of the van. No sooner had the couple started down the road that led to the Formosan Aboriginal Cultural Village than I realized my absent-minded mistake. The vehicle had only gone about 30 metres when I started to wave and shout frantically. All to no avail: the happy family were on their way and were not looking back. "Blast it!" I screamed, or words to that effect. A small agricultural truck came by and I commandeered it telling the driver to follow the van. But the yellow van was well ahead, and at the first three-way intersection it was obvious that we had lost track of it. I shouted some more to let off steam; I just could not believe that I had been so careless. I then hitchhiked back up to the lakeside, hoping the family might come back to that spot to look for me. They did not. I spent several hours by the roadside hoping and waiting, but eventually gave it up as a bad job. I carried on to Shueishe and reported the loss of my camera to the police, thinking the family might hand it in. That was admittedly a long shot, since I knew most Taiwanese people did not trust police. I don't know why not because I saw a whole rack of returned cameras at the police station, all waiting for their owners to come and pick them up. The Sun Moon Lake was not such a big area; I knew the family and had a vehicle description. With my hound-like nose I was sure I could find that family again. The problem was time. How long would it take for me to find them? The answer to that question, as it turned out, was two days.

It made sense to sit tight in Shueishe. The Bunun family would look for me there, if they looked for me at all. I talked to the police and tried to figure out where the family might live, but no one had any ideas, so I camped out in an unoccupied building opposite the police station, necessarily keeping a low profile, and spent my time reading, writing and hoping. It was not a bad place to take a rest, and I once again observed the comings and goings of tourists, most of who seemed to arrive in the village by tour coach, stay for a few hours, and then leave. On the morning of the second day, I checked with the police again, but nothing had turned up. But it was in the afternoon of the second day, just as I was starting to reconcile myself to the loss of the camera and the necessity of making a trip to a city to replace it, that a Taiwanese man walked by my tent, poked his nose in, and said hello. The man, who called himself Jamie, was an architect by profession, and he had been taking a look around the unoccupied building. He seemed quite interested in me too, and we had a long chat about my journey. By coincidence, he was well acquainted with the Dehua village. I told him the story about my camera loss, and it was then that I got my lead. "Oh, they were Bunun. Most of the Bunun who come through the Sun Moon Lake area live over in Tanan, about ten kilometres south-west of the lake", Jamie said, quite casually. As soon as I got this information, I knew there was a good chance of getting my camera back. I asked Jamie if he wanted to make a little trip to Tanan, but he did not. After saying goodbye to the architect at the steps of the empty building, I dashed off to rent a scooter. It was four o'clock in the afternoon, and I had about three hours of daylight to find the Bunan family.

I drove to the turning for Tanan that was located on the lake-side road just south of Dehua. This side road took me over some hills and entered a deeply cut side valley full of mudslides, scarred slopes and huge boulders. It was as if I had entered another land, and in a sense I had because I was now in Sinyi District, a mountainous area that covers the whole south-eastern corner of Nantou County. Continuing along the road it was not long before I came across a Bunun-occupied residence. The people there were surprised to see me, a stray tourist. They told me Tanan was just down the road and I scooted off. I came to a couple of villages. At the first I quizzed a dozen people about the family I was looking for but no one knew them. Near a Catholic church in Tanan, however, one woman I spoke to positively identified the family and told me they lived in Dili, which was another Bunun village a further seven kilometres down the road. I sped off again. By the time I got to Dili, it was getting dark and the village was quite spread out, making my quest rather challenging. After asking around, I narrowed the possible location of the family's home to within a few houses on one street. I even talked to the Bunun man's brother, who somehow did not connect my description of the family to his own relatives. Just as I was knocking on the door of another house, the Bunun family turned up in their yellow van, back from a trip to Taijhong City. They greeted me warmly when they saw me. "God wanted us to know each other, and that is how you came to be here", exclaimed the Bunun man. I put it down to some fine detective work, my dear Holmes.

The Bunun family politely invited me into their home and I stayed with them for a short while. They were a nice family of devout Christians, and I took a photo of them in front of a tapestry depicting the Last Supper, which they had on the wall of their small living room. After exchanging addresses, I then said goodbye and left, covering the 17 kilometres back to Shueishe in good time. The side journey to Dili had been kind of a telescoped odyssey. It is often said Taiwan is small, but Sinyi alone — just one district out of eleven in Nantou County — with its many mountains, rivers and valleys counts as a small kingdom unto itself, and one could have spent many happy days exploring this area alone, never mind the rest of Taiwan, or even the rest of Nantou County. The more I travelled in Taiwan, the bigger it seemed to get.

MY PLAN, as formulated at the Sun Moon Lake, was to climb Yushan, or Jade Mountain. The mountain, a part of the marvellously green Central Mountain Range, was now within easy travelling range — and although not originally on my Trip Two itinerary, I suddenly got the urge to go there again. Camera accounted for; I returned my attention to planning for this hike. Browsing through some maps, I noticed that the Yushan National Park Headquarters was located in Shueili, a town not far from the Sun Moon Lake in Shueili District, Nantou County. I knew I would be able to directly apply at the Park headquarters for a permit to climb Jade Mountain — at 3,952 metres in elevation, the highest land point east of the Himalaya. I had climbed Yushan before with friends and thought it would be interesting to do it solo this time.

Climbing Yushan in the first instance involves navigating Taiwan's national parks bureaucracy. Arriving in the town of Shueili on a bus from Shueishe, I made straight for the park offices, which were quite easy to find. The multi-floor office complex had an abundance of departments, and it took me a while to find the right place to apply for a hiking permit — the permit is necessary as the park authorities seek to limit the number of people entering the park area at any one time. Not used to foreigners turning up out of the blue, the park officers were quite solicitous to me, and we got through all the preliminary paperwork painlessly. When one of the officers heard me speaking Chinese, he gave me a set of nice hiking maps for free; only to be outdone by a colleague, who then gave me a Yushan National Park guide book, which was amazingly generous of her. The moment arrived for us to fix a date for my entry into the park. One major drawback of the national-park application procedure is that permits are only issued seven to 28 days in advance. I was offered a date five days or nine days hence. Thinking I might do some warm-up hiking in advance, I accepted the later date. In retrospect, that was a mistake. The weather had been good, and I should have plumbed for an earlier start.

The Yushan National Park includes within it the sources of three river systems: the Chuoshuei source system, covering 20,810 hectares; the Laonong system, covering 41,440 hectares; and the Siougulan system, spread over a further 43,240 hectares. The park was a big place in other words, but I was actually going to visit only one small part of it. The climbing permit in the bag, I travelled out of Shueili by bus heading directly south on a branch of Route 21 that went all the way to the mountain hot-spring resort area of Dongpu. The ride took me in the general direction of Yushan along the Chenyoulan River valley through the western extremity of Nantou's Sinyi District. Not for the last time I observed first-hand the powerful effects of highly active erosion on the middle and upper reaches of a Taiwan river valley, and also the results of active orogeny in the exposed stratified and buckled lines of sedimentary rocks visible on the steep valley sides. After a 50-kilometre ride, we arrived at Dongpu.

Dongpu is a crossroads in the mountains. The historic Batongguan trail, a 152-kilometre-long trail hewn out of rock in the 1870s, traverses the central mountains and passes nearby. I had hiked a good part of this spectacular, but in places very dangerous, trail before. On this occasion, I was more interested in Dongpu itself and the Bunun villages in its immediate vicinity. The spring weather continued fine and I enjoyed some delightful hours hiking around the area. One highlight of my peregrinations was a giddy walk across the brand-new 201-metre-long Dongpu suspension bridge, a gravity-defying structure that seemed to hang in the air. The footbridge was built a staggering 130 metres off the ground between the main town of Dongpu and a trail leading to a Bunun village on the opposite side of the valley. Crossing the bridge I felt like I was walking on a tightrope, and I could barely look down to the stream below. The footbridge was a solid enough construction, however — another thumb up for Taiwanese civil engineering.

Invigorated by my walks around Dongpu and by the sight of ripening green plums and blooming rhododendrons, I felt ready for Yushan and left the resort. But getting to the Tatajia Saddle between Alishan and Yushan was not going to be as straightforward as I had first thought — nothing ever goes completely according to plan when travelling. According to all the maps, Route 21 went directly up to Tatajia before descending into Gaosyong County. But local people informed me that there was no regular bus service up this road, which was often closed by landslides in any case. This information combined with the fact I had some time on my hands prompted me to make a long 200 kilometre detour via Jiayi City and Jiayi County. This detour, a small adventure itself, involved travelling back to Shueili, catching a train from there to the plains town of Ersui, and then switching to an express train on the main line that ran down to Jiayi City. From Jiayi, I finally approached Yushan up the long drag of a mountain road that runs the length of Jiayi County up to the Alishan Forest Recreation Area.

On the way to Alishan, I tripped and sprained an ankle. It was the injury I feared getting and this sprain could not have happened at a worse moment. Fortunately, I managed to get some ice at a convenience store and pressed it against the ankle, which helped stem the swelling. The injury was nevertheless a real nuisance. Grinning and bearing it, I shacked up in a hotel for the night at Alishan and then survived the unfolding of a typical tourist day at the mountain resort. In the morning I rode out on the scenic railway that joins the main tourist area to a sunrise vantage point along with about 500 other people. Arriving at our destination in 15 minutes, I got out of the crowded train and hobbled about in the cold and dark on a vast concrete viewing platform, a place that had just been a patch of dirt ground when I first came here in the 1980s. Everyone waited expectantly for the sun to rise, hoping for the famous "sea of clouds" view that gave one the feeling of being in heaven. But some people just couldn't wait. A tour guide gave the assembled crowd a running commentary through a megaphone, and there was no avoiding his banal drivel. "Yes, yes, that's right: in only 20 minutes the sun will rise. Amazing; grand; awe-inspiring… only 19 minutes to go now…" I was wondering why people were taking photos of the dark sky when suddenly the first spears of sunlight burst over a distant peak. Alas, the photogenic sea-of-clouds view we hoped for did not quite materialize, the sun quickly disappearing behind altostratus clouds far above our heads. And that was the end of that. The huge crowd of tourists quickly disappeared, and I limped back through the forest to the hotel, where I rested my ankle and tried to psyche myself up for the Yushan hike.

YUSHAN IS one of the most beautiful mountains on earth. The distinctive peak of slate and limestone shines in splendid isolation at the southern end of Taiwan's majestic Central Mountain Range. It has been noted that Yushan is the highest peak in all of East Asia, higher than Mount Fuji in Japan by a margin of 200 metres. But it is the richness of its flora and fauna, the variations in climate zones ranging from subtropical to frigid, and the indigenous cultural backdrop that make Yushan so very special to Taiwanese people and to the East Asia hiking fraternity. I had done my first hike up Yushan in 1999 with an ad hoc climbing association group on a pre-planned trip. Back in those days, joining a group with a qualified guide was mandatory, and this arrangement made a lot of sense in terms of safety and economy. That trip had given me a chance to familiarize myself with the main tourist route up the mountain. Luckily, the March weather had been dry and sunny, and the hike was a relatively easy hike along a beautiful trail some eight kilometres in length. It was this memorable experience that I now sought to relive.

From Alishan, the highway extended 30 kilometres and climbed a further 600 metres in altitude before reaching the Tatajia Ridge. Only chartered buses plied the Alishan-Tatajia segment of the highway. After asking around at Alishan, it became obvious that the only way for me to get to Tatajia would be to hitch a ride. As I stood admiring the tall fir trees standing on the slopes just outside the resort, a family saloon pulled up and offered me a ride to Tatajia. The occupants of the car, a family hailing from Luban in Jiayi County, were very nice. Their infant had just vomited inside the car, but what did that matter? We ascended almost imperceptibly up the long and winding road that cut its way through the Yushan cypress belt. Though most of the cypresses, sadly, had long been cut down, a rich mixture of conifers, spruce and deciduous trees had taken their place, and the ride was gloriously scenic.

At the Tatajia Visitor Centre I got out of the car, said goodbye to the family, and moved off into a thick mountain mist. In the centre I picked up some literature, but the most interesting thing in the centre, actually, was the rather impressive stuffed Formosan Black Bear standing up in a corner of the lobby. The Formosan Black Bear, a member of the Asiatic black bear family, is an endangered species, and this was as close as I was ever likely to get to one of the massive creatures. The stuffed specimen, sporting the distinctive white V-stripe on its chest and owning a superb set of teeth, looked absolutely magnificent. I felt sorry that these bears had become endangered because of some dubious Chinese medicinal theories. On the other hand, a bear-free hike would suit me just fine. What I really wanted to know — and the reason I dropped by the centre — was where I could camp the night. "No camping", I was bluntly informed by a park official. No camping? It seemed ridiculous — I had just come along 30 kilometres of completely empty road, and it would have been a small thing to have built a campsite somewhere. But campsites in Taiwan are poorly managed where they are managed at all and are thus associated in the minds of bureaucratic busybodies with noise and trash. The official at the centre recommended a hostel at a hamlet a little further back on the highway. In the end I spent the night at Shangdongpu not far from the centre.

The forest air at Shangdongpu at an altitude of 2,580 metres was sweet and clean; the location was remote. No one was there when I turned up. It was Sunday though, and later many tourists started to arrive. Some of these people set up temporary camps in empty car parking spaces, whilst others just stopped to enjoy a picnic on the scattered tables and benches. Where on earth had all these people come from? From Alishan, one assumed. Camping in or next to the car park suddenly did not seem like such a good idea, and therefore I set up camp on a patch of flat land a little distance from the highway. Another park official of some kind, who had spotted me from his vehicle, stopped and told me I couldn't camp on national park land. When I gently remonstrated with him something along the lines of "does it really matter", he became angry and by way of making some point he felt relevant to the situation shouted, "This is not America!" To placate the tiresome fellow I told him I would leave, and then crawled back into my tent to take a nap. A car drove up 30 minutes later. I thought it was the park official, or the police. But then three, no four... five... an incredible *ten* four-wheel-drive vehicles rode in quick succession into the tiny clearing where I was camping. It was so weird to be suddenly engulfed by this mechanized column. The cars belonged to a driving club of some kind, out on a jaunt, and they had been given permission to camp on this spot for the night! In no time, the club had a marquee set up and started cooking up a banquet; kids played nosily whilst the adults put up tents to sleep in. I just kept smiling.

At daybreak I removed my ear plugs and quietly broke camp whilst the four-wheeler crowd were still sleeping. I then made my way up to the trail check-in office — the first hiker to hand in their papers that morning — and left a few of my things there to lighten my load a little. Quickly getting underway, I walked the 2.8 kilometres to the 2,610metre-high Tatajia Saddle, the point where the Alishan Mountain Range meets the Yushan Mountain Range. As I walked up to the trailhead, small groups of hikers drove past in two national park shuttle mini buses. They were missing a nice walk, but I would soon suffer for having put in this extra mileage. The giant 3,000-metre-plus peaks of the Yushan Mountain Range were clearly visible from Tatajia. A new access road of some kind had been built on the other side of the saddle, though there was no traffic on it. Finally, after what seemed to have been a long build up, I started walking up the Yushan trail which followed the side of an exposed mountain slope. The sudden thrust into the wild left my brain whirring frantically; the lack of the usual urban prompts and noises caused it to go into remapping overdrive. Readjustment over and senses duly heightened, I proceeded with confidence. I watched my step, however, as I feared a sudden collapse of my dodgy foot on uneven ground. A time flowchart on the back of my map indicated that it would take around three hours and 45 minutes to reach the Baiyun Hut, a distance of only eight and a half kilometres. Although the hike was non-technical, it was far from an easy walk; I had to climb a staggering one kilometre in elevation in a relatively short distance, an average of 117 metres up for every one kilometre hiked.

The path emerged out onto a ridge that afforded clear views of the lowlands and Yushan's satellite peaks. The mountain slopes of the valley below were carpeted with hemlock and firs, a kind of dense Braille telling stories to those who could read it. This forest is one of the last refuges of Taiwan's dwindling species of endemic mammals, including the mighty black bears. Below the forest the bluish lowlands stretched far into the distance. In the opposite direction majestic evergreen oaks and stands of the dwarf-like Yushan bamboo stood next to one another, the trees shading the path. I continued on my way like Hänsel without Gretel. Every now and again the trail became abruptly elevated; staircases and step ladders helped me with yet another ten metres up. Fortuitously Yushan's famous wild rhododendrons were in bloom, adding pleasing splashes of white and light pink along the green trail. I stopped here and there to take photos of scenes along the way and to rest my rapidly wearying muscles. Half-kilometre distance markers went by slowly, emphasizing my sluggish progress. But the ever-changing views and the need to stay alert acted as a sufficient diversion from the aches and pains. At least 60 hikers passed by me as they made their way down the mountain, some of them generously tossing a few words of encouragement my way. The hikers were mostly young Taiwanese people, but some older people and one or two adolescents counted among their number. Higher up the trail, the evergreen oaks gave way to Taiwan firs and Chinese hemlock, tough trees that could survive the harsh high-altitude winter climate. Nestled in among the trees, some footbridges and staircases made of robust tubular steel further eased the way. Near to the main hut, the trail narrowed and hugged a steep rock face. I concentrated on my footwork here, for any collapse of my ankle might have had catastrophic conse-quences: even if one survived a fall down the slope it would not have been possible to climb back up to the path unassisted. The tricky part of the trail behind me, I arrived at the Baiyun Lodge a full five hours after departing from the police station. On a beautiful, warm spring day the hike had been superb, if a bit tiring.

A party mood pervaded the lodge as gaggles of hikers cooked hearty meals and drank rice wine. The small lodge had a full complement of around 60 people. A couple of dozen people camped outdoors whilst the others slept like sardines in the sturdy mountain hut. Most people thought I was barmy to hike alone, but I cherished my independence. There were a group of Koreans at the lodge that had just completed a round of all Yushan's satellite peaks; they looked remarkably unfazed by the rigour of that exercise. I felt respect for a middle-aged Korean man as I watched him bath his feet in ice cold mountain water overflowing from the lodge's water tank, something I could not be bothered to do. Eventually, I found a young Canadian to have a heart to heart with. "Is this your first time here?" I asked him. "Yeah, and probably my last man; did you see how dangerous that path was!" The paunchy overseas student had a guileless manner. He complained about the weight of his pack and about the general lack of safety on the trail. I could certainly empathize with him over the backpack issue, but there was no way I could have got the weight of mine down without compromising my self-sufficiency. The Canadian was a keen amateur photographer, and we had a chat about cameras as we watched dusk settle in over the valley below. "See you at the summit", were his last words to me, almost a challenge. Darkness soon fell on the mountain and it suddenly turned cold.

Huddled in my tent and wrapped up in all my clothes, a sleeping bag and a space blanket, I suffered a sleepless night. The weather had taken a turn for the worse and the wind was blowing strongly outside, so strongly in fact that at 5.00, when I walked out into a murky soup of a morning, nearly all of the tents — unbeknown to their owners who were already on their way to the mountaintop — had blown down. I put some heavy stones on these tents to stop them from disappearing over the edge of the slope. My sturdy little mountain tent had stood the test of the wind very well, the aerodynamic tent ridgeline sticking up proudly like a dinosaur's vertebrae. After anchoring my neighbours' collapsed tents, I dived into the lodge and scrounged some hot water to make tea. Groups of hikers wrapped up in warm jackets, gloves and balaclavas stood about waiting to set off for the summit. They would use flashlights to find the way through the woods in the predawn dark and then scramble up the alpine zone above the tree line. The last section involved ascending a steep rocky path with the aid of chains put in place to help hikers on their way. I suppose I could have tagged along with one of the small groups, but I decided to give it a miss. The cold did not worry me, but the poor visibility meant there would be no views to enjoy at the summit; and the strain of summiting and then walking all the way back down to the Tatajia Saddle in one shot may have been asking too much of my recently sprained ankle. Surprisingly, given the rather dangerous gusting winds, I was the only one to opt out of going to the top of the mountain that morning.

With no regrets, I ate the last of my pasta and then broke camp. After I left the lodge, the poor weather worsened and the rain intensified. Even though I was wearing gumboots and waterproofs, I started to get wet. During the descent, I met a group of Japanese hikers trudging up the mountain in single file. They were all wearing the same, but different-coloured, water-proof suits. "We are 14-people group", announced their guide, a man in orange, by way of introducing the collective entity that was snaking up the path. "I am one-people group", I replied. He asked me about the weather and I remarked that it might improve the next day. After this brief exchange we waved goodbye to one another, my yellow rubber kitchen gloves and sky-blue scooter cape making me something of a sartorial curiosity to the smartly attired Japanese. The last couple of kilo-metres of the hike down the mountain were interminable. The rain did not let up for one minute. Along the final section of the trail on the exposed slope the wind kicked up viciously from around the saddle below. Struggling along I was startled by a small rock that fell and bounced off my head. This happened as I was crossing a landslide pathway and prompted me to run lest the fragment were the harbinger of a major rock fall. Finally, exhausted and drenched, I emerged from the trail onto the access road. A national park shuttle mini bus was waiting there, and I gratefully clambered into it. Storm-like winds buffeted the stationary bus. After waiting a short while to pick up some more returning hikers, the bus drove away from the exposed saddle back to the visitor centre, an oasis of dryness on a very wet mountain. Later in the day I hitched back to Alishan and from there caught a bus back to Jiayi.

As Taiwan's cities go, Jiayi is relatively small despite a vast hinterland that extends all the way to Alishan; its roads are wide, the cityscape low-rise. But I felt alienated there. The weather had suddenly changed again, and in the south it was hot, the city's concrete buildings acting to intensify the heat. Typical of Chinese cities, there was not much civic life in Jiayi; it was one big mush of commercial and retail outlets. Even at the local park, a quite pleasant subtropical space, one could not quite escape the anxiety that radiated from alert, defensive-looking people. Slower-paced than Taibei, the southern city was nonetheless starting to catch the drive-fast sickness prevalent in the northern capital. I walked around Jiayi by night and cycled through it by day, but did not succeed in making any meaningful social contact with anyone.

One place I wanted to visit before leaving Jiayi was the "228 Museum" dedicated to the memory of the victims of Taiwan's 228 Incident, located near the downtown area. The 228 Incident began on 28 February 1947. On that day a fracas between Chinese nationalist anti-smuggling police and a Hoklo Taiwanese woman selling contraband on the streets of Taibei turned nasty. Shots were fired and an onlooker subsequently died of gunshot wounds. The incident sparked civil unrest throughout Taiwan and encouraged Taiwan's native political elite to assert their rights vis-à-vis the high-handed Chinese nationalists who had taken control of the island after Japan's defeat. Before 1895, Taiwan had been a part of China's Fujian province, hence China's legitimate claim to the island, but 50 years of colonialism had put some distance between China and Taiwan. By 1947 tensions between the nationalists and the locals had reached boiling point. The civil disorder was not an organized rebellion, but the Chinese nationalists, already engaged in a no-holds-barred civil war against the communists in mainland China, felt threatened enough by it to send a substantial military force to Taiwan with orders to use force to suppress the unrest. Those troops proved to be undisciplined and badly led, and what followed was an unconscionable massacre of innocents. At first the shooting was sporadic and random, but then Taiwan's political elite were targeted, and many people, including doctors, teachers and writers, were executed. The final death toll has never been authoritatively established, but 8,000 is one conservative estimate. After this brutal suppression, the Chinese nationalist government hushed up any mention of what had happened until 1987, when martial law was lifted on Taiwan and finally an open discussion about what had happened became possible. Jiayi was one of the bloodspots of the 228 Incident, and I was keen to see what the museum had to say about it, but the place was closed for a holiday when I went there, leaving me not much to do in the city.

THE TSOU NATION once ranged over a large area on the mountains of southwest Taiwan. Their traditional hunting culture was similar to that of Taiwan's other 20 or so indigenous nations, but their language, social system and customs were distinct. Unique among the Taiwanese indigenous nations, the Tsou were noted for their production of leather goods and clothes. Today the

Tsou, whose images adorn Alishan souvenir mugs and tea tins, are struggling to keep their old customs alive. A couple of pictures on the walls at Dabang, a village in the hills of Jiayi County I visited on a day trip out of Jiayi, perfectly illustrated the problem. The first picture depicted a traditional Tsou hunter slaying a bear with a long sword. This picture obviously celebrated hunting and was meant to instil ethnic pride in the village children, who walked past it every day on the way to the school. But just around the corner, the Forest Bureau had put up a sign depicting Taiwan's endangered mammals with a reminder not to hunt big animals lest the fauna disappeared forever. Children pick up on contradictions very quickly, and I wondered how "ethnic" the Dabang kids really felt. I also wondered whether I would ever get to experience a hunting trip in Taiwan myself.

Many of Dabang's residents lived and worked elsewhere, but I met a few Tsou people down by the village *kuba*, the traditional large tortoiseshell-shaped grass-thatch hut where clans gathered. These friendly folk had jobs on farms and had just come back from picking spring tea when I met them. They told me that many in the tribe still owned land and that they worked on each other's farms. Over at Tefuye, a village on the north side of the Alishan main road, things were a bit livelier and there were more people and more tourists around. I went there for the ride the same day but did not speak to anyone in the village, which on closer inspection seemed to be in decline. Both Dabang and Tefuye were predominately made up of one- and two-storey houses built with modern materials, and I did not even see a kuba at Tefuye, though there must have been one there somewhere. What impressed me most about Tefuye was the beauty of the valley below and of the lateral mountain road that led to the village. There had been landslides in the area recently, and in places the valley sides were stripped of vegetation, but mostly the valley was green and covered with a really beautiful mixed forest.

After leaving Dabang, I went to Laiji, the most northerly Tsou village located on the upper reaches of the Alishan River valley.

The journey involved hitchhiking from along a mountain road that crossed the wide slopes of Alishan. From Shihjhou, I started walking along this mountain road and enjoyed the stunning panoramic views of the Jiayi plain below, a different world it seemed from this high vantage point. The immediate landscape was dotted with farms and secondary forest that glinted in the bright sunlight. After walking for an hour or so along the road, I got a ride with a local road-construction worker, who took me as far as Fencihu, a small tourist town on the Alishan forestry railway line, where I resumed my walk. Just as I was getting tired of hiking, a Tsou man came along in a pickup truck and offered me a ride all the way to Laiji, which was his home village. I jumped in the back of the truck, ideally positioned for the scenic ride through the tea fields of Taihe and the Alishan River valley. As we crossed over into the valley, the table-shaped Tashan Mountain came into view — a massive, imposing presence.

The Tsou man dropped me off at a lodge in Laiji. Aaron, a short, straight-backed man with a firm handshake, welcomed me to his lodge and home. We sat in the communal outdoor yard under a roof wellcovered from the elements. The place felt like a country homestead, which is exactly what it was. I was tired after the long journey there but soon revived over a cup of tea and a pleasant talk with Aaron, who told me Westerners often stayed at his place on the weekend. Indeed he became quite talkative and immediately set about telling me something about the history of the Tsou people. He informed me that the Tsou originally lived on the plain in Tainan County, migrating to the Alishan area a few hundred years ago. He also told me of the continual struggle of the Tsou people to maintain their land rights, which had been increasingly impinged upon by Hoklo farmers over the years. Sometimes the Chinese would make deals with the Tsou buying their land on the cheap — "for a mess of pottage", as Hancock put it. On one occasion though, the Chinese poisoned the Tsou's water supply, killing a large number of people in one tribe overnight. This black page in the history of Chinese-indigenous relations is not mentioned in Taiwan's school textbooks. "We also dislike the Chinese", said Aaron — who had obviously listened to the whinging of a few Westerners on the subject and had assumed that I would have similar prejudices — "because they are vulgar and greedy: they stole our lands". We then got onto the subject of mountain hiking, Aaron being an enthusiast, as photographs on the wall of the lodge of him guiding rock climbers testified.

The sad case of Reuben Tchernegovski, a New Zealander who came to Taiwan in 1998 with a view to doing some solo hiking in the Alishan area, came up in our conversation. Unfamiliar with the rugged terrain and no doubt putting misplaced faith in a map, Reuben had tried to hike the overland trail from Alishan to Tashan. He was last seen on 24 November and then went missing. Emergency searches for him drew a blank. His father, Phil Tchernegovski, came to Taiwan to help rally search efforts until early the following year. He stayed at the Tashan Lodge several times in subsequent years, but no sign of Reuben was ever found. Talking to Aaron, we surmised that the intrepid New Zealander had not been equipped for a night out, and this may have prompted him to hike in the dark, which is really not a good idea in the best of circumstances and could have been fatal on a trail that had sheer drops along it. At the time Reuben went missing it had been raining over Alishan and the rain would have made the going all the more treacherous. Basically Reuben, who was not an idiot, had been unlucky and had paid the ultimate price for daring to do something adventurous. The talk about Reuben put me off the rock climbing that Aaron proposed we do. I was still getting over the shock of a rock bouncing off my head on the Yushan trail after all, and was in no mood for risk-taking.

The Laiji valley, a boulder-strewn environment with an abundance of wildlife and wild flowers, was astoundingly pretty. The few houses of the village stood on terraces of flat land that had been hacked out of the sides of the high mountain valley. Other valleys further north were more dramatically eroded. One of them was littered with boulders the size of trucks: it must have taken quite an earthquake to have loosed such rocks and sent them rolling into the middle of the river bed. Suspension bridges, vertical rock faces, rock-strewn valley floors and dense subtropical foliage added to the mystique cast by Tashan over Laiji and the nearby area. The sunny weather had given way to clouds and afternoon thunder showers: it looked suspiciously like the beginning of the "plum rain" season. But Laiji was so nice and quiet, and my room so simple and cosy, that I found it hard to pull myself away. The village, isolated and difficult to get to, had a real charm to it; the valley with all its nooks and crannies and ever changing topography was something wonderful to behold. One could never get bored in such a place. In addition, I had made friends with Aaron and his wife and children, and the food served up at the guesthouse was good. All good things come to an end though, and after two days I left the mountain valley and returned Jiayi to end my trip.

As good luck would have it, I got a ride with Peter, a Tsou elder, on the morning of my departure. He was headed to Jiayi to do some volunteer teaching at a high school and to handle some other business. As we slowly drove down the mountain in Peter's car, the Tsou man told me his life story. He had grown up on the mountain but had gone to school in Taichung. His school days were gruelling, and he had suffered discrimination on account of his racial background — his classmates called him "killer", a common taunt sometimes used by Taiwanese kids to tease indigenous children. But Peter, a Catholic and a diligent student, did well enough at school to be offered a government job in Jiayi County, where he worked as a low-level official for 30 years before retiring. He now spent his time informally promoting Tsou culture, especially its music and songs. The killer reference prompted me to ask for Peter's take on head-hunting. "Oh there were rules. Not any head could be taken. The Tsou did not take the heads of Chinese because those heads were not considered to be clean", remarked Peter, a pony-tailed grandfather. Driving out of the valley, Peter gave me an introduction to Tashan, explaining that this mountain was where the souls of the dead were thought to reside. Time flew by as we talked about all this and about Peter's passion for dancing, music and language. After arriving in Jiayi Peter still had some time before taking his class and asked me what we should do. I suggested visiting the 228 Museum and he agreed to take me there. This time the museum was open.

There is a paucity of good-quality information about Taiwan's 228 Incident: much of the evidence of the criminal executions has long been destroyed. But the 228 Museum in Jiayi had assembled photographs of some of the local victims along with background information on their cases. The photographs typically showed mature, respectable men sitting with dignity for standard portrait shots. Men like Wu Shi Shuei, a shoemaker and neighbourhood representative who was held responsible for not disarming the local citizenry with sufficient alacrity. He was picked up by nationalist soldiers on 23 March 1947, and shortly thereafter executed together with ten other people without due process at Jiayi Railway Station. A plaque hanging in the museum with about 180 names written in Chinese gave some indication of the extent of the massacre in Jiayi alone. How did all these people come to be executed? "The 228 Incident was very complicated. One of my brothers was involved. Some people fought back against the nationalist soldiers, but afterwards the nationalists rounded up and killed a lot of Taiwan's elite", Peter explained. We carried on looking at the photographs and reading the inscriptions for a while and then left the museum. Peter dropped me off at the railway station before heading off to his class and, after we exchanged information, I said goodbye to this friendly grey-bearded uncle who had climbed Yushan more than 50 times in his life.

4

TRIP THREE: TAROKO GORGE AND THE HIGH MOUNTAINS

TAIWAN IS A MOUNTAINOUS COUNTRY. ON A COLOUR-CODED satellite photograph, the bulk of it shows up as green folds, and only to the west is there any significant amount of brown that represents agricultural fields. Almost three-fourths of Taiwan is classified as slope land (land over 100 meters in elevation and over five percent slope). The mountains are part of a fault block that runs roughly from northeast to southwest, forming three distinct mountain ranges with over 200 peaks more than 3,000 metres in height. In his book *The Treaty Ports of China and Japan* published in 1867, Fred Myers chose to foreground the island's topography in his description of Formosa by noting that "The bold outline of the Formosan mountain-ranges can plainly be seen on a clear day from the Chinese mainland". Hugh Ritchie, writing in *The Chinese Recorder and Missionary Journal* a decade later, describes the view of these mountains from Takao — present day Gaosyong City in southwest Taiwan — "Several of the mountains are over 12,000 feet in height, and the whole range from east of Takao for 100 miles to the north must stand at near 11,000 feet. In January, 1874, this whole extent was covered by snow..."

Myers and Ritchie noted what to them was quite obvious. But in modern-day Taiwan it is possible to live and work for years in the city without having any conscious relationship with the high mountains of the interior. Indeed, many expatriates and locals lead exactly such citycentred lives, only occasionally making a foray by car or scooter along mountain roads. It seems incredible to me now, but for the first year I lived in Taiwan, in Tainan City, I was not even aware of Taiwan's mountains — so sheltered was my life and so limited the view from the modern, haze-shrouded city. It was only later, when starting to explore Taiwan in a more systematic way, that I appreciated the fact that the island is geographically and culturally dominated by its mountains. The grand tour therefore gave me the ideal opportunity to do some long-planned solo hiking. My hike up Yushan on Trip Two had been the warm up, and now I turned my attention to the mountains of the north.

For Trip Three, a return hike up Snow Mountain, one of my favourite places in Taiwan, naturally suggested itself. I also wanted to climb Nanhudashan, the highest mountain in Taroko National Park, and a hike recommended to me several times. The starting points for these hikes were conveniently nearby each other, but I needed to apply for hiking permits from two separate park headquarters. During what ended up being a two-week break in Taibei, I made a journey to the Syueba National Park headquarters in rural Miaoli County for the Snow Mountain permit. It was quite a long way to go to get a piece of paper, and the headquarters was not easily accessible by public transport, but I eventually got there and got the permit. The paperwork for Nanhudashan would have to be handled later at the Taroko Park Headquarters located on Taiwan's east coast.

WELL-RESTED, I was alert on the train ride down the northeast coast. The smooth and pleasant journey to the eastern city of Hualien on a comfortable train had taken two hours and forty-eight minutes for a ticket price of only US$14.50 — if Taiwan's hotels could match that kind of value for money the island would undoubtedly attract a vast number of backpackers. Hualien Station had been give a bit of a facelift since my last visit. Tourist photographs of local scenic spots adorned the walls of the station's underground walkways — part of the new consumerism. I walked outside to get my bearings. At that moment a flight of ROC air-force jets flew by overhead, a reassuring sight that added to the general feeling of vitality around the busy transportation hub. I got into the queue for the bus to Taroko Gorge.

The bus soon arrived and a short jaunt got us to the entrance to the canyon, a 19-kilometre-long wonder of nature which had steep but negotiable cliffs — little did I know when arriving at Taroko Village around midday that I would climb almost 1,000 metres up one side of this canyon before the day was over. My immediate concern on arrival was to get orientated and to arrange a mountain permit for Nanhudashan, the great mountain found at the north-western extremity of Taroko Park. I therefore walked through the village, crossed a bridge over the Liwu River, and hiked up to the visitor centre. It was noticeable that the centre had been designed not for the convenience of hikers, but for the convenience of those driving cars and buses, and I found this annoying. However, I did very much like the stone sculpture of a Taroko Atayal hunter kneeling beside his hunting dog which stood in the road near the entrance to the visitor centre. The statue was simple but powerful; a reminder of the type of culture we all evolved from and to which our descendents may someday return.

At the centre I set about applying for the climbing permit. I found the relevant department tucked away in a basement of an annex building. They were not expecting me as most applications are done online these days. When I told them what I wanted to do, it took them some time to absorb the information: a lone foreigner applying for a climbing permit was not the standard application. Hikers do actually die on this mountain sometimes, so some kind of circumspection was of course in order, but I felt I knew what I was doing and I wanted a permit.

"But have you ever done any hiking in Taiwan's mountains before", asked a female park ranger, who took the lead in trying to deny me what I wanted.

"Yes", and I smiled as I said it. She replied, "But why don't you apply through a hiking association, and hike with a group". This was so typical: my individual rights getting lumped together with group rights. I said, "No. I want to hike alone. Of course I can do it, why not?" We went back and forth like this for a while. She did not have my interests at heart; she was merely concerned to prevent getting blamed for anything untoward that might happen to me, and I could see all this from her point of view instantly. The situation called for patience and tact. I stared at the wall, sighed, and dug in. Eventually, when they saw I was not going to go away, the rangers relented and agreed to issue me a permit. We set about filling out the paperwork, a task that somehow managed to take a couple of hours. During this time I became friends with the staff in the office, and they were soon offering me cups of tea. One ranger had recently climbed Nanhudashan, and he showed some photos of the trail, which was valuable intelligence. Finally, the lady ranger handed me my copies of the paperwork, approved and stamped, as though she was doing me some kind of personal favour. I left the office exhausted, but happy. Everything was now set, and the trail entry and exit dates ran in a nice sequence with a one-day rest in between the first two hikes, and a two-day rest between the second and third hikes.

The visitor centre had a café and I sipped a soda there whilst wondering what to do next. I could see right away that there was nowhere to camp discreetly in the immediate area, and this suggested a short hike somewhere to find a place. Studying a map of the gorge, I noticed a trail marked in yellow, meaning it was a "Class 3" trail — Class 1 trails being easy and Class 5 the most demanding, according to the map's key. The yellow trail went directly up the side of the gorge and then along a mountain ridge to a couple of villages that had the typically Chinese-sounding names of Dali and Datong. I thought I would give this trail a go and set out to find the trailhead, carrying my full kit of two backpacks and the walking pole. It was four o'clock on a pleasant, warm sunny afternoon in the gorge.

The trailhead was easy enough to find. A few steps brought me onto a raised wooden walkway that joined a dirt footpath. The footpath in turn connected to a staircase that led up into a thick mixed forest. Walking up hundreds of steps with well over 20 kilograms of gear distributed about my body made for a very strenuous aerobic workout, and I quickly worked up a good sweat. On the way up the staircase, I met a king rat snake, a common non-poisonous species of serpent found in Taiwan, China and Vietnam. It lay across an exposed branch next to the walkway, indolent and fat with some just-consumed prey lodged within its length. Knowing it to be unthreatening, I took some photos and then moved on. After about an hour of solid staircase walking, the forest started to thin out as Taroko and the Liwu River Estuary came into view below me. On the other side of the gorge, I could make out a stone quarry of some kind. Westwards up the valley, steep green slopes hemmed in a calm and narrow waterway, the Liwu River.

The staircase had a couple of rest platforms built into it. At one of these platforms a placard with a sketch done in sepia of five anticolonial era Taroko warriors had been placed, a simple memorial. What battle had these men fought and how they died remained unknown to me, but surely they had fought back against their oppressors tenaciously, and it made me sad to think of their doomed struggle. Beyond this placard the staircase continued up the side of the gorge like the stairway to heaven. Eventually it ended at a fork in the path and I was left pondering which way led to Dali. The fact there was no finger sign at the fork was encouraging: obviously this was not going to be a tourist-trap type of place. But which way should I go? I turned left and kept on going up the mountain, hiking for another hour or so. Then the light started to dim and I was obliged to find a place to camp. A water pipe by the trail provided me with fresh water, and with no further ado I set up my tent on the path nearby.

Darkness fell as I prepared a meal under the tent's rain flysheet and sipped a cup of tea. Noises of cars and people travelled up from the gorge below; from the quarry opposite, diggers clanked and rumbled; nearby in the forest, frogs croaked. After a short while an old uncle carrying a small haversack and leaning on a walking stick came climbing up the path like one of the Seven Dwarfs. A resident of Dali he naturally stopped to talk to me and told me the village was only 30 minutes away but that Datong was a further couple of hours hike from there. It was good to get this first-hand information. Uncle had to be getting along as it was raining, and I apologized to him for blocking the driveway; he then disappeared into the night. I wondered how often he made this journey. Surely not every day: it was a really strenuous walk up the gorge, even for a reasonably fit young person, never mind a senior citizen.

The walk up to Dali the next day was immediately taxing, but the top of the gorge was not far away. It was a relief to get onto flat ground again. I passed by a small meteorological station and some old winding gear — which was evidently still in use — and then arrived at a farmstead. Next to an outbuilding a tethered dog barked ferociously, so someone had to be around, I reasoned. I could hear the voices of people working nearby, but there was no one within sight of the farm. At this exact moment it began raining again, but more heavily than the previous evening. I donned my gumboots and rain gear, placed a rain cover over the backpack, gritted my teeth, and started walking in what I supposed to be the direction of Datong. On the way I finally bumped into a farmer who did not bother wearing a raincoat. The man was a Taroko Atayal, and he told me that Dali and Datong were both small villages with few people living in them, something I had surmised by now. He further informed that there was no road up the gorge and that these villages were accessible only on foot. A paved road did exist, however, between Dali and Datong.

The road followed the top of the mountain northwards, away from the main gorge and in parallel with the Shakatang River valley. But all I could see around me from the road was forest. The hike was sort of fun at first, and I enjoyed the feeling of being on top of this isolated mountain with the convenience of an empty and gently undulating road to walk on. Then the rain really kicked in accompanied by thunder and lightning. The gear in my backpacks remained dry as I had taken the precaution to pack everything in plastic bags, but water travelled through the seams of my raincoat and into my boots, turning the hike into a wet, squelching slog. A small patch of ground under an over-hanging rock face was the only bit of dry dirt anywhere, and I stopped there for a while to rest. Another farmer on his way to Dali came by in a motorized wagon and waved to me cheerily, but he was headed in the wrong direction from my point of view. The rain did not let up for one second. I liked the rain but did not like walking in wet boots. A second wagon came along the road, this one sliding off the wet concrete into a rut before my eyes. The farmer, an old Chinese man, dug himself out with a little assistance from me and managed to get going again. He was also headed to Dali though, so I was obliged to continue on foot in the pouring rain. After a long walk I bumped into two farm workers who were napping under a plastic sheet in the back of their small wagon. One of them acknowledged me as I hailed him, casting a sleepy but sympathetic eye on this wet and wandering soul. He told me Datong was just down the road. I thanked him and carried on my sodden way.

As reported, Datong was not much bigger than Dali, basically a few scattered farmsteads and one or two small garbage dumps. The rain eased a little just in time for my arrival at the first farmstead, which stood a short distance down a side path. Here I spotted a man at an outbuilding and waved to him. The man pointed to one of the farm buildings as though to tell me to wait for him there. At this building, a hut, I was greeted by two raging dogs, another man and a woman. The trim middle-aged man was dressed like an urban dweller. I introduced myself to him: I was on a little sally up the gorge, and blast wasn't the rain a nuisance? Takali invited me to sit next to a stove fire set up outside his family's modest but cosy home. It was a great pleasure just to sit down, take off my rain gear, and have a chat. About half a litre of water spilled out of each of my boots as I pulled them off. The dogs quietened down as they saw their master accept me.

Takali handed me a steaming cup of tea and we got talking. I explained that I had come up to the village for the heck of it. The woman, his mother, quietly went about some domestic chores as the Truku (or Taroko Atayal) man told me that very few foreigners came this way; his last visitors had been a couple of Japanese researchers. Takali had a low opinion of the Japanese. What irked him were not the unfortunate historical associations but the fact that the two researchers had repaid his hospitality by asking if him if he would procure a young Truku girl for their pleasure. Such a request betrayed a total misunderstanding of indigenous culture — although many indigenous girls work in the Taiwan sex industry either out of economic necessity or compulsion, Taiwan's indigenous people are actually socially conservative, not least because most of them are practising Christians. I asked Takali to forgive the lascivious Japanese men, just as I was wondering whether there were any young girls at the village. But there were none. I asked Takali about the Atayal resistance, and he had a story to tell.

In the early twentieth century the Truku/Sediq had put up a stiff fight to keep their independence. Armed only with bows and arrows and employing the customary ambush technique, they maintained a stubborn resistance against encroaching Japanese police and army units. The steep-sided valleys perpendicular to the gorge favoured hit-and-run tactics; but once the Japanese got a trail built through the gorge, they were able to bring their heavy weapons to bear on Truku/Sediq villages, Takali explained as though it had all happened yesterday. From then on it was a losing battle as far as the cause of Truku/Sediq independence went. I pulled out my relief map of the gorge, and

Takali pointed out all the places where the Taroko people had once lived and where they were now concentrated. As Takali talked, the gorge came alive; one could imagine large numbers of Truku/Sediq spread out through an area that in a previous era had been a self-contained world. Originally a band of Atayal who had migrated from Nantou County, the relative isolation of the Truku/Sediq in the Taroko Gorge meant that their language had developed into a distinct dialect. Takali pointed out that this linguistic distinction combined with their proud history of resistance to pacification meant that the Truku/Sediq could not fairly be lumped together with the Atayal of northern Taiwan, and indeed the former had attained formal recognition as separate indigenous nations in 2004 and 2008 respectively.

Whilst Takali and I were talking, his mother had been busy preparing duck and ginseng soup, and this was served for lunch in the hut. Having told him I was British, Takali changed the subject of conversation: "Our government were going to buy Tornado jets from Britain, but they were found to be unreliable, so they bought American fighters instead". For someone living on the top of a mountain in a humble abode with no electricity Takali seemed remarkably well informed and worldly; no doubt he caught up on things at church down in Taroko. After nibbling on a bit of rubbery duck, I had another cup of tea before setting off back down the mountain, this time heading directly down the valley side on a trail leading to the Shakatang River. I had thought about staying the night in Datong, but there was not much to do there. Takali and I swapped addresses and I then got on my way, hoping to get back to Taroko by nightfall, something achievable according to Takali's mum. She hadn't said much, but when she did speak it was pertinent to the task at hand.

The heavy rain ceased, but the steep dirt path was very wet and I had to watch my step. For this reason, the five-kilometre walk down to the river valley through the forest took ages. It was a calming and mysterious walk though, like a stroll on a seabed; the trees of the forest swayed in the mist like giant seaweeds and it was eerily quiet. By the end of the afternoon I found myself on the valley floor hiking along a scenic riverside trail back to Taroko. Camping out seemed like it might be a good idea, but by the time I spotted some suitable ground, I had already made up my mind to get back to the village, which involved hiking a further eight kilometres in the dark. The trail was in good condition and flat, and also it was not raining, so the going was good. From what I could make of it, the Shakatang was a spectacular gorge in its own right and very clean. The air was fresh, loaded with negative ions. In places the gorge narrowed and massive boulders almost dammed the shallow river. Eventually I made it to the end of the trail and climbed an unmarked stairwell to get onto a road overhead. By the time I straggled onto the highway, I was totally zonked out, a character out of a survival movie. One or two cars passed by ignoring me but then a vehicle stopped and gave me a ride to Taroko, where I booked into a hotel for the night.

THE NEXT DAY I rested and again visited the Taroko Park Visitor Centre, where I studied maps and relief models of the gorge, carefully photographing them for later reference. The gorge had several peaks ranging from 1,000 to 2,000 metres in height on either side of it; many v-shaped valleys ran perpendicular and parallel to the Liwu River. The mountaintop I had walked along the previous day was a whole geographical microenvironment by itself, and looking at the maps, I realized how several days could have been profitably spent hiking on nearby mountains that overlooked the Pacific Ocean. Also of interest at the centre were the cast bronzes of local endemic species of mammals, such as the gem-faced civet, the pangolin — a small armadillo-like creature, the Reeve's muntjac, the flying squirrel and several others. All of these diminutive creatures were admirably adapted to the local environment. Sadly, the Formosan clouded leopard, an important animal in indigenous folklore, is now extinct. A stuffed specimen of the proud-looking cat sat in a glass case at the centre, a discomforting reminder of the world's diminishing diversity. The muntjac is a kind of small deer, once very common in the mountains, but it was hunted almost to extinction and is now a protected species. Ditto the Formosan sambar, a larger deer. Everything I saw at the centre made me want to explore the gorge further.

In the village, killing time before leaving Taroko, I hung out with a couple of girls who worked in a restaurant. Their ancestral home was on the mountaintop and they were surprised and delighted to learn I had been up to Dali and Datong. One of the Truku girls told me she only really felt comfortable on the mountain and found life on the plain oppressive in some way, an understandable sentiment: I too felt like I had been reborn free when walking on top of the gorge. Whilst we were chatting, one of the women's daughters came home from school. The young girl looked a bit forlorn and slightly awkward, and so I talked to her for a bit about school and what-not. She was shy but obviously very bright. One of the women opened a bottle of wine and offered me a drink — she was alcoholic. The other woman, the mother of the girl, also did not care to drink but took a glass under peer pressure. There was something sad about all this I felt. Soon afterwards I left the girls, resolved to get back on the road. I said goodbye to the women, put my bags on, and walked up further into the gorge.

The gorge was very engaging. For one thing, it was quiet: among other qualities, mountains are great sound absorbers. Below the road, the river — one of the very few left in its natural state in Taiwan — flowed gently. As with the Lanyang River, it surprised me that the water level was so low, given the heavy downpour of the previous day. After walking a couple of kilometres, I turned and followed a side trail that led up to a temple, one of several in the gorge area, and then followed a cliff trail to a small shrine and pavilion that overlooked the gorge road and the river. My destination for the day was Buluowan, an aboriginal tourist village another six kilometres up the schist and marble gorge, but it was not yet in view. To get there I would have to hitchhike up this mysterious valley.

Buluowan, a former Truku village, was appropriated by the state when the gorge became a national park in the 1980s. It was then turned into one of those bureaucrat-inspired phoney cultural villages so popular these days. The location, on an uplifted river meander, was actually really stunning and a natural choice to locate a village. But no one lived there now — the former residents had all been removed to make way for busloads of visitors. The tourist centre — consisting of a multi-media auditorium, a café and some stores — was shutting down when I, having got a ride up the road with a passing salesperson, arrived at around five in the afternoon. The village was pleasant but soulless without a population. The few tourists about soon left and so in the evening I had the place to myself. I set up camp in a discreet spot underneath the auditorium's entrance. For one night in front of my little stove, I lived in Buluowan.

Before the first centre staff arrived the next morning, I slipped out of the village, exiting down some stone steps behind the village. It started to drizzle. Back on the gorge road a tour bus swept past, its occupants staring at me as if I were a wild animal of some sort. Nevertheless, I enjoyed the morning's long walk up the scenic gorge. The spectacular cliffs rose above the side of the road like skyscrapers. The river, now grey with sediment, swirled around hard marble rocks that deflected its course and sent it tumbling. A stream of water entered the gorge from the side of a cream-coloured marble wall, a waterfall in the making. In other places the gorge widened and sunlight shone down, highlighting individual trees and bushes on the gorge's sides that were close and yet so out of reach. At Heliou, a rest station and another former village, I stopped for a break and bought an iced coffee in the small cafeteria there. The workers at the cafeteria were Truku, or perhaps Sediq; but the station itself was owned by the state, and my coffee cost a whopping US$3. Sitting at an outdoor table, I nursed the coffee and spent an hour perusing another map of the gorge. It seemed like Tiansiang was not far away.

Tiansiang, a well-known name on Taiwan's tourist circuit, surprised me a little: it was generally smaller and less developed than I had expected. It consisted of no more than a modest bus station, a post office, a small park station, a few family-run stores and restaurants, and, quite incongruously, a large five-star hotel. Above the road on the side of a hill stood a Catholic hostel, a Presbyterian church and a China Youth Hostel. There was some kind of a temple-monastery on another hill nearby. The sides of the gorge soared high on all sides around the intimate cluster of buildings. Some tourists, who had earlier picked me up when I was struggling, dropped me off at Tiansiang near the park station and I ate a cheap lunch there. Over the rice-chicken lunch box, I got talking to one of the park rangers about the perplexing disappearance of Fryderyk Mieszko Frontier, an American citizen.

"Have you seen Fred Frontier?", ran the poster I had seen stuck on the wall outside the Taibei American School. Together with several photographs of a healthy-looking 28-year-old man, the summary notes of the case read: "Fred arrived in Taipei on 20 May. He checked into the Hualian Tian Hsiang Catholic Hostel on 22 May 2003. He was last seen drawing money from the ATM machine of the Grand Formosa, Tian Hsiang in the morning of 23 May 2003. He was never seen or heard of again…". Fred Frontier had come to Taiwan to teach English and had a contract lined up with a franchise school. While waiting for his job training to start, Fred went to Taroko to do a bit of hiking. No one really knows what happened next. His travel backpack, wallet and camera were all later recovered, but not his passport. The camera had a photograph in it of Fred leaning on a white car somewhere in the gorge. He had no doubt hitched a ride with someone and took the picture as a memento of what for him was a novel situation. He may have made friends with the wrong kind of people; though there is no evidence of foul play, it is rather odd that all his belongings except his passport found their way back to the hostel. The most likely explanation for Fred's disappearance, however, is that he went for a walk off-trail and had a catastrophic accident that left him in a very difficult situation or killed him outright. The park ranger I quizzed in Tiansiang about the case told me he had been involved in the official search for Fred and that in his opinion it is most likely that the American had got lost and starved to death. I found it hard to believe that a strong and evidently intelligent young man with experience of the outdoors could have got lost, but who knows? In a rock fall scenario Fred's body should have been easily found, but that of course depends on where such an accident may have happened. One of the unfortunate facts of the case is that the alarm was raised late, and a proper search for Fred was not organized until well over a month after his disappearance, making his rescue statistically unlikely. Fred's mother, Barbara Klita, has been in and out of Taiwan ever since that official search ended, trying to track down her missing son; the ranger I met told me he had met her many times. Since 2003, several private searches for Fred have been made in the Taroko area, but the park is large, the terrain rugged, and nothing was found. By now, if indeed he died near a trail, Fred's body would be decomposed, covered by foliage, and hard to spot. The park ranger told me he had found a man from Hong Kong in just such a state. Hiking alone in the wilderness presents obvious dangers, and I thought long and hard about Fred's case wondering what the hell could have happened to the poor guy, but ended up as puzzled by the disappearance as everybody else.

The Catholic hostel, where Fred had stayed, was deserted when I tried to check in, so I took accommodation at the nearby Presbyterian Church instead. Using the church as my base, I did some easy hikes in the area. On the afternoon of the first day, I tried the short Baiyang Trail that joins the Liwu River valley gorge with a parallel valley via a long tunnel. The trail had been built as part of a planned hydroelectric development that was abandoned after Taroko became a national park. The entrance to the tunnel was one kilometre up the road from Tiansiang. The main path started on the far side of the tunnel where it crossed a treacherous swirling river. It could have been my imagination playing tricks, but the gorge did start to take on a slightly sinister aspect at this mid-level altitude, and the Baiyang Trail, although basically flat and easy to walk, felt very dangerous. The tributary river dropped altitude at an incredible rate so that within a kilometre or so, the level path was well above the water trace. The valley was wet, hazy, heavily foliated and wild. But what worried me were the overhanging rocks above the path on either side of several short tunnels: they looked like they would collapse at any moment. It seemed extraordinary that this unstable trail was a popular walk with day-trippers, including families with children. The trail came to a dead end on account of a disused bridge that once allowed people to cross the river and visit a distant waterfall on the other side of the valley. I was quite content to view this waterfall at a distance without risking a walk over the damaged and taped off bridge.

Back in Tiansiang, I checked out the five-star hotel, an oasis of vulgar luxury in the midst of a torrid and isolated natural environment. The hotel felt like one of those ludicrously well-appointed lodges you might find in a safari park in Kenya that cater to middle-class tastes and expectations. The restaurant and bar in the lobby looked out onto room windows, a weird design that seemed to suggest exhibitionism. At the hotel, I contrived to lose my walking pole whilst using a computer in the business centre. Despite making immediate inquiries and looking high and low, my pole was gone — somebody at the hotel evidently had sticky fingers. The walking pole was an important part of my kit, essential for serious hikes, and I had no choice but to rush back to Hualian City on a bus and hunt down a camping shop to buy a new one. This I accomplished in short order, getting back to Tiansiang late at night by chartered taxi. This expensive detour at least served to demonstrate the sharp contrast between the dry plain and the wet and, in some ways, forbidding gorge.

The church bordered a small tributary of the Liwu River.

From the rear of the church, one could observe wildlife, including fleeting glances of sambar deer, on the steep terrain opposite this powerful stream. When I told the pastor of the church, a Truku man who had lived in the gorge all his life, of my plans to hike on Nanhudashan, he got quite excited. The mountain was an old Truku hunting ground, and he told me — as if anyone needed telling — that the indigenous people loved hunting. He counselled me to hike with a companion, but I told him I would be okay, and if the rain got too bad I could always turn around, which were prophetic words in retrospect. On a rest day, I read more of *War and Peace*.

In this classic work Tolstoy alternates between well-paced narrative, folk psychology and philosophy, and the effect is usually edifying; he had a unique critical mind, and in the Second Epilogue — an essay on history sometimes lopped off in abridgements of the novel — he makes an interesting critique of bourgeois history that foregrounds the role of individuals. As a Russian, it was natural in some ways for Tolstoy to downplay Napoleon's skilful marshalling of his armies and to criticize the commonly held belief that Napoleon was some kind of military genius. I think Tolstoy is right to be sceptical though. After all, many people had Hitler marked down as a military genius until he started losing the Second World War; but Tolstoy's point is that there are always limits to what any single person can do in any given set of circumstances. Tolstoy intimates that there are laws at work in history, though he does not define what these laws are or how they work, and suggests that what transpires in any epoch cannot be explained by reference to the will of any one particular individual no matter how powerful that person may be, and in this belief he seems to anticipate Marx. As Tolstoy pithily puts it, "…modern history, like a deaf man, answers questions no one asks". Tolstoy's discussion of history and how it is created in the imaginations of historians got me thinking further about the accounts I had read of Truku history and their anticolonial struggle, and how this history had also to some extent been romanticized or partially distorted at least. The original Truku had come into the Taroko Gorge around 1200 CE, but there had been other people living there at the time. Those "original" people were undoubtedly pushed out, assimilated, or annihilated by the Truku — a process that smacks exactly of the kind of process that oppressed the Truku/Sediq in later years. Tolstoy would have understood the irony. He perceptively deconstructs history, for example, when he demolishes Thiers's interpretation of Bonaparte's fateful meeting with a Cossack before the battle of Borodino, but one wonders if Tolstoy's version of that event has any more veracity to it. As I read, the pastor busied himself with chores, such as endlessly sweeping the veranda where I was sitting, but chores I would not do on a reading day.

The Taroko Gorge had fascinated, exhausted and scared me in turn, and in the end I found it to be a rather mysterious place. The gorge keeps growing, being uplifted a few millimetres every year by highspeed orogeny. Every now and then an earthquake shudders through the deep-cut valley, sending massive rocks smashing into the rivers below, and these forbidding rocks are in turn worked on and broken down by all-powerful erosive processes. The gorge was yet another place in Taiwan where one would never feel bored, and a proper exploration of the area would keep an adventurer, or poet, happily occupied for weeks. But by the time you would have got to know the gorge well, it would have changed, and you would have changed, and the river would never be the same again.

"WAIT A MINUTE, don't film me! This won't look good..." I had ambushed Ms Wang and was taking a short video clip of her messing about behind her desk. Mandopop played on a radio as I panned the camera. "Are you really filming me?" She became slightly flustered. "Don't film me; it's dark in here and it won't look good!" I carried on filming her, our relationship close enough for me to tease her in this way. Finally, she sat down and put a piece of paper in front of her face, once again demanding I desist from filming her, at which point I stopped. After travelling up from Taroko Gorge by taking a bus from Tiansiang to Dayuling, and from there another to Lishan, a journey of over four hours in a cramped bus, I found myself once more in the Lishan Visitor Centre talking to my friend Ms Wang. She had not been overwhelmed with joy to see me again, but she kept up a very pleasant front, which was good enough and very professional of her. My filming had been a deliberate ploy to see whether she could maintain her convivial mask under a bit of pressure, and she did fine.

The visitor centre, deserted the month before, was now a hive of activity. Local school kids came in to change for a dance performance. The cultural show had been arranged long in advance and involved inviting local bigwigs and county-government officials along. Ms Wang got her revenge on me for videoing her by making me guest of honour at a table in the visitor centre, where a group of Taijhong City tourist officials were having a picnic dinner. The bureaucrats, predictably, were tiresome in the extreme. They erroneously saw me as some kind of kindred-spirit outsider. How did I think tourism could be improved in the area? Answer: I don't know, and I don't care; I'm not trying to carve a career for myself in local government. What I actually said was "hoteliers should not be so short-sighted", a vague criticism that was taken for Solomon-like wisdom by the city-government functionaries. I thought I might get stuck with the bureaucrats all night, but later managed to give them the slip and went off to watch the dance show.

On a small permanent stage opposite the old Lishan Hotel, a procession of dancers and singers performed in front of the assembled audience. Most of the dancers and audience were local Atayals. The first performers I watched were a group of aging mums who moved very nicely. They sported the red headbands and the dark blue and purple woven cloth of the Taijhong Atayals. The Lishan Atayal women went on next, dressed in the red and white costumes of their tribes. Not overexerting themselves, they danced in the easy and natural sway of the Atayal. Next up the elementary school kids put on a very spirited performance, dancing in a modernistic style and singing a Hoklo Chinese folk song, which the crowd loved. As the evening progressed so the audience grew in size to perhaps 300 people including many teenagers home for the weekend: Lishan had finally come alive. Some teenage Atayal girls, who were not falsely shy or modest, chatted freely with me. Meanwhile, the show continued with a polished performance by an Amis group, who had come down from Taibei especially for the occasion. The Amis female dance troupe — dressed in traditional red shirts, multicoloured skirts and long socks — danced in an energetic high-kicking style reminiscent of the Highland fling. The evening also hosted drama, which was narrated in the local Atayal dialect, plus some singing and the playing of a single-string harp by an Atayal man. The harp player also sang, and his voice was as gentle and divine as a choir boy's, though of course a little lower down the scale. Some singing by an elder then ended a worthy celebration of Atayal culture. That night I camped on the roof of the derelict Grand Hotel in Lishan. It remained dry during the night and I slept well in the unbounded fresh air of the mountains.

In the morning I hitched a ride to Wuling. The driver of a small, empty chartered bus picked me up and asked me many questions about my travels. He usefully got me into the state farm free of charge, the ticket price now demanded at the gate being an outrage, especially since any hikers travelling to Snow Mountain necessarily had to pass through that gate. At the Mount Snow National Park Centre just inside the farm, I got out, thanked the driver for the ride, and sniffed the air. With nothing to do — my climbing permit was not valid until the following day — I strolled around the park visitor centre and the state farm in which it had been placed. The farm was quiet with only a few passing tourists wandering about. I went into the national park centre to ask about camping. On a wall opposite the reception, a poster-sized photograph of some hikers walking through a snowy forest in winter intrigued me. For Taiwan-born people, snow is something of a novelty — the temperature on the plains rarely dipping below ten degrees Celsius — and local hikers made a point of hiking on the mountain in winter to seek it out and make snowballs. How many days of the year Snow Mountain's peak was covered in snow these days was not stated on the poster or anywhere else in the centre, but fewer, I would venture, than when Hugh Ritchie wrote his description of Taiwan's Central Mountain Range back in the 1870s. For me, hiking in winter was out of the question because I was not equipped for it. After finding out where the campsite was, I left the tourist enclave.

The large campsite, located in the protected Cijiawan Creek valley, was a prime location surrounded by fantastic green mountains. When I arrived, however, the place was completely empty. It was Sunday night: I had deliberately planned my entrance to the trail for Monday morning, when there would be few hikers going up the mountain. The site attendant, a Truku woman, let me camp on the well-kept field nearest the site store and office, usually reserved for car owners, upon a bit of gentle urging. The clear evening left me feeling optimistic that I would have a good hike, and although it got rather cold during the night, there was never any question of it snowing. A few transient car tourists checked in later in the evening, but mostly the site remained quiet and peaceful, which was great relief, all things considered. I greatly looked forward to my hike.

The early birds at Wuling broke into song in staggers. Every five minutes a completely new singing pattern emanated from the nearby trees. As one unidentified bird hooted loudly, I got up. It was 5.50. I was fed, packed and ready for the off by 7.00, leaving my tent and some spare clothes at the campsite office. It was a beautiful sunny morning and I slowly walked the one kilometre through the campsite to the trailhead, a cool and fresh breeze making the place feel like a European wood. As the sun rose higher in the sky, it got much warmer and I was even obliged to slather some sunscreen on my face. The Syueba Park area has a staggering total of 51 peaks over 3,000 metres in height within it, and I could clearly see some of these mountains in the distance up the valley. By the time I got to the trailhead, the scene started to look familiar, though the small office building there was something new. It seemed the purpose of the office was to check hikers' climbing permits before they entered the trail, but no one was there checking when I turned up. I excitedly began the ten-kilometrelong trail that would eventually lead me up to the summit of Snow Mountain. Syueshan — meaning Snow Mountain — at 3,886 metres in elevation is the highest point of the Syueshan Range, and it is a very popular trekking destination for good reason. The forest environment on this mountain is simply sublime; a fantastic and magical natural world unspoilt in any way. It was thrilling to be there alone. As I climbed up through the forest, the air cooled, counteracting the heat my body was generating; my heart felt fine and I was breathing very smoothly: it was really a great pleasure to feel my own vital organs functioning well. Around me the forest of Taiwan spruce, Taiwan red pine, Taiwan alder and Taiwan juniper was intensely engaging, changing in colour and density all the time. The spruces were covered in green mossy lichen that made them look like decorated Christmas trees; one red pine had fallen down near the trail, but its still-living trunk had grown vertically again, making it look like a giant set square. After walking for an hour and a half through these magical trees, I arrived at the Chika cabin. I stopped at the hut and made a brew, the first part of the hike completed.

Beyond the Chika hut the trail steepened and the forest became both denser and damper. On a rock I saw a mottled green lizard crawling slowly; a brown laughing thrush pecked away lazily at the trail ahead — one is actually never alone in a forest. There was only one really challenging part to the trail, a steep section exaggeratedly known as the "Crying Slope". Before climbing this craggy incline, I stopped and made a pasta soup, the ideal battery recharger on such a walk. Thus fortified and hiking at an easy pace, I got up the slope in less than an hour with almost no sweat. By now the forest had completely changed in character. The trees had become anaemic-looking, mountain mist hung in small depressions all around restricting visibility, and the colours looked a little faded. Far down the trail behind me, thunder rumbled in the valley, though it would not rain on the mountain. By early afternoon I was up on the ridge and at the five-kilometre marker. Carrying a lighter load than on Yushan, I had made good time and the rest of the trail was an easy, if rather long, walk through grassy woodland. The mist blocked out the panoramic views, but the fir trees, dwarf bamboo and blooming rhododendrons were a pleasant-enough visual distraction, the rare flowers adding welcome splashes of colour in among the subdued greens, browns and greys of the high mountain.

The "369" shelter sat in the middle of a slope covered by Yushan cane, an odd species of hardy dwarf bamboo. As I approached the hut, I was surprised to see quite a few people were already there, weekend hikers on their way back down the mountain. In a small outbuilding mountain guides were busy cooking rice, vegetables, and tins of pork and fish in aluminium wash bowls. The mountain hut looked almost exactly the same as when I had last been through ten years before, though the immediate area about had been cleaned up, I noticed, and a proper outdoor latrine dug nearby. Though only a rudimentary dormitory bunk awaited me, staying at the hut allowed me to dispense with the tent, which considerably lightened my load. I cooked a meal for myself after arriving and then watched a spectacular sunset over the plains below with everyone else. Soon after sunset, clouds fell down all around us and I sat there content like a dreamy zeppelin passenger. During the evening a group of tired hard hikers turned up at the hut. They had just completed a huge circuit around the Snow Mountain ridge that I had been dissuaded from attempting — due to the necessity of using ropes in places — by the Syueba park officials back in Miaoli. The pained expressions on the faces of these gallant hikers said it all as they collapsed on bunks and onto the floor. It seemed this would only be a pit stop for them though; they continued their hike down to the Chika hut later the same evening.

Shaking off the cold, I stepped out of the hut early in the morning and observed with some elation that the day was fine. I packed a small bag, ate a quick breakfast, and then hit the trail up the mountain. The summit was only four kilometres away, I knew the route, and the sun was shining in an arching blue sky: things could not have been set up more perfectly. From the hut I followed the switchbacks up the mountain through dwarf cane and the "silver forest" — a patch of burnt-out fir trees. The trail then entered the truly majestic "black forest", a large area of tall, unmolested Taiwan firs. This forest was just staggering to behold in the morning sun, as shafts of golden light glimmered through and bounced off the upright living trunks. Walking through the trees — there was no path — I felt like a child who had discovered some wonderful playground. In places, one could see more glimpses of the same type of forest around the side of the mountain, and it was gratifying to see so many of the same species of endemic tree in one place. This forest is a refuge to mammals such as the muntjac deer, wild boar, Taiwan serow and Taiwan black bear. The mammals on the mountain clearly understood that people represented a threat, however, and kept well away from the hiking route, although some squirrels were less shy. At the end of the black forest, the path got a little steeper and wound through an area of wind-contorted Taiwan junipers, the surrealist trees. Through the stand of junipers I got my first glimpse of the distant summit; Everest in my imagination. The path up to this summit was treeless and rocky, and this combined with the thinning air made the walk if not exactly Himalayan-like, then nonetheless fairly strenuous. The origin of the upper cirque valley near the summit of Snow Mountain is a bit of a mystery, but in the smoothed-out sides of the valley rhododendrons thrived magnificently.

Stripped of vegetation by forest fires, the summit afforded a fantastic clear rooftop view of the surrounding mountains, a sea of green humps, slopes and peaks. I almost jumped for joy simply because it was not raining. The view along the Snow Mountain Range and across to the parallel Central Mountain Range through 360 degrees was completely unobstructed, a view that could not be bought but had to be earned — and even then, you needed some luck. Staring out over the far side of the summit, I took in this amazing panorama. Clouds threw patches of darkness over distant forested slopes; in other places brown, scarred ground revealed landslips of varying ages. Each angle of this scene revealed another fascinating variation on a theme, a geological cubist painting that required more time to study than I had available. After staring at the mountains for a while, I sat and had a picnic, eating a tin of salmon in chilli sauce that I had saved for the occasion. Three hikers — two young girls with a male guide — arrived at the summit shortly thereafter, and the magic spell was broken as they hailed me to take their group photograph, not that I minded meeting this request. The mountains and forests looked so beautiful beyond the summit of Snow Mountain, but survival out there for the average person would be impossible for more than a couple of weeks. We were actually in some danger, and there was never any question of straying off the trail on this mountain. After a brief chat with the girls, I started to walk back down the mountain eager to keep ahead of any rain. On the way down the side of the exposed valley, I saw the other three hikers disappear over the ridge on the opposite side of the valley on their way to a small lake. I had been to that lake before and thought about the bashing their knees were about to get on the nasty scree slope below them. Not this time, I thought, as I hoisted my walking pole in the air to acknowledge the girls waving goodbye.

The air remained cool and fresh on the descent; the sun was pleasantly diffused by a light mist and, crucially, it did not rain. I frequently stopped to savour the moment, knowing it would be a long time before I would come back here, if I ever did. From the bottom of the eroded cirque I re-entered the juniper thicket and then trekked back through the fir forest, all at a slow pace.

There was only one small stream where drinking water was available, and by the time I got to that water I was pretty thirsty. How sweet the mountain water, filtered through moss, tasted. My thirst slaked, I ambled back to the hut past the glistening burnt-out tree stumps of the silver forest and through the aggressive dwarf bamboo that was encroaching onto the path in many places. The mountain shelter was deserted when I arrived, the boisterous weekend hikers long gone. But according to intelligence I later received from a guide, 20 more hikers were on their way up the mountain. I resolved to leave the 369 shelter before that group of hikers arrived, which I did after cooking a quick meal. At first I bounced along the ridge path, energized by the morning's successful summiting. No fewer than 40 local hikers passed me on the ridge — Snow Mountain had become more popular than ever. But everyone was extremely friendly, and the walk back to the Chika hut went well, even though I was tiring by the minute. The last two kilometres down to the farm were inevitably a strain after the long hike, and by the time I got back to the Wuling campsite at dusk, I was struggling to stay on my feet.

My NEXT TREK would take me up the Ciyou Trail, an obscure path that leads up to Snow Mountain's long eastern ridge. The five-kilometre walk up the picturesque Cijiawan valley the next day actually took some time; it was not possible to hitch a ride as there was almost no through traffic at the farm. At a roadside stall I asked about the price of some oolong tea, thinking to replenish my stocks. A small bag of the fine tea cost US$55 a farmer informed me. The tea was no doubt wonderful, but no amount of fancy packaging could persuade me to part with that amount of cash for it. New consumerism had arrived elsewhere at the farm. After a two-hour walk, I made it to the Wuling hostel. There were some people milling about outside the large government-run hostel. These tourists had obviously stayed overnight and were returning from a morning walk along the Taoshan Trail. Out of interest I asked about room prices at the establishment and was quoted US$45, which was in line with rates in the cities and much more than any student could afford. I walked out and past the hostel and started hiking up a mountain road through a planted forest. Combined with the walk up the valley, I had covered ten kilometres before getting anywhere near the target trailhead. After a brief detour to a waterfall, I finally found the start of the Ciyou Trail tucked away beside the road and began walking up a true crying slope.

The trail went directly up the side of the mountain more or less at a 45-degree angle; in effect the path was a three-and-a-half kilometrelong staircase. Starting at midday, it took me about an hour to cover the first kilometre, some indication of the rigorous nature of the trail. To better cope with the extremely strenuous walk, I adopted a system that involved taking 100 paces as briskly as I could, resting 30 seconds, and then repeating the cycle. By this method I was able to break down the hike into manageable packets. The warmer climate on this side of the mountain encouraged a mid-elevation forest growth that was quite dense, like jungle; but I paid little attention to my surroundings, focused as I was on the business of getting up onto the ridge. On the one and only tiny bit of off-trail flat ground, I sat down for lunch, hungrily eating two corned-beef sandwiches before getting back to work: I felt like I was in training for an Olympics. By mid-afternoon, a sign indicated I still had two kilometres to go before reaching my first objective, a fact I found difficult to comprehend. On and up I went, a hundred at a time. The temperature finally started to cool and wispy clouds enveloped the forest; the trees began to thin out as Taiwan red pines and grass replaced the chaos of the mixed forest. Far below, resting between steps, I caught glimpses through the forest of the Wuling Farm lit up in the afternoon sunshine. At exactly 17.25, five hours after leaving the trailhead, I reached Snow Mountain's eastern ridgeline and took a long, deep breath.

To the east, I could clearly see a mountain cabin atop Tao Mountain, which would be my goal the next day. But after reaching the ridge, my next task was to walk westwards and get over to the Sinda Cabin, which according to a time-flow chart on the back of my map was only about a 30-minute hike away. Because I had overshot the time-flow schedule by only a small amount on the hike up the Ciyou Trail, I assumed this information to be reliable. I felt tired, but the real problem was a lack of water: I had used up all I had hiking up the trail. The ridge was isolated, rugged and overgrown with head-high bamboo. In places, the ground was open and woodsy, but nowhere was it a particularly easy for walking. I pushed my way through the foliage, scampered over rocks, and pressed on in my increasingly desperate search for water. After about 40 minutes I came to a river of rocks that cut across the path, but there was not so much as a dribble of water to be seen anywhere. A tree festooned with climbing tags marked the turning for Ciyou's 3,239-metre-high main peak. Although not far away, climbing up to that peak was no longer on my agenda. Dehydrated and with the day about to end, I needed to find water. Where the heck was that cabin anyway? The path followed a line just south of the jagged ridge, going up and down a misty high-altitude forest of Chinese hemlock. The hike became a curious other-worldly journey. Bunches of white rhododendrons blooming among the twisted hemlocks now made it feel like I was attending my own funeral, and in a panic moment I blew my whistle for assistance, a point-less act since the nearest person was several kilometres away down at Wuling.

Recovering my mental balance I weighed my options and decided to keep going; the cabin couldn't be far away after all. I clambered up and over huge cracked and broken rocks, around promontories that stuck out into thin air, and over fallen logs and exposed tree roots. After a full hour of walking, a finger sign for the Sinda Cabin finally came into view. My morale consider-ably bolstered by the sign, I now walked at a clip knowing that my problems would be solved once I reached the shelter. But half an hour later and to my intense frustration, there was still no sign of the elusive cabin. The path finally arrived at some flat grassy land, where stagnant pools of rainwater had collected. By this time I was so thirsty I had no qualms about gulping down handfuls of the water, which had evidently been recently replenished with rain water and so luckily was not brackish. The water-supply problem thus solved, I thought about making a makeshift tent with my rain gear and roughing it near one of the ponds. Just as I was considering doing this the cabin came into view a little further up the trail.

The cabin turned out to be a grand palace fit for kings, it was something way beyond all my expectations, something the likes of which I had never seen in Taiwan before; a well-built modern hut with a sloping roof. It even had double glazing and its own electricity supply powered by solar panels. At a pinch, the cabin could have accommodated 50 people, but no one was about when I arrived, and it seemed as though the place had not been used in a while. I strode up to this great house in the grass one hour and 40 minutes after starting out along the ridge. In other words, it had taken me three times the amount of time to cover the distance that had been indicated on the back of my map. In other circumstances, my reliance on this information could have been fatal, and that is why one must always treat maps and time-flow charts with a certain amount of circumspection. I was of course happy to have found a place of shelter for the night. Best of all, the cabin had a full tank of fresh rainwater next to it, an incredible resource that made me feel rich and secure. There were no beds in the cabin, but a varnished wooden floor was quite homey; I made myself comfortable, cooked a meal, and wrote up my journal. Bad weather closed in during the night and it thundered red and angry over the cold mountains — certainly not conditions for roughing it outside.

Getting to the Sinda Cabin had put me well within reach of 3,524metre-high Pintian Mountain, a toothy intrusion of folded rock that in some ways resembles the more massive Mount Tapa located further to the northwest. Pintian had fascinated me on my previous trip to Snow Mountain, and I had long thought about climbing it. The hard walk of the night before, however, spooked me and I had second thoughts about pushing my luck on a peak I knew nothing about; recalling that someone mentioned rope work being involved, I decided to give it a miss. Instead I chose to enjoy a leisurely morning by the cabin, quaffing water to my heart's content. It was actually a really beautiful spot, and when the sun came out, the mountains on all sides were clearly visible: wave upon wave of mountains — where did they all come from? A pair of eagles flew about in the morning sky overhead, making for an unforgettable hour on the grand tour. If I did not climb up to the top of Pintian, I certainly got closer to it than I had ever been before. Through some trees on the north side of the ridge, a clear view of its massive angularity held my attention some time.

Later I left the cabin and hiked back along the ridge, a relatively straightforward walk in ideal conditions. The trail stuck out over the side of a precipice in one place, the danger of which I had not been aware of the night before. Past the sheer drop, I began to breathe easily again. Snow Mountain's 369 Shelter and the black forest were clearly visible across intervening wooded valleys, looking like part of an architect's scale model in the far distance. Passing the river of broken rocks and wind-twisted trees, I finally arrived back at the three-way point on the ridge. A finger sign indicated the direction to Mt Tao; it read *Tao Mountain 2.3k*. How difficult could it be to walk just over two kilometres along a ridge? The sometimes unreliable time-flow chart on my map had it down as a 200-minute walk, which suggested that it was not going to be that easy.

Things began well enough, and I felt confident. It was only 11.00 and I had the rest of the day to cover the relatively short distance over to the Taoshan Cabin, which I could actually see in the distance. The path was rugged but not overgrown, and it all seemed doable. But not long into the hike, the first rope appeared besides the path, a sight that set off alarm bells in my head. The ridge had suddenly dipped steeply and actually

151

became almost vertical; the rope was there to lend assistance. This first rope was merely the precursor of a score more. With huge boulder-like rocks dominating the path, it became a labour to walk along the ridge. Up and down the jagged trail, I went sliding down dirt runs in places, disappearing into thick foliage elsewhere. More than once I had to stop to get my bearings, and more than once I fell down a steep section of path on my back. About a third of the way to Taoshan, I stopped for lunch. It was hard to find any flat ground, but a small rocky protrusion of ridge was rounded off sufficiently for me to be able to sit down. It was a nice spot, exactly level with some burnt scarecrow-looking trees opposite where another pair of eagles sat like vultures. Far in the distance I could make out Wuling Farm cooking in the sun. Ominously, the air was close. Just as I was finishing off a hastily made sandwich, it started to rain. The unmistakable signs were that this was the start of a thunderstorm, and so it turned out to be. Quick as a flash I pulled on my rain gear and hit the trail. The rain of course made things even more stressful. I now had to contend with slippery mud and misting spectacles in addition to the rock obstacles and steep drops. Moreover, the trail was not always clearly marked. Luckily, some hiking tags had been left by previous hikers, and these helped me to find my way. By the time I reached the bottom of the slope that approached the Taoshan hut, I had lost the trail completely, but intuition and the occasional shred of a tag got me back on track. The trail snaked up through a dense bamboo forest. The rain poured down and I got soaked below the knee and around my waist. The walk up the steep approach-slope took an hour or so, and then the path broke out onto open ground, where the gorgeous cabin stood unperturbed. Just as I dived through the cabin door, the heavens opened up and ball bearing hail shot down in a heavy barrage.

A glance at my watch told me I had done the hike from the threeway point in only 150 minutes. My elation at making such good time soon turned into mild anxiety as I wondered just how I was going to get off the mountain. The shelter, a smaller version of the one I had stayed in the night before, was great and its water tank was brimming with the very finest rainwater; although situated on a very exposed slope at an elevation of 4000 metres, I was basically safe. The cause of my anxiety was that my maps did not show in sufficient detail where the Taoshan summit actually was, or exactly where the trail to Wuling met the ridge. I spent a couple of hours poring over the maps and even some documents that had been left behind by a previous hiking group. The summit of Taoshan could not be far away, and apparently the Taoshan Trail that led to Wuling joined this summit, but that was all I knew. Later in the afternoon after the thunderstorm subsided, I sallied out on a reconnaissance but was beaten back by soaking foliage. It amazed me that there were no sketch maps or finger signs near the cabin to orientate hikers. A previous visitor obviously felt the same way and had written some direction indicators with opaque correction fluid on the metal frame of the cabin. But these directions did not tell me what I wanted to know. In the end, I just stopped worrying about it, prepared a simple meal and went to bed early after writing up my notes.

The next day, another glorious morning brought clarity to the air and peace of mind. I still had no idea where the trail back to Wuling began, but surely it could not be far, and no way was I going to backtrack along the ridge to Ciyou. Neither, I had decided, would I be tackling Mt Kalahei in the other direction. After drying my clothes out in the sun, I headed up to the summit of Taoshan, which was in fact only a short walk away. There I found a wooden finger sign indicating the way to the cabin, to Mt Kalahei and to Wuling, which answered all questions in one stroke. From the summit of Taoshan — literally "Peach Mountain" in Chinese, but known to the Atayal as "Babokoba" or "Tisl" — the whole of creation came into view in the form of the ridge behind me, the ridge beyond, the trail to Wuling and the amazing mountain ranges all around. I stayed on the 3,325-metre-high summit, a rounded patch of open ground, for over half an hour admiring this astonishing unobstructed vista. Here Taiwan did not look small at all; rather it looked infinite and mysterious like the night sky. Reassuring was the fact that the way back to Wuling was clearly visible and would obviously not present me with any difficulties, indeed it looked like it would be a fine walk. Mt Kalahei could be tackled another day — beating myself up on another ridge walk was not obligatory, and I wanted to save some energy for Nanhudashan.

A long walk down the Taoshan Trail eventually got me back to the Wuling Hostel. At first the path meandered through woods overgrown with Yushan cane, and then dropped down over an extended rocky slope. The path was always clear, however, and there were no major obstacles or nasty sheer drops to negotiate — plain sailing in the Solent basically. Clear views of Snow Mountain provided a pleasant diversion on the walk through the endless sea of dwarf bamboo. A light, wispy cool wind, nature's air-conditioning, blew down the mountain. At a lower elevation the path took on a zigzag pattern that would be maintained all the way down to the valley floor. Down and down I went. In places, fences had been emplaced to prevent hikers from taking short cuts that might inadvertently create erosion channels. A campsite halfway down the mountain had not been used in a while, possibly due to a lack of a reliable water supply. I stopped around this campsite and felt the presence of previous generations of hikers, all of whom would have experienced the same expansion of time and space that I was feeling at that moment; I sat quietly and did nothing much, enjoying the coolness that flowed around me. Later on I reached a forestry trail of planted pine trees, which eventually ended at the Taoshan Creek. The hostel was not far away from the glittering creek. Hitching a lift from the hostel, I arrived back at the Wuling campsite, my legs sunburnt rhubarb red.

At the campsite I gathered my things and then hitched a ride back to Lishan with Daniel, a Bunun mountain guide. He had just come back from his trip on Snow Mountain, where we had met briefly a couple of days before. I piled into Daniel's van and off we drove. It materialized that the Bunun guide was from Dili;

a neighbour of the family who temporarily owned my camera no less. A youngish man but experienced and married with two children, Daniel told me he was a musician, but worked as a mountain porter for extra income. We shared a bottle of beer and a meal at Lishan before he continued on his long drive back to Dili. Daniel checked over my Nanhudashan itinerary and provided me with some useful information about a confounding unmarked fork in the trail on that remote and forbidding mountain.

THE TYPHOON SEASON had begun early. I attentively watched the weather reports on television at a guesthouse in Lishan; three typhoons out in the Pacific were interacting with one another like elements in an unstable chemical. One typhoon that had been heading directly towards Taiwan now appeared to be veering south, towards the Philippines, but the path of any storm is notoriously unpredictable, and a sudden change in direction could not be ruled out. It remained dry in Lishan, however, and I idled about for a couple of days making friends with the family who ran the guesthouse. I also took some time out to catch up on the Atayal cultural festival that was winding down. As part of the closing festivities, participants were invited to pound rice into a gooey mix with the traditional Atayal large pestle and mortar. I had a go and found it surprising how much the mortar weighed and how much hard work it was to mash rice. On my second day in town, I called Alex and she warned me about the typhoon. I told her it was heading away from Taiwan and that there was nothing to worry about; trek on.

The Nanhudashan trailhead was connected to a forestry road accessible from the Sihyuan Pass on Highway 7, the road I had previously travelled up on from the Lanyang valley. From Lishan I took the bus, a 50-kilometre ride, back down the road. After getting off the bus in the middle of nowhere and looking at a map on a signboard, which was useless, I started to walk along a track perpendicular to the trailhead. This old forestry road was mostly in pretty reasonable condition and the walk was generally easy going. In some places, however, the road had been washed away or badly damaged by storm runoff. Some of the worst damage to the track had occurred near its start at the confluence of two mountain creeks. Here the ground was smashed and turned over as if it had been dynamited. Not long after getting underway, I bumped into some forestry bureau officials, who were coming down the disused road. They warned me to expect rain and one asked me if I had a raincoat. I assured him that I did. Satisfied that I was properly equipped, they went on their way wishing me luck. I also met several small groups of hikers retreating down the mountain on the old forestry track. A German man was in one of these groups, the first Westerner I had seen for a while. I asked the burly fellow if he had had a good hike, and he answered, "Ja, good but tough", which was basically the end of our conversation. A group of local hikers greeted me politely, but they looked all in — apparently these overachievers had just completed a 21-hour non-stop hike over all Nanhudashan's satellite peaks.

The trail proper began about eight kilometres down the forestry track. I took the turning and began a steady ascent through a pine forest. The path seemed to follow a watercourse of some kind and was strewn with fallen trees and puddles, the latter growing larger by the minute, for it had started to rain again. About an hour into the hike, I came to a sign that indicated I had covered 1.75 kilometres and had 3.7 kilometres to go before reaching the first mountain cabin — I was making good time considering the rain, which inevitably slowed one down. Despite deploying an umbrella and wearing all my wet-weather clothing, I started to get wet; it seemed like no amount of waterproof clothing would keep me dry for longer than about 40 minutes in continuous subtropical rain. With no let up in the downpour, the hike turned into a long, wet trudge; but for all that it was not a drag, and the wooded mountain kept changing in all kinds of subtle ways, which made the walk interesting and engaging as all walks in Taiwan's mountains prove to be. Where the path forked ambiguously, I took Daniel's advice and presently came upon another sturdy shelter.

The Yulin Cabin was deserted. I made myself at home and hung up my wet clothes like a ghost. I was shivering with cold and knew that my clothes could not possibly dry before morning, and this meant my trek was off. I only had one spare set of dry clothes, which left me no safety margin: if it rained the following day, as seemed likely, I would have no dry clothes at all to wear on top of a 12,000-foot-high mountain. It was already cold on the mountain, and even in dry clothes and a dry sleeping bag I could not get warm during the evening. It rained intermittently throughout the night and the wind blustered. Early the next day I took my time to assess the situation. At one point the weather looked like it was clearing up and the sun even poked its head out, but tellingly the air pressure remained low. A clear view of Nanhu's main peak could be seen in the distance along a ridge, but it was probably much further away than it seemed, and it would require grit to attempt this hike solo. I put my clothes outside on some grass, hoping to get them dry, but the sun was not strong enough to dry them — and then the atmospheric pressure dropped another notch. Reluctantly, I decided to turn around and get off the mountain: the high chance of more rain was a complication I could not deal with. Only under blue skies would I have risked hiking to the summit of Nanhu alone. On the way back down the trail, it rained heavily and continuously, the type of rain associated with tropical storms — the typhoon that had veered previously away from Taiwan had, unbeknownst to me at that moment, changed direction and was heading up through the middle of the Taiwan Strait. If I had continued up the mountain, there is no question I would have got into trouble.

Passing through the pine forest on the way back, I disturbed a huge bird that rose startled, lifting its wings clumsily like a flying boat, a mysterious encounter. The bird flew off deeper into the woods before I could get a proper look at it. Near the end of the old forestry road, I spent a nervous half hour trying to find my way back to the main road. It seemed ridiculous to get lost at the last hurdle, but the dirt road was so badly mashed at its end that it was unrecognisable as a road. Finally, I got on the path that led back to the Nanhu Creek, and from there it was but a ten-minute walk to the highway. Relieved to be off the mountain, I drank a soda from a little stash I had hidden beforehand and stood by the road ready to hitch a lift. A pickup truck duly came along and gave me a ride to Lishan. As I sat in the back of the truck, my mobile phone rang. It took me a minute to locate the phone, buried as it was deep in the folds of a damp pocket, but I managed to answer before the caller rang off. It was Alex. She told me that a typhoon was on the way and that Taroko Park officials had been calling her to tell me to get off the mountain.

STRANGELY, the typhoon hardly affected Lishan. The storm seemed to be distant and below us: though the sky was in constant turmoil and the wind howled, it rained far less than one might have expected. Everyone was surprised. I sat it out back at the guesthouse, bored to death with the inactivity. Before the storm blew completely out, I resolved to escape the rising damp hotel. I called the Hehuan Lodge to book a room, or a bunk, or whatever they had available. "Have you booked?" a man on the other end of the line asked. I said, "What do you mean; I'm calling to book, aren't I?" The man was dull. "Did you book online?" he then inquired. He just wasn't getting it. I was *calling* to make a booking. Had telephones gone out of fashion as a means to book a room? The man dithered, and after finding out I was an independent traveller and not part of a group, he started to lose what little interest he had in me. He vaguely promised me a space in a dormitory, but only for one night. Better than nothing, I thought, ringing off.

Travelling up to Hehuan by bus, I repeated Trip Two's roller-coaster ride — the road was in pretty good shape considering the recent storm; in fact, it was no more damaged than it had been the month before — but this time I got off the bus just the other side of Hehuan's black-slate summit and walked over to the colonial-era lodge. The lodge's caretaker deigned to give me a space in one of the empty dormitories. After dumping my gear in the room, I went outside to survey the scene. Hehuan was dry but cold. The spot was effectively a major crossroads in the high mountains; from the lodge one could follow paths in all directions. Across the road, the trail for Cilai Mountain began. I could just about make out the jagged line of Cilai's dramatic ridgeline in the distance through a break in the clouds. Below the highway, dwarf conifers and a few ponds dotted a carpet of grass that stretched away into a distance dominated by yet more high mountains. Hehuan East Peak was a mere 40-minute walk away up a trail that started next to a large unoccupied building near the lodge. I walked up this trail and ambled up onto an open grassy slope that had once been used for skiing in the winter months. I reached a summit marker that indicated the East Peak's height: 3,421 metres. Pink rhododendrons bravely bloomed in bunches on the cold mist-shrouded peak. Through gaps in the mist, one could see the lodge below and the road to Dayuling. On the way back to the lodge, I made a small diversion to take in Mt Shihmen, one of Taiwan's famous "Hundred Peaks". In reality, Shihmen was just a bump on the other side of the highway. In the distance stood the giant peaks of the Snow Mountain Range, among them Nanhudashan, which I had left in such a hurry just a few days before.

Back at the lodge people were arriving. The visitors were mostly city people out for a bracing drive through the mountains, but one or two hikers turned up plus a number of people intent on photographing Hehuan's famous wild rhododendrons, which I had seen for myself shortly before. I shared my dormitory with a posse of young male photographers, all obsessed with capturing the perfectly focused rhododendron. The amateur snappers quizzed me on the state of the bloom, but I had no idea how to analyse what I had seen; they just looked like flowers to me. I chatted with one 50-year-old man who was on his own. He worked for Taiwan's state-run telephone company and travelled to the mountains in his spare time to photograph flowers, using a large-format camera. He told me he had been to Nanhudashan, his favourite mountain in Taiwan, dozens of times. He remarked, "Nanhu is dangerous, and people die on it", and there was no doubt he knew what he was talking about. When I told him the story of my trip there, he congratulated me on my decision to abort the hike.

At Hehuan, the popular place to watch the sun rise was on nearby Shihmen, but the next day I found a place on the slope behind the lodge, which served the same purpose and was much nearer the canteen. With the morning light highlighting it, Nanhudashan was again visible in the distance, and I rued my choice of spring to attempt to climb it; I would not get the chance to go there again soon, I knew. Toying with the idea of illicitly camping somewhere in the Hehuan area, I eventually decided to quit the place and hitchhiked back to Lishan.

Before leaving Lishan, I called up a Bunun agricultural worker who had befriended me on a bus ride. He had invited me over to his place, and I thought I would take him up on that offer before returning to the plains. I was curious to know something about his life and how things were for the workers in the area. When I called Dongla, he told me to come over to Songmao; and a little while after taking a local bus, I arrived at the Atayal village just north of Lishan, where I waited for Dongla in the street. He was still not back from work, so I just hung out and talked to a couple of local people. The village, which clung to the sides of a steep mountain road, livened up later in the afternoon, and I recognized a few faces from Lishan. The Atayals owned houses in the area and seemed to keep themselves apart from the agricultural labourers, the latter forming a kind of social underclass. Sequestered in cheaply made dormitories on the hillsides, these seasonal workers seldom left their places of work and only travelled home infrequently. The body language of the local Atayals was confident and unrestrained, but the almost invisible workers kept a low profile and seemed to avoid the street.

Eventually the diminutive Dongla turned up, dressed in gumboots, a thick sweater and worn canvas jeans. We went back to his dormitory, a real dump of a place about 100 metres away from the road down a side street, and here I met his roommates; a married couple from the Philippines, two Rukai men and an Amis girl. They offered me a cup of some kind of spirit, which I sniffed at and sipped a little; we then sat and chatted for several hours. The married couple, slightly resenting the intrusion, I felt, soon retired from the makeshift living room, leaving Dongla, the two Rukai men and myself in the room. One of the Rukai men who had long hair was impish, natural and intelligent. The other one, tall and well-built, was more intellectual and held a thick medical book in his hands as we spoke. Dongla prepared some kind of loaf to eat but he burnt the thing and ended up tossing it away. The Amis girl briefly piped up, puffing on a cigarette and speaking Chinese coarsely in a loud voice. But she was obviously shy and could not bring herself to talk to me directly; presently she also left the impromptu soirée.

The two Rukai men told me a little bit about their lives: they came to Lishan to work every spring and worked through the summer months until harvest time; the pay was US$40 a day, including free board and lodging. The money was not great, but it was at least some kind of work. Of the ten significant landowners in the area, nine of them were ethnic Chinese, the land having been acquired from the Atayals over a period of time. This meant that the rates of pay were more or less fixed, and it was hard for the workers to get a better deal. Did they like their work? The tall man spoke, "Yes, but our pay is low. It is very hard for indigenous people to find work in our home villages, so we are forced to come here…" — adding, by way of trying to say something positive, "…in the summer it is nice here". Nice if you are driving through in a car, I thought, but not so nice if you have to work seven days a week as these labourers did, only stopping when the weather turned bad, and then not getting paid for the lost time. It had been good to meet these workers in situ, whom it would have been easy for me to ignore, but they had to go to work the next day; and not wanting to overstay my welcome, I left the hillside dormitory before it got late. I camped out in Lishan one more time. The next day I retraced my route through the Taroko Gorge by taking the bus to Hualian and then caught the train back to Taibei thus bringing Trip Three full circle.

5

TRIP FOUR: THE EAST COAST AND THE SOUTH

SITTING ON A SOUTHBOUND TRAIN, I NOTICED TWO WOMEN WHO were speaking Japanese. They were impeccably dressed as if they were about to attend a board meeting. Both of them had long, slim, attractive silk-stocking-clad legs, which I couldn't help but admire. Where had these women come from and where were they going to? Making a conscious effort not to stare continuously at the women's legs, I instead looked out the window. The sight of workers busily constructing new rail infrastructure just outside the city served to jolt me out of a hangover and lascivious gawping: the job, my job, was travelling, and I had to get on with it. Shuangsi, Fulong and Yilan all fell past in short order. The stale air of the air-conditioned train was making me feel drowsy, but the passing rustic scenes were invigorating — fast-flowing creeks here, fields of healthy rice there, and mountains and ferns all converged to make a statement about life itself: that life goes on and is renewed every year. Summer had arrived and the trees and plants outside were a translucent green, their pulsating colour slightly offset by a light haze; by the time the train arrived at Suao, I was almost fresh.

The Japanese women, who also got off the train at Suao New Station, piled into a taxi and disappeared, gone like mannequins in a dream. I lumbered out of the station with my two backpacks and an additional bag that held a large pair of 10x50 Porro prism binoculars — thought they might come in handy — and wandered up and down the highway outside the station. A worker at the cement works opposite the station was able to direct me to downtown, which was about one kilometre away. In town I got my bearings and then walked over to the harbour area. There was little to do at the port, and so after supping an iced coffee at the local convenience store, I hit the coast road. The highway climbed steeply out of the harbour area, and once more I found myself enjoying the feeling of not knowing quite what was going to happen next. Just as I was revelling in this freedom, a man stopped his vehicle beside me. "Where are you going?" asked the middle-aged man from inside a slightly battered Swedish-made car. "Hualian", I told him. The man waved me into his car, clearing some junk off of the front passenger seat to make room for me.

Mr Liu chatted to me all the while in Chinese as we travelled along the dramatic coast road. The coastal highway between Suao and Hualian City, he told me, was about 100 kilometres long. It had been rebuilt and widened over the years and passed through mountains and along sheer cliffs, a fascinating journey. We drove along this famous road slowly and passed one or two villages, one of which was an Amis village, Mr Liu said; this came as a surprise to me as I had assumed the territory between Suao and the Taroko Gorge was entirely Atayal. As he cruised along, my new friend interrogated me about my trip and my future travel plans. Asking my own questions, I learned that Mr Liu — a television repairperson by trade — had upped and left the big city, moving to rural Hualian 20 years ago. In Hualian he had started his own business raising goats, and more recently, he had become an apartment landlord. He lived in Hualian County not far from the new Donghua University, and he offered me a room for a couple of nights in his student dormitory free of charge, an offer I accepted.

As Mr Liu was talking, I was tried to concentrate and observe the road. The only industry en route appeared to be the cement factories of eastern Taiwan; there was no tourism to speak of, even though the coast was stunningly beautiful. We stopped at a couple of scenic locales along the way. At one viewing platform overlooking a picturesque bay, I put my binoculars into action for the first time and was rewarded with a wonderful close-up of an osprey flying in the sky overhead. Backlit by the sun its wings shone golden like a drawing of a mythical beast on an ancient temple wall. We made another stop further down the road near the Cingshuei cliffs before eventually reaching the small delta in front of the Taroko Gorge about an hour later. Here we stopped and bought purple-fleshed baked sweet potatoes from a roadside stall. Mr Liu knew the stallholder — he knew everyone in these parts as I would discover. After eating our tasty snack, we resumed our journey and soon crossed the short distance from the Taroko Gorge to the Shoufong District, where Mr Liu lived.

Considering Taiwan is the second-most densely populated country in the world — second only to Bangladesh — it is surprising how expansive and laid back some of its eastern rural townships feel. Before taking me back to his dormitory home, Mr Liu took me on a tour of his properties in the Shoufong backwater. First though, we dropped by to see his mistress and one of his sons. The mistress, an Amis woman who lived in an ordinary rural suburb, was a nice-enough woman. She was wary of me since I could speak Chinese, which made me a kind of fifth columnist in her eyes. She need not have worried though: I had no plans to blackmail my benefactor. Mr Liu next proudly showed me his herd of goats that wandered about freely on some open land nearby. Apparently this land was strewn with rocks and not really suitable for agricultural use, but the high and quickgrowing grass made for excellent grazing. Poaching was an ongoing problem and profits were not easy to make, complained Liu. We dropped by a dilapidated farm house on his land. A dead fish floated in a large pond next to the building. In the driveway sat an old Frenchmade car slowly disintegrating. Mr Liu used this house as a store room and gathered some things there. We then drove over to another plot of land where

Liu was having a new goat pen built. This pen was quite a structure, certainly big enough to house 200 goats. Three of four Amis workers were busy putting in some wooden slating on the floor of the pen as we walked in. The workers were friendly to me, surprised to see an American — of course I was an American — tagging along with Mr Liu, their boss. From his car, Mr Liu pulled out a crate of booze and gave it to the workers, who were moderately pacified by this display of munificence. On yet another plot of land, the industrious Mr Liu had planted night-blooming cereuses — a sprawling cactus plant grown for its seedy 'dragon fruit' — in rows, supported by concrete posts, wooden supports and heavy-duty steel cable. "I'm not very good at growing things", the entrepreneur confessed. But I for one could not see how he could have done anything more for the cactus plants. We then went on a drive through the 250-hecatre campus of Donghua University, a new school that had only been open six years and had a small student body. The green campus was abundant with rabbits and birdlife and had been fenced off to prevent Amis people and others from poaching at night. Telling me this, Mr Liu went on to admit without a trace of irony that he had once poached on a regular basis himself. We finally arrived at the dorm. Most of the self-contained apartments were still empty, and I was shown to one of them. Later in the muggy evening, Mr Liu delivered a platter of succulent durian fruits to my room, which was really above and beyond the call of duty, and informed me that we would be making a road trip the next day.

Liu knocked on my door early in the morning wanting to know if I was ready to go. "Yeah, sure", I shouted, sitting on the end of the bed in a daze. It had been a wet, muggy night, and I had slept badly. Not wanting to disappoint my friend, I got up, dressed, grabbed my maps, camera, umbrella and binoculars and clambered into the boxy car. It was the top part of Taiwan's rift valley that Liu wanted to show me. Much of Hualian, a large county, is mountainous and inaccessible; to the west it is dominated by Taiwan's backbone Central Mountain Range, and to the east stands another range of mountains next to the ocean. The rift valley lies between these two mountain ranges. After departing from the dormitory and filling up with gas, we started by visiting an Amis village at the foot of the East Coast Mountain Range, a place where Mr Liu had contacts. He made conversation with the local mayor whilst I surveyed the scene. The village was typical of indigenous villages, made up of a few rows of fairly simple one-storey houses and a sprinkling of three-storied concrete apartments. From the village we drove down Route 193, keeping close to the eastern mountains, which gave us a clear view of the Hualian River and the whole rift valley that stretched over to the magnificent Central Mountain Range. After leaving the village, Mr Liu gave me his take on the Amis. Taiwan's indigenous peoples were not really great agriculturalists, he said, and they did not like to study. Consequently, they had ended up selling most of their lands to Han Chinese settlers like him, and were now obliged to work as wage labourers. He spoke with respect for the indigenous people's physical endurance and knowledge of wild plants and evidently had a soft spot for Amis girls. But what Mr Liu did not mention was the outright theft of indigenous land, which had been grabbed by cement companies and other business interests, an inconvenient truth that he had subconsciously suppressed. Later we passed through a pretty river valley that cut through the coastal mountains and then drove back up the scenic coast road back to Shoufong making a circuit.

The outing down the rift valley was the precursor to a longer journey. We had tried to talk him out of it, but Mr Liu wanted to take us — his mistress, his son and me — all the way down to Taidong by car. Liu, whose wife had returned to Taibei for the weekend, seemed to have set his heart on this trip, and so on a Sunday morning we all rallied, piled into the car, and travelled right down the whole length of Route 9, the main road that runs the length of the rift valley, almost without stopping. It rained in Hualian, but got warmer and drier as we moved southwards; near the Tropic of Cancer line about half way to Taidong, the temperature increased at least a couple of degrees. Although the passing scenery was a pleasing diversion, we were going too fast to see anything well. Mr Liu's son was bored, understandably, and kept asking where we were going and why — a child is guaranteed to come up with critical questions like these, and perhaps that is why adults are always telling them to shoosh. The boy was bright, and it saddened me when Mr Liu told him to shut him up, further calling him a "little devil". The question remained: where were we going? Our breezy trip took us across, in short order, the Shoufong River, the Wanli River and the Mataian River. Driving at speed across wide bridges, it is easy to forget how not long ago these rivers were considerable obstacles that hindered land communications. One of the biggest and most powerful rivers in eastern Taiwan is the Siouguluan River. The view of the mountains was partly obscured by clouds and rain, but I did catch a glimpse of some helmeted tourists rafting in the Siouguluan's tumbling waters.

After driving non-stop for two and a half hours, we stopped for lunch in Jhihsing, Taidong County. Jhihsing rice is famous in Taiwan for its purity and great taste. Naturally we ordered rice box lunches at a roadside diner and sat down in the crowded restaurant to eat. Junior scoffed his meal down; Dad ate whilst reading a newspaper and ignored his son. After lunch, we drove back to Shoufong more or less the way we had come, not bothering to explore any of the many Amis villages in the area.

The stressful road trip had exhausted everyone. After dropping his mistress and child off, Mr Liu and I retired to our rooms. But I sensed the day had not been completed quite to Liu's satisfaction, and he was still inclined to go out and gallivant, a 60-year old gamely resisting his aging. I must have disappointed my benefactor because I was not interested in going out with him again, and it was not long before his friendly attitude towards me started to shift. I wanted to hang around in Shoufong a few more days and offered to help Mr Liu with his work, but first thing the next day, the boss wanted me out. He was quite nice about it, but also quite insistent. When I asked him for his mailing address so I could send him some photos taken on our trip together, he would not give it to me, afraid his wife might get to see the photos first no doubt. Seeing the lay of the land, I thanked Mr Liu for everything and quickly packed. When he realized that getting rid of me was not going to be difficult after all, the ex-television company worker became his affable self and offered me a ride over to the coast road, which of course I accepted. Outside the East Coast National Scenic Area visitor centre, on the empty coast road next to a garish amusement park, Mr Liu dropped me off and said farewell before swinging his car around and rocketing off in the direction of Shoufong.

THE EXHIBITS at the visitor centre presented the east coast as a playground where one could windsurf, paraglide and raft. I had gone there to get a map of the coast road, and they did have a basic sketch map printed out on a sheet of A4 paper available, but the map had been designed for motorists and lacked detail. My rough plan was to walk as much of Route 11, the 170-kilometre-long east-coast road that connected Hualian and Taidong cities, as I could and then visit Green Island and Orchid Island, two of Taiwan's most popular offshore islands. A phone call lined me up with a camping spot at Jicih, a beach resort 37 kilometres down the road, and on that successful note I left the almost-deserted visitor centre. After stopping to chat to an Amis woman selling cigarettes and drinks from a roadside stall — I needed to put some social distance between me and Mr Liu — I started hiking along the incomparably beautiful coastal highway.

It felt good to be out on the road now that the interminable plum rains had eased, and walking allowed me to see and hear all the things one normally misses driving around in a car. Through binoculars I straightaway observed a close-up of a black-headed shrike bobbing on a nearby tree and many other birds, which sat obligingly still on branches and overhead cables.

I used to think birding was for nerds, but I found it relaxing to observe this varied fauna by the coast. Next to the roadside beautiful evergreen plants and bushes glowed with vitality in the summer sunshine, and from time to time oleanders, hibiscus and Cana lilies brightened the greens. On one side of me, a steady trickle of tourists in cars, a few cyclists and the odd truck passed by, but the density of traffic was low compared to the city. Off road, the Pacific Ocean lapped calmly like a somnambulant cow, its vastness concealed by the curvature of the horizon. Most houses by the side of the road were old and weather-beaten, but some of them had latterly been converted into guesthouses; nonetheless, they all seemed to be empty. The walk, my first for a week, went well and I made good progress covering about ten kilometres in approximately two hours. On the way I stopped for a picnic lunch at a roadside shelter that overlooked the ocean. Here I put my feet up and stared up at the green foothills facing the road. I imagined making a secret camp in among the trees, but the crenulated vegetation would have posed a formidable obstacle to any casual exploration.

During the early afternoon I walked about seven kilometres down the coast road, passing a couple of small settlements before switching to hitching mode out of exhaustion. I was just about on my last legs when a happy band of people came down the road in a miniature bus. The slow-moving vehicle screeched to a stop when I flagged it, the driver evidently used to picking up stragglers. There was hardly any room for me to sit in the crowded minibus but I squashed in anyway. Two married couples, assorted children and a baby were on their way home after a picnic trip. The men were road workers and lived in temporary housing near their place of work. The driver, a burly, strong man sporting a crew-cut hairstyle and tattoos, was partly drunk but drove very slowly and carefully as though to compensate for his condition. He drove a darn sight better than many apparently sober people I had observed careening about on the road that day. His brother, or friend, held his drink less well and had sort of collapsed into the dashboard. The two women were lively, merry, unreserved and constantly giggled, but the unspoilt and neatly dressed children were, I noticed, quiet and well-behaved. The shirtless driver drove cracking jokes all the while. A few kilometres down the road, we arrived at the workers' camp, a collection of converted shipping cargo containers plonked down in a field. Here I mingled with the assembled company. One of the wives handed me her newborn baby to look after and walked off not worrying about a thing. Some photos were then taken, several of them featuring the joker gesturing to cut off my head with a knife, but within a short while the group lost interest in me. A worker at the camp, a huge and quite serious fellow, offered to take me down to Jicih in his car. I was sorry to leave so soon, but it was probably a good idea to get me away from those pretty wives. We arrived at Jicih 50 minutes later.

At the small club house by the sea, a resort attendant duly ushered me to a camping spot. For ten bucks I got a space on a wooden platform and the use of the washrooms. I felt this was a terrible waste of money — why pay to camp? — but the resort looked as though it might make a good place to hang out for a couple of days, and it would have been rude to have left after booking. Therefore I settled in and then went on a reconnaissance of the area. A number of young people staying at the government-owned camp congregated on the grey beach near the club house and played volleyball. After only half an hour at the camp beach, I wanted to roam outside its domain, something that would never have occurred to those young people to do. I took a walk up a cliff promontory to the south, climbing a path up and over it. Numerous signs warned of snakes and killer bees, but the common swinhoe's japulura, a small lizard, was the only creature I came across on this walk. From the top of the cliff, I could clearly see the beach resort and the gaggle of students on the beach. On the other side of the cliff, an equally clear view of the road south presented itself. On this south side I spotted signs of permanent settlement next to the coast road and followed the path down onto the highway to investigate.

The Amis nation, with a population of around 140,000, is the largest indigenous ethnic group in Taiwan. They have always lived on the eastern plains of the island and are distinct from all the other nations in terms of culture, language and history. No one knows where the Amis originated from, but their ethnicity is closely related to the Austronesia / Pacific Islander cultures. In contrast to many Han Chinese people and some of the other indigenous nations, Amis men tend to be tall and well-built — the dark-haired road worker who had given me a ride to Jicih had almost certainly been Amis. Along with the Puyuma further south, Amis society is typically matrilineal with women occupying positions of social superiority in extended clans. Amis girls, many of whom work in Taiwan's hospitality industry, are self-confident, healthy and good-looking. The traditional Amis village was quite large, and Amis summer-harvest festivals are still notable gatherings of the clans. Significantly, traditional Amis society is highly stratified with strict social hierarchies and ranking according to seniority, and this perhaps explains the Amis' relatively easy assimilation into Han Chinese culture.

The first thing I noticed about Gueishan, the Amis village next to the highway I had stumbled across, was the plethora of election banners that festooned every corner of an outdoor yard. Some kind of party was taking place here, and I gained my entry to it after being hailed by a strong, late-middle-aged man who was dressed in a white vest, track-suit bottoms and sandals. This man was in fact the village headman. Receiving the headman's invitation, I was immediately accepted as a part of the group. The purpose of the gathering was to drum up support for Mr Chang, candidate number twelve on the ballot paper, in an upcoming local election. There were about 20 people at the small rally, casually feasting on food that had been laid out on round, collapsible banqueting tables. I was invited to sit down by a drunken man who had decided to make friends. I sipped on some of the rice wine he offered me to be sociable. The drunk was quite harmless, even likeable, but he had the annoying habit of speaking quite unintelligible English to me. It was interesting how he refused to speak Mandarin, which was hardly a neutral lingua franca after all. I patiently tried to communicate with my new friend. In more lucid moments he would talk to others in his native language, and it was heartening to hear the Amis language — a sing-song high-pitchedsounding tongue to a native English speaker — being spoken by all present in the yard. The man also impressed me when he hauled in a loose toddler who had strayed dangerously close to the main road; he may have been drunk but he was responsible and paid close attention to the psychological atmosphere of the gathering. Just as he was boring me with yet another monologue about some fishing job he had had overseas, we were joined by a teenage girl who had been informed of my presence. She told the man quite directly that his lousy English was an embarrassment and then invited me to eat with her. We ate some rice, green beans and leafy vegetables. The girl, a child carer, was typically self-confident as I discovered when she made a very forward proposition to me that one would not normally expect to receive from a teenage girl on a first acquaintance. Brushing aside her intriguing suggestion, I let her introduce me to some of the children of her extended clan and played with the kids for a little while inside a house. The house was plain, but adequately furnished — the kind of home you might find anywhere in rural Taiwan. Catholic iconography and family portraits hung on the otherwise bare walls.

Back in the yard, the formal segment of the election gathering began. I left the kids and sat in as guest of honour near the village headman at the meeting. Some wine was handed around, as is the Amis custom, before the speeches began. Political meetings are usually dominated by one or two leading speakers who make lengthy speeches. This Amis meeting followed the classic pattern and the village chief and his subordinates spoke for an inordinate length of time without making any attempt to interact with their audience. The villagers sat in a sexsegregated circle, and the women, mostly middle-aged and late middle-aged, were visibly bored. If women were powerful in Amis society, it was not apparent by what was going on at this village gathering. To be sure, many young people were absent from Gueishan, and some families in the village made a point of not attending the partisan rally, but the pattern of politicking was taken straight from the dominant culture. Even the drunken man had sobered up and was on his best submissive behaviour. It is possible that at traditional ceremonies Amis women asserted themselves, but this is not something I would get a chance to see. In fact, leaving the meeting early, my investigation of Amis culture had more or less come to an end. The village kids followed me a short distance out of the village and then waved goodbye as I walked away down the highway.

Though less than half a kilometre away, the beach resort may as well have been in another country. No one from the resort visited the Amis village, and the villagers — though they did keep a few boats on a slipway near the resort's property — likewise stayed away from the resort. In the evening it was pleasantly cool by the ocean and I took dinner at the club house, where I ate fried noodles and drank ice-cold lager. After dinner I sat at a table outside. The sound of waves gently rolling up the beach made for a pleasant atmosphere conducive to scribbling. I slapped my journal onto the table and wrote copious notes. The atmosphere and my mood reminded me of a passage in Christopher Isherwood's *Goodbye to Berlin*, where the protagonist, Isherwood's alter ego, reflects on how liberating it is to sit in a café writing in a notebook while sipping a beer. At Jicih I felt something similar: I felt pleasure in what I was doing and felt that it was right to be doing it.

A heat wave woke me early the next day and I exited the tent in a stupor. The fresh morning air perked me up though and I proceeded to read in a chair as the resident young ones played volleyball on the narrow beach. In the afternoon, I went for a swim. The seafloor dropped away quite steeply from the beach, and the breakers were far more powerful than they looked. Not venturing too far out, I put in a few lengths using the extent of the resort's property as my length marker. After this moderate exercise I clambered back to the beach and crashed out in the lounge chair. From the beach I watched a flock of sea birds landing and taking off from a rock platform as though the rock were an aircraft carrier. The Taiwanese students, who were on a post-exam vacation, swam in the sea, wisely sticking close to the shoreline. Later in the afternoon a convoy of cars with candidate number twelve's banners attached to them drove by and I waved to them, but I doubt anyone saw me. The second night in the club house was far less exhilarating than the first had been, and suddenly the place seemed tatty and confining — the students were well-behaved but dull.

Determined to get a head start on the day, I hiked out of the resort briskly early the next day. The morning was warm but cloudy; the coast was evenly lit by the diffused light. A local fisherperson from Gueishan drove his boat out into the ocean as I walked by the slipway. The Amis fishing style was low-stress: some net traps were left in the sea near the shore overnight and hauled in the next morning; if the catches were not massive they were plentiful enough to feed the clan. Opposite the village next to the ocean, a large fish farm stood abandoned and ravaged by the tides and time. One wondered why this farm was no longer operational. My guess was that the original investors lost interest as Taiwan's economy became more developed and fish farming relatively less profitable; I would see many such abandoned fish farms on my travels. As I passed Gueishan, spotting a few birds by the way, I noticed a lanky man sitting in a chair staring at me. The villager's motionless face expressed understanding, an acknowledgement of the fact that there was no turning back for either of us.

My goal for the day was to walk to Fongbin, a town about 15 kilometres south of Jicih. The coast road, passing through an occasional short tunnel, closely followed the rocky shoreline and I hiked along it happily enjoying the warmth of the day. About half way to Fongbin, the narrow coastal plain widened out a little. On this small plain I came across a large operational fish farm next to some extensive areas of rice paddy. The bright green cultivated fields and pools of the fish farm looked very picturesque against the mid-blues of the distant mountains. I entered another village, this one larger and more spread out than Gueishan. To my surprise the village, which went by the Chinese name of Sinshe, was a Kavalan settlement. The Kavalan, another of Taiwan's indigenous nations, once lived in Yilan County but got pushed out by encroaching Han migrants. It had been my impression that this nation was small and almost extinct, but here was a living and breathing Kavalan settlement. By now I was in need of a rest and refreshment, and after finding a little restaurant, I sat and bought a soda there. The owner of the store was Kavalan, and so I was able to ask her a few questions about Kavalan people and their culture. The woman told me she still spoke Kavalan with some of her neighbours and that the locals still took pride in their Kavalan ethnicity. Inside the restaurant some Kavalan garments and other cultural artefacts had been put on display. But the Kavalan's numbers had been greatly reduced by assimilation, and one sensed that the culture had reached its critical phase. The government had given the Kavalan formal recognition, and this meant they could get some funds for cultural and economic development, but I felt it would take a miracle to prevent yet another language death.

From Sinshe, I carried on walking down the coast road, occasionally declining the offer of a ride from passing drivers: there was simply too much to see to jump in a car and let it all rush by. The road eventually climbed in elevation, thus affording much better views of the fantastic coastline. Beside one stretch of cliff top road, I came across a couple of huts that had nice gardens attached. Curious, I went over to take a closer look. The dwellings were traditional Amis houses made of bamboo, wood and grass. One of the houses functioned as a small store and sold betel nuts, cigarettes, soda drinks and some snack foods to passers-by. I went over to the store and talked to the owner, an aging Amis man. He told me he had built the house himself in the old way, using materials taken from the nearby mountains. He told me that the traditional Amis house is designed to last five years, after which time it is burnt and a new house erected. In traditional Amis society, the building of a house was a communal undertaking, the completion of a house occasioning a big party. Inside the small hut-like structure, the owner had pinned up some photographs of the house being built. By looking at these photographs, one could share just a little in the community spirit of the Amis. I asked the store owner to teach me some Amis language. He recited "mama", meaning father. So, what was the word for mother? Answer: "inu". The cliff top garden was filled with blooming hibiscus and canna lilies and I took a little stroll around its borders before kitting up and getting back on the road. The old man said goodbye to me, in Chinese. Later I entered Fongbin district after an excruciating final hour of walking; my leg muscles were by now torn to shreds. I set up camp near the Baliwan River and rested as the weather took a turn for the worse again; it rained during the night and my tent leaked for the one and only time on my travels.

As soon as the rain stopped the next day, I broke camp, drying my things as best I could before rapidly packing. I then hiked out of the area along the coast road, basically giving up on the idea of making a detour inland. My legs were stiff from the previous day's hike, but it was not raining; the air was fresh and the coast road long and deserted. All in all it was great to be alive as a densely populated roadside graveyard that I passed served to emphasize. I got into my stride and walked the stiffness out of my legs. The settlements I came to along the road were small and generally uninteresting, and many annoyingly noisy election convoys passed me by, but on the whole the day's walk was pleasant and rewarding. Well-clear of Hualian City's gravitational pull, the road was almost devoid of traffic, and visibility was crystal clear. But given the weight of my backpacks, the summer heat and the length of the coast road, it was inevitable that I would have to resort to hitching, and at some point later in the day, I hitched some rides that got me many kilometres down the highway. At Shihtiping I was able to spend a night camping at what must rank as one of the best campsites in the whole of Taiwan. Nestled in among wind-eroded rock formations and subtropical flora right by the seashore, the camp had fine open-ended wooden shelters on which campers could pitch their tents. I took a rest at the campsite, limiting myself to a short walk and a bit of birding, and then got a good night's sleep.

The next day I resumed my journey southwards. Not far along the road, I arrived at the Jhanghong Bridge, which crossed the powerful Siouguluan River, and slowly walked across, entering the subtropics proper. The Basian Cave complex was ten kilometres down the road, and I took a bus there to save my legs. Getting off the bus at the site, I left my gear at the small visitor centre, bought a ticket, and started a tour of the site. The caves, raised by tectonic-plate movement, sat empty well above the ocean. To see them one had to walk up a steep trail that climbed up and around the side of the cliff. The walk was pleasant, but there was nothing at all to see in the caves, and this left it all to the imagination. Paleolithic people would have followed the game that migrated to the forests of Taiwan at the end of the last ice age — it has been suggested that these ancient peoples were the ancestors of Taiwan's indigenous peoples, who later spread south and east populating all of Austronesia. On the east coast of Taiwan, these Paleolithic people lived in the caves, fished in the sea, and foraged. Physically very similar to modern people, they nevertheless would have had relatively short life spans and probably witnessed more violence in their everyday lives than most Taiwanese people do today. But they had not thought to paint images on the walls of the caves — too much to do in the warm outdoors, one supposes.

The sun shone brightly as I walked down the road away from the caves of time. It was the first really hot day of summer, and I wondered how much more I could take of the heat. From Changbin onwards the heat rather than the rain became the main source of stress for me. But I continued walking along the road regardless. Changbin village was completely lifeless at high noon; the local people sensibly kept indoors out of the sun. I walked right through the village, finally stopping at a convenience store at the far end of the street where I sat in the shade outside together with a tramp and waited for the day's temperature to peak before heading off again. Beyond some hills south of Changbin, I definitely felt as though I had entered another realm: the colour around me became more washed out, the vegetation more truly tropical, and the heat even more relentless than during the midday march from the cave complex. I walked in a semi daze wondering how much more ground I would be able to cover when a local man kindly stopped his car and offered me a ride. And to think I had been turning offers of rides down the previous day! My next planned stop was Sansiantai, a couple of small volcanic islands attached to the mainland ten kilometres down the road, and the Amis man who picked me up kindly took me there. I dumped my gear at a visitor centre and walked out to the quiet, isolated islands over a long bridge.

The black honeycombed islands afforded great views of the sea and of the whole spectacular east coast, northwards and southwards. From the outer island the coast looked particularly magnificent, scenes worthy of any tourist magazine cover. The small islands would have made a great place to camp, except that this was prohibited. Also, a typhoon was apparently headed in, and the sea and sky had started to take on the dramatic patterns associated with an approaching storm. Walking back across the eight steeped arches of the Chinese bridge that connected the islands to the mainland, I observed the ocean getting rougher almost by the minute. I looked for my Amis pal at the visitor centre where I had left him talking to friends, but he had disappeared. This left me with a long walk into Chenggong, the nearest town of any size. I walked for about an hour along the highway, feeling the winds about me strengthen as I did so, and then hitched the remaining couple of kilometres into town.

I had no choice but to sit it out in a guesthouse in Chenggong and wait for the typhoon to pass — the first lazy day I enjoyed, tired as I was from my strenuous walks along the coastal high-way. On this day it merely rained steadily without any accompanying high winds. I therefore took the opportunity to visit the National Taidong Oceanarium in town. The aquarium housed a variety of fish specimens including a giant shark whale that swam peaceful, but demented, circuits in a huge tank. As it was explained on some information boards in the aquarium, Chenggong was, from a fishing point of view, ideally located at the interface of two ocean currents, and this explained the enormous abundance of fish in the seas just offshore. A walk around the town's harbour brought me into direct contact with that abundance: a fishing trawler had just landed a huge catch of dolphin fish. When I strolled by, a crew of people were busy processing this catch of monsters; some filleted the fish whilst others hauled the fish up with large hooks, throwing them into the bucket of a mechanical digger, which presumably took them away for further processing. The fish were each about a metre long and must have weighed at least ten kilograms apiece. Watching the fish butchery was about the only excitement to be had in Chenggong, however; and my second and third day in town proved to be a total washout. I watched television at the guesthouse but the political debates in the local government legislature made for tiresome viewing and sent me into paroxysms of boredom.

Eventually the storm subsided and after paying my bills, I left the Chenggong guesthouse, swearing to myself not to watch any more television if it could be avoided, and walked along the coastal road in the cooling drizzle of the typhoon's tail. The main East Coast National Scenic Area Administration headquarters was located twelve kilometres down the road. Before starting to hitch, I walked a couple of kilometres to keep my legs in; after all, the typhoon had cleared the air and the mountains of the East Coast Mountain Range stood out massive, clear and imposing — a tremendous sight — and it had to be enjoyed on foot at least for a while. By the roadside, water trickled away everywhere and stands of coconut trees thrived in the warmer southern climate. I finally hitched my first ride of the day with a kindly local Taiwanese woman who went out of her way to take me to Scenic Area offices.

At the modernistic park headquarters, I accidentally walked into the administration-department part of the building. Ringing a bell at reception drew a blank. Realizing I was in the wrong place, I then made my way over to the visitor centre next door. But the people working in the centre lacked a concept of service. Two young girls, the children of bureaucrats most likely, struggled to communicate with me even in their own language. I asked if I could leave my bags at the desk: yes, that was okay even though, they made it clear, this was quite irregular. They also took my request as a cue to ask me with whom I was travelling and where I was going. No, I told them, I was here to ask the questions and they were here to answer them, and not the other way around. They did not like that and even said to me that I should smile — the employees of a visitor centre were *telling a visitor* to smile! Suppressing a scream I went off to tour the building before our "misunderstanding" got any worse.

The centre's exhibits covered topics such as plate tectonics, local ecology and Amis culture. In one thinly occupied area of the building, a wind-surfing board and a mountain bike had been deemed worthy of display, a bit ahead of time one felt. But the centre had no real focus, and the inevitable result was an exercise in superficiality. The controlled air-conditioned environment of the building was completely out of context in the subtropical environment; and what is more, this huge money-consuming bureaucracy had not produced a decent map of the area. I left the centre after about an hour resolved to make my way down to the port of Fugang as quickly as possible.

Ironically, it was an East Coast National Scenic Area park ranger who picked me up shortly after I left the air-conditioned nightmare of the park headquarters; a case of hitchhiking bringing people together. After driving for about an hour around a wide bay and past more Amis settlements with this nice man, I arrived at the port of Fugang, gateway to Green Island and Orchid Island. I thanked the ranger for the ride, stepped out into a broiling heat, and made a beeline for the ticket counter in the terminal building, where I paid for my passage to Green Island. The boat, an aging but powerful hydrofoil, was just about to leave, and it looked like I might miss it when one of the terminal staff took the initiative and gave me a ride on his scooter to where the boat was moored — for every one unhelpful person I met on my travels in Taiwan, I would encounter at least ten really helpful people.

AT FUGANG I found myself back on the tourist circuit. The hydrofoil boat at anchor in the harbour was filled with about 100 young Taiwanese people who were in party mode. A former fishing centre and home to political and high-security prisons, Green Island had become a popular getaway tourist destination for students and youngsters like these ones. I got on the boat. It took only 50 minutes to cover the 33 kilometres out to the small island, but curiously, given the calm sea, this was long enough for some people to get seasick. Fit and sick, we all bundled out of the sleek boat at Nanliao, the island's main harbour, upon arrival. Most of the tourists headed off to meet tour guides and mount scooters, but I had other ideas. Green Island, or Samasana Island as it is called by the Amis, was only about 20 kilometres in circumference, and this was an invitation to walk it, I felt. Outside the small fishing harbour, I started my hike.

The day had clouded over but it was still pretty warm, and I sweated profusely as I passed by a long line of stores and restaurants contiguous to Nanliao's waterfront. The place was quiet, as though waiting for people to arrive. I walked atop the sea-wall promenade and passed gaggles of scooterists swarming like locusts at the local gas station. Further along the promenade a small airport runway joined the seafront — only a large wind sock flying next to a fence gave it away. Just as I looked over this fence, a little passenger plane landed bringing in another tranche of tourists.

At the Green Island visitor centre, which I popped into by the way, some photographs of birds caught my attention. It is a little-known fact that hectare for hectare, Taiwan is one of the most ecologically, not to mention ethnically, diverse countries in the world, and apparently there were more than 500 species of birds to be found on Green Island alone. Many of these species were migratory but no fewer than 15 were endemic to Taiwan, and many more were unique, local versions of regional species. I had already seen the crested serpent eagle and the black-headed shrike on my travels down the coast, but there were so many more I did not know or could not identify. Leaving the centre I bought some provisions at a village store and then edged my way around the coast past another small harbour and on to the Green Island Detention Centre.

The detention centre held political prisoners during the 1949 to 1987 martial-law era. Latterly it had been turned into a museum dedicated to the struggle for human rights and democracy in Taiwan. I had read references to this detention centre — euphemistically named the "Freshman Disciplinary Camp" and "The Oasis Villa" by the authorities — many times and was eager to see it for myself. From a distance of a couple of hundred metres, the detention centre did indeed look a bit like a shabby holiday villa, but upon closer inspection, the barbed wire on its walls confirmed its former function.

In the post-war era Taiwan went through an economic boom, widely labelled an "economic miracle". A complex interplay of factors helped Taiwan to develop a modern economy; US aid and advice given to the nationalist government was of great importance in the early years. But in what came to be known as the 228 Incident, the nationalist government opened its rule on Taiwan brutally by murdering thousands of people; with US knowledge, authoritarian rule was extended long after the emergency conditions of the China civil war had ended. As the economy boomed, the nationalists set up a system of political control, modelled on bolshevism that reached down to every level of society. Once this system of control was in place, it only required the occasional murder to keep the citizenry in its place. Political opposition voices were silenced, and those who dared to speak out against Chiang Kai-shek, or his son Chiang Ching-kuo, soon found themselves on Green Island, or worse. As a text inside the museum summarized:

The rulers of that time [...] proclaimed draconian laws, dispatched their military, police and agents to tightly control society, contort the human spirit, and destroy human nature. All this was covered up, and no one dared talk about it.

Considering the sensitive nature of the topic, and the potential for getting it wrong, I thought the museum did a pretty good job of presenting the White Terror period, as it is known by historians, on Taiwan. On the walls of the museum, there were a lot of portrait photographs of the former inmates of the prison, some of whom went on to become leading figures in Taiwan's democracy movement and, later, government. One of them, the redoubtable Annette Lu, was still the vice-president of Taiwan at the time of my visit to Green Island. But there were many photographs of individuals I did not know; so many untold stories. The sentences of the prisoners were listed under their photographs: "10 years", "15 years", "12 years", "executed". Some people got ten years in this shit-hole prison for making a loose critical remark about the nationalist government. But what had one pretty, confident-looking young woman named Shih Shui-huan done to incur the wrath of the authorities? Apparently she had protected her younger brother, who had been sought by the police at the time of the 228 Incident; and for this action she received the death penalty — this is what is meant by "contort the human spirit and destroy human nature", because helping a sibling in trouble is the most natural of human instincts, most especially among people of ethnic Chinese descent. It is notable that many victims of the White Terror were women.

A group of people who had just arrived on a tour bus walked

into the museum as I was looking at the portrait photographs. They took only a perfunctory interest in the display information, but I suppose this is normal. It is usually intellectuals who feel a direct connection to political persecution, whilst the "average person" might regard it as something apart from themselves. But this museum contained everything one would need to conduct a valuable political educational programme, and it seems to me that Taiwan's authoritarian era could not be talked about too much. Unfortunately, the political practices of that era still negatively affect Taiwanese culture, and authoritarianism often rears its ugly head at the institutional level; the way the two receptionists at the East Coast National Scenic Area had tried to construct me into an ideal visitor being a case in point. Many Taiwanese people go along with this kind of subjection, not daring to answer back or rewrite the script. What the brave and hardy souls who ended up at the Green Island detention centre proved is that there is an alternative to being subjugated by authority, but that you have to fight for the right to define yourself, and to speak your mind. The battle for democracy is never won and must constantly be struggled for in the present. On the way out of the museum, I noticed closed-circuit television cameras on the walls of the prison. They were not part of an archaic system of oppression but modern operational surveillance equipment emplaced to monitor innocent people — authoritarianism has taken on new and disguised forms, and in fact it is all around us.

Another prison, a former high-security centre for convicted criminals deemed to be dangerous, stood next to the former detention centre. The prison was locked and boarded up; apparently not open to the public. But I had seen enough of prison cells and barbed wire for one day and was quite happy to pass it by as I continued my walk along the delightful coastline of Green Island. The road wound up to a high promontory and from there followed the cliffs south. After walking for about an hour or so on top of these cliffs, I started to scout for a place to camp but — as though my mind had been read — just off-road a sign declared *No Camping*. I naturally ignored the sign and, after collecting some water from a roadside vending area, followed a grassy path along the cliffs, fully intending to pitch my tent harmlessly somewhere in the rough. An ideal camping spot presented itself in the form of an abandoned military observation post nestled in among thick twirling screw-pine plants. I put my tent up inside the crumbling barracks, which was dilapidated but still had an intact roof. A lengthy walk from the coast road, no one bothered me, and I spent the rest of the evening observing sea birds through my binoculars.

In a reversal of roles, a herd of wandering water buffalo closely observed me as I left the military post in the morning. Obviously concerned to protect their calves, they even clubbed together to stare me down when I looked back at them. Further along the cliff top road, yet another abandoned fish farm came into view down on the shoreline — this one in quite an advanced stage of decay, and black as the ace of spades. Pyroclastic intrusions, also black in colour, stood up like miniature mountain ranges in the water just in front of the farm. There were no beaches to speak of on the exposed eastern side of the island; just exposed wave-cut platforms and lumpy outcrops of rock that few tourists bothered to venture down to inspect. After a while I hitched a ride in a farmer's truck to the island's official campsite in the more sheltered southwest corner of the island. Here I reserved a wooden shelter that stood among a stand of planted beefwoods — a haven for birdlife — unpacked, and took a rest. The campsite, which overlooked another wide seashore rock platform, was deserted save for a couple of Amis attendants.

Green Island's hot springs are quite famous in Taiwan, and the photographs I had seen of people luxuriating in the hot geothermal waters by the ocean in the middle of winter had been rather enticing. The springs were just 15 minutes away on foot back down the road, and so this was my chance to enjoy them at long last myself. A hot summer afternoon was probably not the best time for a soak in what was effectively a heated swimming pool, but I knew they would be crowded in the evening and so it was now or never. I got to the springs, bought a ticket, and headed down to the pools. The hot-spring baths were circular and carved into the wave-cut rock platform, their boiling sulphuric water made tepid by the addition of fresh water. After roasting in one of these baths for 15 minutes, I retired to a sheltered indoor pool for the rest of the afternoon. Less than half a dozen people were at the springs; the enervating heat turning everyone into lounge lizards. After bathing, I sat under an outdoor shelter. The bathing had succeeded in easing the chronic soreness in my leg muscles.

The ocean had been moody all day; a hot wind blew from the southwest, but only the occasional slap of rain made it to terra firma. Later in the evening it became damp and misty, but it also remained warm making sleeping difficult, even in a stripped down tent. The campsite attendants had left for Nanliao by the time I returned from the hot springs, and I spent the evening alone cooking and listening to birdsong. The woods were alive with birds but it was very difficult to spot any of them: they were small and flitted about like insects. Was that a streak-breasted scimitar babbler or perhaps a grey wagtail? No idea. The cacophony of sound coming out of the woods added to the aura of magic that is Samasana, and in the end, names were not really needed.

The next day I walked back to the harbour, where I spent an hour slumped in a chair outside a sailors' drop-in. Overhead, frayed blue awnings rustled in the wind like storm waves at sea. All was quiet at the harbour until the hydrofoil arrived and a roughly equal exchange of inbound and outbound passengers took place. I got on the boat and it soon roared off, cutting its way through a big ocean swell with impressive vigour. I had thought of taking a couple of seasick pills as a preventative measure, but when I opened the packet I had stored away for just such an occasion, I discovered that the pills had somehow melted.

To GET TO ORCHID ISLAND, known locally as Lanyu, one was obliged to take a dedicated boat from Fugang — there were no connecting boats from Green Island. It was also possible to fly there, but the sea passage was cheaper and on the whole more fun. After getting back to Fugang, the first thing I did was check the boat schedule: there were three departures per week on Monday, Wednesday and Friday. It was Wednesday, but the boat for Orchid Island had already left, so that left me a couple of days to visit Taidong City. From the harbour I hitchhiked the final few kilometres down Route 11 into Taidong.

A provincial subtropical city, Taidong is undoubtedly Taiwan's most laid-back urban centre, a place made up mostly of one-storey buildings and green space. When I got there the small shops and stores that sold cheap hats, rubber shoes and rip-off pre-recorded cassette tapes reminded me of 1980s Taiwan. There was not actually much to do in Taidong, but I rode around the local municipal park on a rented bicycle after checking into a business hotel by the railway station. Carefully landscaped, the park was actually a tract of land next to a river that had been lassoed in and bureaucratized. The trees there included some planted beefwoods and rare specimen trees, such as the magnificent orange-blossomed Madagascar flame tree. As I cycled around the trees, an armed military jet flew overhead, its long sleek fuselage and armaments pointed towards the ocean. There was a big artificial lake in the middle of the park. About a kilometre in length, the lake looked like an ancient Angkorian reservoir; there was no one about and very little infrastructure around the lake. A notice there read:

Warning Danger! Deep Water (at least 2 metres) No playing in the Water. The notice went on to say that visitors were responsible for their own safety. Fair enough. But what was the lake for if not to play and swim in? I rode the length of the mysterious pool, headed down to the nearby ocean, and then rode back into town along a driftwoodfilled shoreline. There was little else to do in Taidong other than mark time.

On the day of the boat ride to Orchid Island, I got up early and caught a bus from my hotel out to Fugang. After getting to the harbour I got on the boat, another hydrofoil smaller than the one that I had taken to Green Island, but big enough to carry a fair-sized contingent of people 150 kilometres southeast into the Pacific. I sat back in a cramped window seat and got ready to enjoy the ride. I was looking forward to visiting Lanyu; by all accounts the island was remote, unspoilt by mass tourism, and covered in a rich flora. About three times the size of its neighbour to the north, it was also home to a unique ethnic group, and I had a feeling that going there would be one of the highlights of the grand tour.

THE PORT of Kaiyuan was smaller than Nanliao; the harbour infrastructure was modest where it existed at all. The arrival of the boat, however, did excite a sudden flurry of human activity. As I clambered out of the hydrofoil, boxes and supplies were rapidly loaded and unloaded on the craft. Meanwhile, locals and tourists alike disembarked to meet their friends, lovers and tour guides. In no time, a group of 20 vacationing students were helmeted and queuing up for petrol at the nearby state-owned gas station. But Orchid Island was a decent size and easily absorbed the 100 visitors who had turned up; I was soon on my own. Kaiyuan lay on the west side of Orchid Island facing Taiwan; most of the tourists seemed to be heading south to the main village and administrative centre of Yeyou. After walking around trying to get my bearings and admiring the crystal blue waters of an apparently unpolluted ocean by the way, I tried to find a place to buy bottled water. Incredibly, there was none available at the gas station. At the small harbour offices a kindly man offered me a oneand-a-half-litre bottle of water from stores, a gift more precious than gold.

Once again I found myself walking anticlockwise around a Pacific volcanic island. It was a thrilling moment and it felt good to be striding out along a dramatic and quite beautiful coastline.

Compared to Green Island, Lanyu was mountainous. The mountains were not especially high — not more than 500 metres in height — but big enough to make hiking them a serious proposition. I therefore followed the coast road around the northwest headland. On the way to the headland, I got a good view of the mountainsides, which were cultivated in places; by the ocean, leafy taro plants grew in small flooded fields; further inland, banana trees lay scattered in among the root vegetables. Simple, raised sun shelters offered those who worked the land a respite from the fierce sun. As I walked along the road, a warm wind whipped up the waves in the deep blue ocean beyond the rocky shoreline. Sipping from the bottle of water, slathered in sun milk, and wearing a bandanna to cover my head, I sauntered along, contemplating the scene before my eyes, and time itself slowed down. After two or three kilometres, I came to the north-western corner of the island, marked by a rocky protrusion. A natural tunnel in the form of a raised cave afforded me some shade and a chance to take stock of the western bay, which looked very picturesque now that clouds had formed on the mountaintops. Resuming my hike, I walked through to the other side of the tunnel and stumbled straight into a very stiff onshore wind. Blown this way and that, I passed along a narrow cliffhugging section of the highway that eventually merged into a widened road after a couple of hundred metres. Although the village of Langdao had by now come into view, it was still some way off and when a truck came along, I hailed it and got a ride with some villagers who were transporting supplies back from the harbour.

The Tao people originally migrated to Orchid Island from the Batan Archipelago eight centuries ago. Culturally they are completely distinct from both the Han Chinese and Taiwan's other indigenous nations. Although the Tao hunted, they have never engaged in the practice of headhunting. The Tao developed a peaceful and harmonious relationship with their surroundings and with each other, social disputes being resolved by the use of symbolic, rather than real, violence. The Tao are expert fisherpeople, and fish in the offshore waters of Orchid Island in skilfully constructed wooden canoes. The fish-based diet is supplemented with taro and wild fruits and vegetables. This traditional diet is very nutritious and the resulting good gene pool is evident today in the excellent bone structure of the people and the longevity of its senior citizens. Until 1954 Orchid Island was off-limits to Taiwan's general public, but in the Chinese nationalist era, modernization arrived in the form of a penal colony, compulsory education for the local people, and later, a nuclear waste disposal facility. Although numbering only about 3,000 people, the remoteness of Orchid Island has at least served to limit inward migration, meaning that the Tao have up to now been able to keep their language and traditions alive. The culture killer in Taiwan is, ironically, formal education. It is the implanted desire for secondary and post-secondary education that draws young indigenous people away from their ancestral lands towards the cities. Once this happens, local social demographics and the local economy will start to become unbalanced, and any local language will start to die out — a process now in full swing on this paradise island.

The first thing I noticed in Langdao was in fact its elementary school. It was much bigger than it really needed to be, as though to accommodate the children of future generations as well as the presentday population. A model Tao home and statue of a Tao fisherman stood in the grounds of the school, a token cultural gesture, one felt. After leaving my backpacks at a roadside store near the elementary school, I went for a walk through the rest of the village. Half of the settlement, the part nearest the ocean, consisted of traditional dwellings built half underground to protect them from frequent tropical storms. Store rooms and rest shelters were close to one another above ground, and the gaiety of the village children testified to the intimacy of traditional village life. Further inland the village transmogrified into something like a clone-city suburb. Modern two- and three-storey houses made out of rebar and cement stood in two crowded lines like a street of two-up two-down houses in the north of

England. At the end of this street, I came to a traditional wooden sun shelter, the only one in this part of the settlement. I sat in the shelter a while. A young village girl returning from school joined me, as did an aging Tao woman who had been working in the fields. The pretty and confident young girl was curious about the Other I represented, and asked "Where are you from?" This was a learned question. When I gave her an evasive answer, she persisted in trying to stick an identifying label on me. In her hands the girl held a gun made out of rubber bands and chopsticks that she had been taught how to make at school. The old woman showed no interest in the girl, and was more at ease with the communal situation. Interestingly, she asked me all the questions I had come to expect to be asked by Chinese people, questions pertaining to my social and economic status. We struggled to communicate though as her Mandarin Chinese was far from standard and I knew no Tao language at all. Bored with me, she soon left the shelter, hauling her elderly frame and a basket full of vegetables back home. I then noticed all the fish hanging up to dry outside a nearby house, a reminder of the traditional economy. "Are you American?" the young girl asked me, changing tack slightly. "No I am not", I said, at loss for a better reply and immediately regretting my words. "I have to go now. Nice meeting you", I added before heading off back through the village to the harbour. As I went down the path, some more kids came along toting their chopstick weapons: "American!" they cried happily.

At a store down by Langdao's harbour, I tried to engage the woman who worked there in conversation, but she was not interested in me at all. She seemed depressed. A man, possibly a teacher or a police officer, came by the store whilst I sat outside drinking a soda and asked me what my business was there. By now I was losing patience with nosy state apparatchiks and told him quite bluntly that I was a traveller and that was all he needed to know. Taken aback by my aggressive changing of the script, he then tried to insinuate that he had only wanted to help me, which might possibly have been the case in the sense that he was probably angling to offer me some overpriced accommodation. But I was not in the mood for answering his questions and immediately left the village. Walking out of the Langdao, I noticed the village children enjoying an unsupervised swimming session in the harbour. Seeing the children at play near the talismanic white and red wooden Tao canoes laid up on the shore was heart-warming, and it was noticeable how open their body language was compared to their stiff and adult-like Hoklo contemporaries. The rocky shoreline beyond Langdao was honeycombed and sharp, and there was no level ground on which to camp. I therefore followed the Langdao Creek upstream about a kilometre into the island's interior, eventually finding a good place to camp. No one came up the creek path that night; I had been careful to put my tent in a position where it would not be spotted from the coast road.

But early the next morning, I was awoken by a man's voice. "Hello, hello...", at first I pretended to not hear, hoping the man would go away, but there was something innocent about the voice and whoever he was, he could not have been a state apparatchik. Realizing the little cub was not going to go away, I decided to put my best foot forward. "Good morning!" I said brightly, popping my head out from under the tent fly. The modestly dressed man looked like a labourer of some kind. He carried a small haversack and a long hooked knife. I made him a hot drink, which he politely accepted, and we sat in front of my tent and chatted in Chinese for an hour or so. The man was a 58-yearold Langdao villager. For a few years he had served as a ship's captain in Brazil, memories of which lit up his eyes and prompted utterances like "Hey baby!" as he reminisced. But the hardscrabble nature of his existence on Orchid Island was apparent in his dress and by the fact that he was going on a foraging expedition. The former captain told me he could sometimes earn US$25 a day cutting grass for the local government, but the work was not steady; and for the past two days he had been searching for a hard-to-find, special tree-plant that could be exchanged for cash on the open market. We got on to the subject of the nuclear-waste storage facility. The building of the facility had been strenuously opposed by the Tao people, but the local government were bought off and the site, suspected of leaking radioactive materials, now held around 100,000 barrels of semi-solid radioactive waste. "It's very dangerous — one sniff and you're dead", was the Langdao man's unscientific but not inaccurate assessment of the dangers of this waste material. Whilst we were talking, it began to rain lightly. Unprepared for the rain, I gave the man one of my small umbrellas, which he proceeded to break by continually opening and closing it; so then I gave him a disposable raincoat, and on that note our tête-à-tête came to an end. Reluctantly, the man walked off into the island's forest in search of the elusive high-value plant, and later I wondered if I should not have accompanied him.

One or two bonneted women were clearing foliage and tending taro plants in the fields as I hiked down the creek path back to the coast road. The mountains rose steeply from the coast here, as almost everywhere around the island, and they provided an interesting counterpoint to the empty ocean and limitless sky offshore. Telephone poles drove a line between mountain and sea and served as my road markers; I hiked eastwards towards them. After walking for a couple of hours along the quiet road, I arrived at the north-eastern extremity of the island. At a disused roadside bus shelter, I took a break and cooked a simple meal on my stove. As I was looking at the rock formation in the sea known as Lion-rock, a coast guard vessel approached and came in close to the shore. It appeared to be looking for something, though exactly what, I could not fathom. I ate my food and then carried on walking through the heat of the day. Around a corner I came face to face with the austerely beautiful east coast of Orchid Island: a barren road accompanied by only telephone poles wound around a deserted coastline made dramatic by the mountains, jagged rock formations out to sea, and bunching cumulous clouds hanging in the wide sky. The mountains and wave-cut rock platform were covered in lush green vegetation dotted purple with morning glories in full bloom. I stood for a few minutes admiring this vista, which was worth making the trip to Orchid Island for alone. Given the abundance of fish in the sea, there was obviously no need for fish farms on the island, but I did pass a disused chicken farm, perhaps a relic from the days when Lanyu hosted a penal colony. Apart from this old farm, the road was empty until Dongjing, known as Ranmeylek in Tao. Dongjing, actually two amalgamated villages, sat in a curvaceous bay on a small amount of flat ground at the foot of green mountains. As I walked into the settlement, I noticed a few male villagers sitting in the sun shelter opposite the harbour, but strangely there were no children swimming in the harbour on what was a hot day. At a small oasis of a roadside restaurant and café, I introduced myself to a Chinese girl who called herself Sophie, and ordered an iced coffee. I would visit this café several times over the next two days and often chatted to the kitten-loving Sophie, who seemed slightly melancholy despite having landed herself an excellent boyfriend and a goldengoose business. The rest of the village had a weather-beaten look to it, the result of frequent Pacific storms. There were no traditional homes in this part of the village, but neither were there any really large houses; the place looked a bit like a Cretan mountain village, except for the filleted fish hanging out to dry all over the place. Some wooden canoes sat in the front yard of the houses facing the ocean and along the stony shore, but the modest harbour was full of small, sleek boats equipped with powerful outboard motors.

Later in the day I discovered a great place to camp on the sandy beach of Dongjing Bay. Having found the spot, I settled into Crusoe mode, shaping the environment to my immediate needs — a pile of stones made for a table, a pine branch for a washing line, and a dugout sandpit for a tent platform. A quick swim in the bay told me why the beach was empty: the riptides were very strong, and there appeared to be jellyfish in the water. During the evening a fierce onshore wind nearly blew the tent away despite my careful placing of it.

Leaving my tent where it was, I spent the next day exploring the village more fully. Yeying was about the same size as Dongjing proper but enjoyed a slightly better aspect and was probably the senior part of the amalgamated village. Arriving there after a short walk, I rested at a communal shelter and observed the sea and the village. It was basically quiet, even though a cross-island road exited onto the coast road not far from where I was sitting. There was almost no activity at sea; most fishing was done at night. I walked to the far end of Yeying, where traditional houses had been sunk into the ground. Nearby these houses stood a whitewashed Catholic church that had been decorated with an abstract Tao mural. It was Sunday and I watched as a small, aging congregation left the church after morning mass, sort of hurriedly, as though to get away from somebody. There were very few young people about, and the village seemed to be in decline despite the presence of a guest-house and evidence of tourism in the form of a diving-gear rental outlet. After strolling about I bought some water and then hiked back to the main harbour and Sophie's restaurant, where I read and lazed about.

In the afternoon some village children came by and I gave them my binoculars to play with. Just as I was settling down to sketch some traditional Tao armour on display at the restaurant, two of the boys returned with the binoculars, which they had been told to return to me, an adult intervention. Feeling sorry for the bored boys, I took them on a little outing onto the nearby ridge promontory that overlooked Dongjing Bay. Sophie supplied us with a bottle of water and three plastic cups, and that was all we needed. The two boys made for lively company. They accepted me as an uncle, implicitly trusting me because I treated them as equals. The elder boy, who was maybe ten years old, told me his father had died and that he was living with his maternal grandmother in the village; his mother worked on the mainland. Like many children who have lost a parent, Remak was mature beyond his years and took good care of his younger cousin, whom I called Bob. As we walked out of the settlement the village lads, young muscular fishermen in the prime of life, passed us and walked on ahead, climbing swiftly up to the top of the promontory. I followed them with the two eager boys in tow, pulling them up in places where the path was too steep for them. Little Bob alternated "thank you, Uncle" with "no need, Uncle" as he scrambled up the slope. After reaching the flat ridgeline high above the village, I urged the boys not to run, accidents being apt to happen when walking in haste on mountain paths. But it was hard to control their excitable natures and they ran about forgetting my warnings. We made it to the end of the promontory, which afforded fantastic views of the bay, the village and the big blue sea. It was a hot afternoon and we guzzled several cupfuls of water after reaching the end of the cliff. The young men of the village were already there scanning the ocean with a powerful, but damaged, pair of binoculars. They were passionate about soccer. One of them said, "If Orchid Island formed a soccer team, we would win the world cup no problem", and the others concurred. They were proud men who had worked hard on the mainland to raise the funds to buy their expensive motorized boats. They sat together and drank a medicinal drink, offering me a cup. But they showed no interest in the boys, and so after a short while, I took my charges back down the hill, finishing the outing with a quick walk down by the sea. Curious to find out why none of the village children swam in the harbour, I asked the boys if they liked swimming. Remak then mentioned something about someone dying; when I pressed him for more details, he clammed up. After getting back to the village and sending the boys home, I sat at the café and sipped a beer. It was then that I learned from Sophie that a 39-year-old fisherman from Dongjing had recently been lost at sea. The coast guard, who I had earlier seen scanning Orchid Island's coastline, had been searching for him, but he was now officially missing, presumed dead.

That evening I walked back to my tent in an altered frame of mind. I wondered why no one was looking for the missing man; why a number of powerful boats sat idle in the harbour. "But the ocean is huge, where should we look?" replied one of the men at the village sun shelter when I queried him about the lack of an extended search. The community had already written off the missing man, and there was apparently nothing to be done about it. A tragic accident happening at sea is always a possibility for the Tao fisherpeople, and the village that would have felt this loss painfully nonetheless remained stoical about it. Later that night Zeus visited the Pacific, and the sky echoed with deafening thunderclaps. Continuous lightening splayed across the heavens, spewing deadly bolts down to the ocean. Only a little rain licked the beach, but the powerful lightening flashed for over two hours and scared the living daylights out of me. I lay huddled naked in my tent, not daring to move until morning. The dangerous thunderstorm had been a reality check; also writing off the missing man, I packed and left Dongjing early the next day.

The rest of my walk around Orchid Island went smoothly enough, and I covered the last dozen kilometres or so of the coast road in good time, stopping only once at a bus shelter by the sinister nuclear-waste storage facility for a picnic. The Taiwan government has repeatedly stated that this facility is perfectly safe, but the local Tao people have reported increased rates of cancer among the island population along with an unusually high incidence of deformities in newborn children. For these reasons the Tao continued to fight to have the facility removed, and the government has now put in place a plan to relocate it to the mainland. But would the people ever be able to plant taro again on the fields that were taken over by the state? That was the question in my mind as I nibbled on some bread. I then followed the starkly beautiful and almost completely unin-habited coast road from the nuclear storage facility around to the southern tip of the island. An occasional tourist minibus came by as I poured buckets of sweat on another hot sunny day. But I seemed to be walking faster, or at least better, than on the first day of my round-island walk and soon reached the Yeyou Creek, where I made camp for the night on a bed of rounded stones and bathed in a small, clean waterfall.

The next morning I walked past the local airport and the village of Hongtou and entered the main village of Yeyou early. This village was a bit more commercialized than the other villages; it served as a maintenance depot for buses, scooters and mechanical diggers. It was also the only village on the island where I saw teenage children and a hotel, the latter a rather rundown affair. With little to do, I finally walked up to Kaiyuan a little way up the coast road and waited for my ride back to the mainland. The hydrofoil arrived on time and left the harbour mid-morning. Only six passengers got on the boat for the return leg to Fugang. I was satisfied with my reconnaissance of Orchid Island but sad not to have got to know the place and its people better, and I hoped I'd be able to return someday.

AFTER A BRIEF STOP IN TAIDONG, I hiked out of the city on Route 9, which headed west and then swung north. The road up to Haiduan would take me through Taidong's suburbs and the Beinan, Luye and Guanshan Districts — I wanted to get to the Southern Cross-Island Highway. It was still very hot and walking was a chore; my backpacks weighed down on me like leaden bricks. In Beinan Town, about five kilometres west of Taidong, I dropped by a convenience store to stock up on bottled water and met a couple of local Puyuma ladies there. The indigenous Puyuma Nation, which inhabit the Taidong plain, number about 10,000 people today, but I had never talked to any of them before. The lady I met — a fat, dark-skinned beauty — was accompanied by her daughter, a pretty girl of elementary school age. As I sat taking a rest outside the store, I chatted with the young girl who sat down beside me. She proudly told me that she was off to her elementary-school graduation ceremony. I congratulated her on graduating, even though I had my doubts about her schooling. Her self-conscious mother then joined us and asked me where I was going and so forth, but she had little concept about individual travel and wondered why I would be alone. I did not bother to try and explain it. This brief interaction was my only contact with the Puyuma of southeastern Taiwan, traditionally a matriarchal society that apparently used to put its male youth through rigorous warrior training. Further along the road I did pass a Puyuma cultural village of some kind. *Wa a Dukan Da Dekal I Puyuma*, read the sign above its gate, but when I entered the village, the bamboo and grass huts appeared to be locked and no one was home.

After walking about ten kilometres up Route 9, I hitched a ride with a couple of men who hailed from Taidong City. They were out carcruising on their day off. When I told them I wanted to go up the road, they told me to get in the car. The two men seemed to have no idea of where they wanted to go and adopted my travel plan as their own: wherever I said I wanted to go, they offered to take me there. And in this way I briefly got to see the Luye plateau and one or two other scenic spots on the way up to Haiduan. The Taidong plain was fertile, attractive and completely laid-back. But in the distance the everpresent high mountains brooded and beckoned. Shortly before reaching my destination for the day, one of the men offered to put me up at his family's home in Taidong, but returning to that city was not on my agenda, and I told him I would soon be heading up the Southern Cross-Island Highway. He offered to take me at least part of the way. But I declined this offer since the afternoon was drawing on and I wanted to stop somewhere.

Chulai is a Bunun village, gateway to the mountains surrounding the Taidong plain. We got there late in the afternoon. The settlement was small but had a police station and a small elementary school. Leaving my bags at a roadside store near where I parted company with the two men from Taidong, I took a quick walk around and said hello to some locals, who greeted me warmly in return. Back at the store I bought a soda and mulled my options. I could always camp at the elementary school…but maybe I could find a quieter spot further up the road? As I was thinking things over, the store owner, an aging Bunun man, came out and chatted to me in a civil way. He was a former school teacher and spoke standard Mandarin Chinese fluently so communication was easy. He told me that the Bunun Nation, around 35,000 in number, lived over a widespread territory and basically "owned" the mountains above Chulai. I told him I would cross the mountains in the morning, and I planned to camp out nearby that night. The friendly ex-teacher offered me a room for the night, free of charge. At first I declined the offer, but eventually accepted it, not wanting to offend the nice man. It was all arranged quickly and without fuss, and soon I was unpacking in a tidy furnished room on the second floor of the store. As I was unpacking, the store owner's resident son, a young artist, introduced himself to me. The Chineseeducated man was diffident in the Confucian manner but evidently felt great pride in his clan bloodline. After we had chatted a little while, he showed me the ethnographic study on his home village that he had authored. What struck me — flicking through the book's many pages of photographs — was how long and how deep the process of cultural assimilation of the indigenous peoples of Taiwan had been: there were no photographs of hunting parties or people wearing traditional dress, but rather snaps of young people attending school graduation ceremonies and portraits of young Bunun men in national military uniform. The storeowner's son, a fine-arts graduate, told me that Bunun households had the right to keep their ancestral homemade rifles at home and still used them on occasional hunting trips. Of course, the hunting was not what it used to be, and these days the authorities were serious about stopping poaching, but he had been hunting himself on many occasions. He told me by way of a slight reprimand that he would never leave his home village.

I left Chulai early the next morning. The storeowner could have arranged a ride into the mountains for me, but I wanted to get a walk in first and so slipped away before the morning rush hour began. And what a beautiful morning for a walk it was — the sun shone in a blue sky, but it was pleasantly cool in the shade. A white and black bird sat perched on a fencepost as I hiked past, which augured well, I liked to think. Just outside the village stood a tremendous statue of a longhaired Bunun hunter carrying an animal on his shoulders. Such statues are a relatively new thing in Taiwan and represent an emerging aboriginal pride: Taiwan's indigenous cultures, though irrevocably assimilated into the economic mainstream, are nonetheless negotiating a new relationship with the dominant culture, one that demands more respect for cultural differences. Opposite this statue a road sign indicated that Tainan was 204 kilometres distant across the mountains: not much respect for the intervening Bunun villages there. I marched off up the valley that reminded me in some ways of the Lanyang valley. There was the same sense of the dramatic; the telescoping of multiple mountains beside a wild riverbed, and the same sense of an alternative world and a previous time. I continued walking up the quiet valley road, covering about five kilometres in one hour. A little pickup truck eventually came along and I waved it down. The driver, a Paiwan man, stopped and told me he was on his way to Sinwu and would be happy to take me there.

The Paiwan are another of Taiwan's indigenous nations, and they inhabit a wide territory in southern Taiwan. They are an ethnic group that I had had little contact with over the years, and I knew almost nothing about them except what I had read in books, so it was interesting for me to meet this man. A former major in the Taiwan army, he spoke Chinese perfectly, but he also had an aboriginal character and identity, expressed partly in his easy-going manner. He was interested in how much my kit weighed, how far I had walked that morning, and how long it had taken to cover this ground. I was not surprised to learn from the major that my pack was about equivalent in weight to that carried by infantry, and my walking speed was about equivalent to that of a soldier on exercise, the difference of course being that soldiers on exercise do not have the option of hitching a ride when they get tired. The canny retired officer, who seemed quite adept at extracting information from me, had got himself a supervisor's job at a small construction site in Sinwu. On the way there we stopped at another small village for drinks. The

Bunun villagers treated the Paiwan man cordially, as they would any outsider, but clearly relations were not especially warm. In the pre-modern era the Bunun and Paiwan were deadly enemies, but it was actually the Paiwan man's status as a boss that marked him apart. We presently left the village and then, after a brief visit to the construction site where he worked, the major took me to a spot beyond Sinwu, where we said farewell and where I resumed my walk.

In reality Sinwu was just a small village, and almost none of it could be seen from the road. I carried on walking up the mountain highway without bothering to explore the settlement. Having quickly gained several hundred metres in altitude, the air on the high road was cool and therefore the walk less oppressive than it might have been. Staring across the narrowing valley, I spotted my first eagle of this cross-island journey. The great bird glided about effortlessly high in the sky, no doubt searching for a quarry. Not far ahead I noticed that the road climbed at an impossible rate in tight switchbacks — hitchhiking was definitely the order of the day. The driver of the next vehicle that came along slammed his truck to a halt beside me when I waved him down; he told me to jump in and off we went, just like that. The lively 50-something Bunun man went by the name of Dilong. He had been on a shuttle run to Taidong to pick up lunchboxes and newspapers for a team of workers who were reinforcing slopes further up the highway. Dilong, an open-hearted and good-natured fellow, was one of the most loquacious people I met during my travels around Taiwan, and within half an hour or so we had talked about many things. I asked him about the workers' pay and he told me it was down to US$60 a day from a high of US$150 per day five years previous; the opening of the Taiwan economy to foreign labour had effectively depressed wage levels. We passed Lidao, the last major Bunun settlement in Taidong County that sat on some flat land tucked away in the mountains, like a miniature Machu Picchu; it was Dilong's home village. Dilong told me it was characteristic of the Bunun to site a village at any altitude and in any place, unlike the Atayal, who traditionally always chose lower elevations on which to build. After driving for 50 minutes up tight hairpin bends, we finally arrived at the road works. Dilong introduced me to his aging father, a spry 70-yearold man who seemed to fulfil some kind of leadership function at the site among the mostly Bunun workers there. I remembered the photograph of Bunun men practicing archery that I had seen at the museum in the Formosan Aboriginal Culture Village in Nantou and felt the same spirit of equality among these tough workers. The ever solicitous Dilong invited me to stay at the workers temporary camp for the night, but the day was still young and I wanted to push on with my journey. The talkative supervisor then took me to an isolated area a couple kilometres beyond the worker's camp, where I donned a raincoat and prepared to start hiking again, but not before Dilong insisted I take a photograph of him. "Gairay, hey Gairay take a picture of me!" I had in fact taken a few candid snaps of Dilong as we had driven along and was happy to take another one. After exchanging addresses, we then parted company.

From Lidao, the Southern Cross-Island Highway climbed westnorthwest high into the mountains; I suddenly found myself walking at an altitude of over 2,000 metres. At this elevation the forest smelt boreal, and it started to rain. Not unhappy, I hiked up the forested road through the downpour. Roadside streams choked with boulders and fallen logs gushed like fountains. Tall skinny hemlocks gave the forest a magical artificial appearance in the rain. I was not far from the famous 2,772-metre-high Daguanshan Tunnel, which marked the boundary between Taidong and Gaosyong Counties. Just before the Yakou, or mountain pass, I was wondering how I might get up and through this tunnel when a young couple driving up the highway stopped and offered me a ride. This was a generous offer, considering I was loaded down with gear and soaking wet. Talking to the young couple, I did not really pay attention to the road, which was fogged in at the Yakou in any case. The Taiwanese man, in his early thirties, had recently returned from studying in the US; his girlfriend worked for a telecommunications company in Taibei and spoke to me very politely as though I were a relative of her boyfriend. They had been driving around Taiwan in his new car for five days and were now headed to Tainan City. I liked this couple, who epitomized Taiwan's emerging middle classes, because they had done something adventurous by themselves and because they were in love with one another. When I told them that I was on day 95 of a grand tour, they were quite surprised, and so was I. We soon hit the long, narrow and bumpy Daguanshan Tunnel and, after a five-minute drive, emerged out on the other side of it into Gaosyong County and Yushan National Park.

At first, nothing much changed and it remained wet and foggy, but a kilometre or two down the highway the weather miraculously cleared up. I wanted to start walking down the road at Tianchih, a scenic mountain resort, but we overshot the poorly marked site and I ended up getting out of the car ten kilometres further down the highway at Jhongjhihguan. As we both stood beside the car, the girl did not quite know how to end our association. I smiled at her, said thanks, turned around, and walked off.

The highway at Jhongjhihguan was dry, the forest dense and full of impressive tall trees. Walking past a small deserted rest station, I contemplated camping out but ironically, given all the streams I had passed only an hour before, the lack of a reliable water supply forced me to abandon this idea. As I was walking down the slightly misty road, a cyclist appeared from nowhere riding up the steep incline. His Taiwanese-made road bike was laden with panniers, and it looked like hard work getting up the gradient. Barely acknowledging me with a nod — or maybe just the regular movement of his head in time with the downward push of one of his legs — he passed me and rode relentlessly on towards the Yakou. Good luck to him, I thought, and then carried on hiking downhill. Not feeling particularly tired and in a relaxed mood, I stopped here and there to admire the splendid trees. I had no idea what lay ahead, but the going was good.

A while later a couple of Bunun road workers riding 125cc motorcycles came hurtling down the highway. One of them stopped and asked me what I was doing. I told him I planned to walk an indeterminate distance down the highway before hitching a ride. A little concerned, the man assured me that there would be few vehicles passing by later in the afternoon, and the weather forecast was for rain. He more or less insisted I get on the back of his motorbike. When I mentioned the fact that my backpack was heavy and that this might upset his centre of gravity, he seemed quite unperturbed and again told me to get on; if I did not go with him, there was every chance of me getting caught out in a storm. It seemed prudent to heed his warnings. The short but stocky and strong man took my small backpack and slung it over the bike's petrol tank whilst I somehow managed to squeeze onto the back of the motorcycle seat, still carrying my large backpack, a more or less balanced arrangement. What followed was a hair-raising ride down to Meishan, the next major settlement on the Southern Cross-Island Highway 30 kilometres distant. I yelled at the man to slow down more than once. He slowed each time I made such a request, but speeded up again out of every corner. He was at least driving very well, if too fast by my own conservative standards. The wooded landscape sped by, and I rued the missed chance to walk a bit more along this scenic highway that cut through Jade Mountain's backyard, but the atmosphere was getting close and it was right to seek shelter in such conditions. We made it to Meishan in less than an hour. The Bunun man lived in Taoyuan further down the road and so dropped me off at the local Youth Activity Centre in the village. I was completely exhausted from holding a static position for so long with so much weight on my back and struggled to lift my leg over the bike. Finally, I got off and gave a "Phew" look to the man. "Are you afraid of me?" he suddenly asked — I must have looked a little shaken up. "No, but I was afraid we might have had an accident. Anyway, good driving", I gasped. The Bunun man smiled and left for home and I blew, quite literally, into the YAC.

It poured down with tropical rain during the night, but next day the sun shone again, casting its warm light on the steep wooded slopes opposite the YAC. I immediately set about packing, intending to make a detour to visit the ethnically Bunun part of Meishan, which was located about a kilometre and a half away. Outside the hostel I glanced into the sky and spotted another eagle circling over a distant valley. It seemed to point the way to the Bunun village. Following a sign, I hiked over to the settlement, which was not difficult to find. The walk took me along a narrow mountain road — partly protected from rock fall by a reinforced concrete colonnade — and across a high bridge that overlooked a picturesque mountain river. The small Bunun village — composed entirely of modern brick and concrete homes — was neat, tidy and quiet: but it was the wrong time to visit a village and no one was at home. I walked past a church, across a suspension bridge, and around an old forestry road before returning to the main highway. In the morning sunshine, the surrounding steep mountains looked most inviting in a picture-postcard kind of way; a lifetime's worth of exploring was available right on this village's doorstep. Another eagle, or perhaps the same one I had seen earlier, screeched exquisitely as it flew off into its hunting grounds over those green heights.

My last contact with Bunun people came when I entered the much larger village of Taoyuan, eight kilometres away down the Southern Cross-Island Highway. I had walked along the scenic highway that snaked down from Meishan. Taoyuan was at least half ethnically Han Taiwanese and functioned as an administrative centre. When I arrived, tired, it was lunchtime and groups of Bunun workers ate and boozed in party mode at small restaurants around town. Later they would troop off to their hard manual labour on the highway and in nearby fields. Though there was still some distance to travel before reaching the plain proper, by the time I got to Taoyuan, I sensed my trip across the mountains had ended. After sitting on a stool outside a store in the shade watching the lunch hour unfold, I hitched a ride travelling on the back of a truck that left the village headed southwestwards. The driver and his friend were Bunun workers and they were going to Baolai, a rafting centre, about 20 kilometres down the road in Gaosyong County. They dropped me off in Baolai after a pleasant cooling ride down the mountain road, and from the river town I walked another ten kilometres or so along the highway downwards until night fell whereupon I set up camp by a disused roadside shelter.

The next day I continued my journey down into Gaosyong County, reaching the outer limits of the plain. Mangos, lemons, bananas and betel-nut trees grew everywhere here, watered by the fast-flowing Laonong River — another Eden-like scene. The plain was hot, and after walking only four or five kilometres, I elected to hitch. By a series of short rides, I tacked over to the Hakka Chinese village of Meinong to the west of the Laonong River valley; and from there, after a short break, hitched directly to the bright-lights big city of Gaosyong.

———

COMPARED TO THE MOUNTAINS, Gaosyong was like New York, a beehive of anonymity and a permanent revolution of activity. The sudden shock of being in a city again was momentarily overwhelming, and I naturally sought the sanctuary of a hotel on arrival. A downtown hotel near the railway station looked okay and I booked into it. No sooner had I entered my room than someone knocked on the door. I opened it and a brash woman strode in uninvited. She stood in the middle of the small room near the vanity table all business. "Yes, you want massage?" She said this giving a little mime massage in the air with her flabby, wrinkled hands. It was not exactly a Cleopatra moment, and I was rather taken aback by the woman's brusqueness. Did I not pay for this room? Did she really have a right to walk in like that? It seemed extraordinary. "I don't think I called room service", I replied quickly, trying to figure out how best to deal with the intrusion; one needed to proceed with care because behind this woman stood the mafia. "You want a girl, yes?" she added, seeing me hesitate. Err…, no actually. Well, not under these terms anyway. "I'm sorry, you have the wrong room", I said gesturing gently with my hand for her to exit the room. Perhaps used to such rejections, she left promptly without comment. Gaosyong is quite a handful. It has a population of around one and a half million people, possibly the only city in Taiwan with a numerically significant industrial working class, and it feels big. Having visited the city only in the summer months, it is a place I associate with heat, traffic and dirt. A first glance of my surroundings on a foray out of the hotel seemed to confirm all these impressions: it was hot and steamy outside, the roads were teaming with vehicles, and the air quality left a lot to be desired. During my first day in town, I went out shopping; I urgently needed to get fresh reading material — I had finished *War and Peace*. I hunted down the local branch of one of Taiwan's largest chain bookstores, which I eventually found in a downtown department store. The store, with its stylized window dressing, polished floors, elevators and high ceilings seemed quite surreal to me. After a quick search of the English-language bookshelves in the starship-like bookshop, I selected *The Motorcycle Diaries* by Ernesto "Che" Guevera and *Death of a Revolutionary* by Richard Harris for purchase. The books were a bit on the slim side, but the upside of this was that they would not be burdensome to carry. After leaving the department store, I looked in vain for a bar to have a drink. Taiwanese people do not, generally speaking, socialize at bars, which tend to be thin on the ground, and after searching fruitlessly for about an hour, I gave up and returned to my hotel feeling somewhat lonely — which explains why there had been a pimp working the eleventh floor when I had arrived in town that afternoon.

The next day, determined to get to grips with the southern metropolis, I rented a scooter to explore the city. Gaosyong, heavily bombed during World War II, was rebuilt according to a grid system and is therefore a city designed for car use. But the city's streets all looked fairly similar, making orientation for me quite difficult at first. Out riding around on the bike, I turned this way and that, not really knowing where I was going. I eventually drove north towards the city's suburbs and surrounding hills for no other reason than it was somewhere to aim for. After a short drive I arrived at a park area known as Chengcing Lake. This lake, an oasis set in some green space, was almost completely enveloped by the surrounding city, and it seemed like the shallow water of the lake might evaporate before my very eyes. After a quick circuit of the lake, I drove westwards towards the coast. Getting to the coast road required driving through the city's western hills, where the swankiest properties, a large temple and a campsite, were located. I dropped by the temple for the views over the city and even checked out the campsite, which turned out to be a pathetic patch of unused land that evidently no one took much interest in. The northern part of Gaosyong Port, abutting a nearby university and some former colonial buildings, is the most popular part of the city for tourists, and I went there next. Arriving at the former British Consulate, which stood on a cliff just south of an entrance to Chongshan University, I parked my bike and went to take a quick look around. The consulate was similar in feel to the one at Danshuei; it had the same excellent position overlooking a waterway, and the same irrelevance to the contemporary era.

Driving beyond the consulate northwards, I found myself on a nice little cliff-top road that overlooked the silver sea. This road eventually led to a no-through barricade marking the outer perimeter of the Zuoying naval base. I drove back along the road, stopping to scan the silhouettes passing by on the sun-bleached ocean with my binoculars from the top of the cliff. Sweeping the magnifying glasses around, I was surprised to spot three Taiwanese marines swimming naked in the sea below on the shoreline, which was perhaps not a bad idea on such a hot day. In an amusing drama, an officer turned up on the scene and reprimanded the soldiers. The officer looked up at the cliff where I was standing as though to check if anyone were watching; when he did this, I waved to him. My binoculars were not powerful enough to make out his facial expression, but he did not wave back, and so maybe did not see the funny side of things. I quickly drove back along the cliff road past a hilltop radar station and some kind of urban warfare training ground. I circled back to the university to see if I could sneak onto the school's private beach, but it was better guarded than the Zuoying base, and at this point I gave up on Gaosyong. It was too hot and there was too much traffic and dirt for me to enjoy the place, and my chances of making a friend there were about zero. On the way back to the bike rental, I dropped into the railway station and bought a next-day oneway ticket to Pingdong City.

THE WINDOWS of the local train to Pingdong had been sealed to keep the air-conditioning in, a bit of a disappointment. I had deliberately chosen the "ordinary" class train, wanting to poke my head out into the rushing slipstream, but the *putongche* had effectively become a regular semi-express train, except that it stopped at all stations. I took a window seat in the mostly empty, chilled carriage and sat back to try and enjoy the slow 25 kilometre journey inland anyway. The landscape was drier and browner here than in the north, but no less fecund. The land drifted by like an old film, one yellowing, rural, tropical still image blurring into another — all palms, fronds and rice. About halfway the train crossed the sun-drenched Gaoping River, the boundary between Gaosyong County and Pingdong County. The remnants of an old bridge stood parallel to the railway line in the shallow waters of another deceptively gentle-looking river. Sitting in the cold carriage, I felt like a piece of meat being transported to a supermarket. But before long I got my chance to warm up; after storing my bags at Pingdong Station, I went on a brief walkabout in the county capital.

A sleepy provincial city, Pingdong was quite different in many ways from its burgeoning coastal neighbour, but similar in one respect: it was absolutely broiling hot outside. The streets of

Pingdong with their 1960s five-storey concrete buildings, Cuban fern trees and obscure local banks reminded me of Tainan City, where I had lived for a couple of years in the late 1980s; there were the same kind of clone retail outlets, temples, and streets named after places in China. The place was laid back, relatively speaking, but not civic in any way — a frontier town essentially. Pingdong sits in the northwest corner of a large elongated county that includes a mountainous northeast sector and the flat Hengchun Peninsula further south. It has many more districts than any other county in Taiwan, perhaps reflecting its geographical and ethnic complexity — a colour-coded map of the county was an amazing patchwork quilt. My original plan had been to travel directly south through the length of Ping-dong, but after studying the map, I spontaneously decided to make a little detour through the nearby mountains first. My motivation to do so on this occasion was a desire to make contact with the indigenous Rukai Nation, who inhabited a relatively small but very rugged area north-northeast of Sandimen (the larger Paiwan Nation occupied villages immediately to the south and all the way down to the Hengchun Peninsula). After wandering around the city for a while, I found I could no longer cope with the heat, or the déjà vu. I bought some provisions, picked my bags up at the railway station, and then headed over to the county bus station, where I caught a bus to Sandimen. This would be my only chance to meet the Rukai, the hundred-pacer-snake-worshipping people.

The 15-kilometre journey to the outlying district of Sandimen Town took about 40 minutes, the bus frequently stopping to drop kids off at the many small villages en route. The plain was thriving, the genius of Taiwanese culture guaranteeing successful farming outcomes and healthy social communities. Then the other Taiwan came into view: mountain Taiwan — the mountains, of course, represented a completely different culture; a different way of being. I got off the bus at Shueimen, the major crossroads village at the foot of the mountains in Sandimen District. From this starting point I would enter the mountains three times along different access roads in the next couple of days. The first of these forays involved following a road east out of Shueimen along the South Ailiao River valley.

A sign indicating the *Indigenous Peoples Cultural Park* led me up one road, which headed south-eastwards along the valley, a natural border between Rukai and Paiwan territory, a border matched by the modern administrative boundary between Sandimen and Majia Districts. When I got there, I found the entrance to the 83-hectare cultural park was barricaded, and there was a charge for entry, whereupon I flashed my old and invalid press card, which got me in for free. A vast amount of money had obviously been spent on building the large visitor centre, reception and a hotel just beyond the gate, but the rest of the park was a scatty affair. In the visitor centre some general information and artefacts about aboriginal culture had been put on display, but it was mostly general stuff that did not relate to the immediate environment or to the Rukai and Paiwan nations specifically. After taking a peek around the visitor centre, I strode outside into the hot sun and walked into the park proper. Multiple replica, traditional indigenous houses had been placed on slope land by the road, in much the same manner as at the Aboriginal Culture Park in Nantou County. The difference was that this park was owned by the government, looked a little neglected, and was not making any significant revenue. The whole idea of the park had one fundamental flaw: it had been put on either side of an access road, which meant that most visitors would drive through without stopping. This was a pity because the replica houses were actually very authentic and interesting to study. But without people or models, they were also rather static and lifeless, and therefore unattractive to the average Taiwanese visitor. I walked through the park along the main road, taking a close look at some of the houses by the way, and then hiked up over a hill above the road. The fantastic views of the valley and of the high mountains made the effort of ascending the hill trail worthwhile. I was again struck by the contrast between the mountains and the plain as I glanced back at Shueimen Village, now a dot on the low-lying land behind me. The valley, so different from the plain, was covered in moon-like grey alluvial deposits and ringed with betel-nut trees. The hill trail led back down to the access road and, appropriately enough, some traditional Rukai and Paiwan houses made of slate and thatched grass. It occurred to me that the inside of one of these houses might make a good place to camp for the night, and so I started to inspect their interiors. Eventually I found a roomy thatched hut not too far from the road, which seemed ideal. After getting settled in and eating a meal, I went down to the road and spent the remainder of the day mountainwatching.

My goal, which I formulated overnight perusing a tourist brochure, was to visit "Old Haocha", an abandoned Rukai village located somewhere in the mountains up the valley. The slate houses of the Rukai with their carved lintels and roof posts interested me, and I thought it might be interesting to seek out an "authentic" village. With this goal in mind I left the park and began walking up the valley. Before long I came to the first road works, and although the partial collapse of the road was quite negligible, it did sort of announce the mountains. After a pleasant hour's walk along the shaded, narrow mountain road, I hitched a lift with a road engineer who was going to work. He told me that the road above (New) Haocha was badly damaged and that he was a part of the crew currently patching it up. I asked the driver about the trail to Old Haocha, but despite having worked in the area for many weeks, he could not tell me much about this trail; he was merely aware of its existence. I got out of the engineers' pickup truck at the entrance to Haocha and walked into the village.

The secluded village was quiet and there was little activity going on. The houses were mostly simple stone and wooden dwellings, but some used slate extensively in their walls. There were several three-storey villas in the village, which was clear evidence of income inequality. In fact, traditional Rukai and Paiwan society was class-based, and so some kind of inequality in property was only to be expected. The houses and the village were neat and tidy. Depictions of a talisman showing a hundred-pacer snake, a highly poisonous pit viper that used to be common to southern Taiwan, adorned some doorways, and door and window lintels. The lack of children's voices was noticeable, however — and this seemed to indicate that the village was in decline; it was no surprise to find the local elementary school looking sad and neglected. Near the school I bumped into a man who introduced himself by a common Chinese surname. I asked him about the trail to Old Haocha. "Won't you get lost if you try to go there?" he answered by way of a reply. Well, honestly how should I know? I could not be bothered to interrogate the man any further and walked away.

The road out of Haocha wound up a steep incline. I followed the road for about half a kilometre, where I came across the engineer who had given me a ride that morning. Not far away the engineer and a crew of workers were busy repairing the mauled road. The engineer was busy looking at plans, and so I continued on my way without stopping to talk to him. The driver of a huge digger politely halted his actions for half a minute whilst I squeezed past the giant machine. I then walked up to the top of the hill and around a bend and came face to face with a tremendous vista. The mountains in the southern section of the Central Mountain Range, particularly tough walking terrain known by Taiwan's hikers as "South One", dominated a wide horizon. The trail to "Old Haocha" actually began where the road ended nearby; a small finger sign pointed the way. It was still early, the sun was shining, and I had food and a tent: what was I waiting for? I hit the trail thinking I might cover the five kilometres or so to the old village — known to the Rukai as Kochapongan — before lunchtime.

The trail turned out to be a challenging obstacle course. The first 100 metres took me past the landslide that had taken out the road, and it required concentration to keep my balance on a steep scree slope. This was probably the most dangerous part of the hike — right there at the beginning — but it was certainly not the most strenuous section. After walking along the side of the slope for about 20 minutes, I bumped into a Rukai couple who were doing some running repairs to a homemade reservoir and water-supply system. They asked me where I was going, and when I told them Old Haocha, they warned me that it was a difficult three-hour trek away, saying, literally, "Not good walk". I thanked them for their information and moved on, not yet discouraged. In no time I came to the first of a series of deeply eroded gullies that had to be negotiated by climbing up and down their steep sides. Climbing over the first two gullies was sort of okay though rather exhausting work, but the third one was really tricky. For one thing, the trail was difficult to discern in the lunar-like landscape. I had to stop and search for climbing tags and other hints to try and determine the route. I got lost, but retrieved the situation by back tracking and starting again. So far, it had taken me an hour to walk less than one kilometre — no wonder they moved the village. After the gullies, the path levelled out and turned into a reasonable walk along the side of a valley. Around a corner a farmstead stood in the middle of some semi-cultivated land. The farmstead, a small low-rise dwelling made out of slate and wood in the Rukai style, had a terrific view of the South Ailiao River below and of the high mountains in the distance.

There was evidence that someone still lived at the farmstead: clothes had been put out to dry and a serviceable long knife hung from a nail by the doorway. But whoever lived here, they were poor and, judging from all the old spirit bottles lying about, alcoholic. I sat down and brewed a tea in the dwelling's tiny yard. Too bad I did not meet the person or people who lived there because by now I had given up on the idea of visiting Old Haocha. The walk across the gullies had been mentally taxing and who knows what other obstacles lay ahead even if I did find the trail; there were just too many unknowns and I did not fancy it anymore. Instead I spent a lazy hour at the farmstead gazing into the mountains, admiring the blooming wild lilies and catching the breeze. In the distance, beyond the river, the majestic and beckoning twin peaks of Dawu Mountain glistened in the sun. I was in the realm of the Rukai. But hardly anyone lived here anymore, and nature was already reclaiming its lost ground. Leaving the farmstead forever, I returned the way I had come.

Walking back through the village of New Haocha, I finally met some identifiably Rukai people in the yard of a store. Two dignified ladies sat embroidering some snake-head patterns onto cloth. To establish a relationship, I asked one of them if I could have a go at the embroidering and she let me do a little bit. She teased me for my poor effort, but I argued that my needlework was good enough. The women were curious about my little jaunt out into the hills. The lady who let me embroider her cloth told me she had lived in Kochapongan during her childhood. She used to walk to school every day along the trail, but in those days the gullies and other natural obstacles had not yet made the path such a difficult hike. An aging Rukai man who joined us in the store's yard remained diffident, but he listened with interest to our conversation. These Rukai people were quite assimilated to modern ways, but exercised the kind of reserved social etiquette one finds in monarchical class-based societies. After chatting for a little while longer, I left the women and man and hitched a ride back down to Shueimen with a local who was going that way.

Back at Shueimen I crossed a major road bridge that took me to the administrative centre of Sandimen District beyond the Ailiao River. The plains-style village was of little interest to me and so I started walking along Provincial Route 24, which led eastwards towards the Wutai District, an exclusively Rukai village. Before getting to Wutai, I took a small detour to Dewen, a Paiwan village made up of several churches, an elementary school, and clusters of wood and brick residences, some of which were nicely kept. The late afternoon view, through betel-nut palms, across the mountains had a certain charm, but when I tried to talk to some locals, I found them to be uninterested. I sensed that this was another village divided. There was no suitable place for me to camp in the cramped settlement anyway, and so I hitched back to Sandimen with, of all people, the pastor of the local Presbyterian Church. The pastor was a friendly Paiwan man. He told me that there were other interesting villages to visit further up the road. But a lengthy and quite superficial conversation about the contrasting personalities of Rukai and Paiwan people suggested to me that the pastor was not a reliable guide to authentic indigenous culture — whatever that may be. The pastor dropped me off at Sandimen before heading off in his swish car to some pressing engagement down on the plain. It was getting late and I either had to go down onto the plain myself or try hitching a ride up to Wutai. Calculating that I could get a ride with someone returning from work, I started to hitch. My luck was in and before long, a four-wheel-drive vehicle stopped and the occupants, a Rukai couple, offered me a ride up the road.

In the short time available to me, I tried to learn something from this couple, but they were reticent in the Confucian manner: I was a complete stranger and we were speaking in Chinese, after all. The woman did mention something about the Bunun being their traditional enemies, but that they were all friends these days, a story I had heard before. Judging by their vehicle, the couple were relatively prosperous. By their manner, I guessed that they were Christians. The woman asked me if I had faith, a question that always leaves me somewhat flabbergasted since it presupposes there is only one valid faith, which is palpable nonsense. I said something about believing in everything, my stock response to the faith question. We got onto the issue of where I would stay for the night. The couple ran a guest-house in their ancestral home and, for an exorbitant amount of money, offered me a room. It annoyed me that they were trying to take advantage of me in this way, but to reward them for giving me a ride earlier I took a room at a reduced rate. It was dark outside when we arrived at the couple's house, an old slate building that had been converted into separate apartments. The small room given to me was odd to say the least: it was essentially part of an old barn full of bric-a-brac, including framed bad sketches, various household items, old brass instruments, and some aboriginal hunting trophies in the form of boar jaws and muntjac horns. The couple became solicitous to me when they realized that I was not a roving moneybags. But the damage had been done, and I did not really trust them. Retiring to the slate house, I closed the wooden shutters and crashed out on the black floor.

The next morning, the mountain road looked nothing if not inviting, and I soon left the village to hike up it. The highway climbed into the hills above Wutai, passing a slate graveyard, where an empty row of graves had thoughtfully been prepared for the soon-to-be-departed. The road then evened out and wound along the side of a pretty but largely deforested valley. It was not long before I encountered a series of road works, where a group of workers were busy placing stones inside a wire frame, laboriously building up a strong reinforcing wall. The side of the valley was very steep, affording a terrific bird's-eye view of the snaking river below, but its steepness also made the road vulnerable to landslides, especially during the typhoon season. I carried on past the workers through clouds of dust, and reached another long clear stretch of road. The walk that followed was one of the most enjoyable I would do on the grand tour: neither strenuous nor dangerous, it was yet tremendously romantic to be out walking along on a quiet high mountain road in the middle of summer. Keeping to the main highway, I walked for hours passing the turnings for several satellite villages, happily daydreaming as I went, the occasional cry of a primate in the forest breaking the silence. By the time I reached Aili, the district's innermost village at the end of the highway, I was very tired but pleased to have made it there under my own steam.

Aili was almost completely depopulated — the only two stores in the tiny settlement were closed all the time I was there. On arrival, I walked to the far end of the village, where I met a couple of aging men sitting outside their homes chatting. As I walked by, one of them asked me where I was going, and I told him that I had already arrived. Seeing my backpack, he counselled me not to enter the mountains alone. He need not have worried. I was not up for any more Davy Crockett-like excursions into the wilds, not after my failed attempt to find Old Haocha. Leaving the oldies, I looked for a place to stay the night. A disused bus station above the village made for a good place to camp, from which I had a commanding view of the mountainside opposite the Aili enclave. Studying this mountainside in the evening through binoculars, I noticed the trace line of what appeared to be a disused road. It must have been the old forestry road extending from Aili deep into the east that was marked on my map. It occurred to me that this old forestry road must somehow connect with Taidong County, and this was confirmed to me later by some locals and also by Transportation Ministry officials. But the condition of this road was anyone's guess. How long would it take to get to Taidong? Again, it was guesswork.

The walk back to Wutai the next day took a considerable amount of time and helped wear a second pair of boots out, but was rewarding for the chance to enjoy the valley once more in a way that would not have been possible from the inside of a speeding vehicle. On the way back to Wutai, I took the opportunity to drop by one of the smaller Rukai satellite villages that lay just off the main highway, entering the deserted village of Jilu at eight o'clock in the morning. Not a single person was about. My guess was that most of the absent residents were away working in Pingdong; and if anyone was still resident, they had either left for work early or were housebound. It was eerie to walk through this empty village on a windy day, the first time I had come across such a quiet settlement in Taiwan, or anywhere else for that matter. Rukai wall murals hinted at a lively village life; the village must have been a vital hub of life not so very long ago. The valley near the village was steep, stark and denuded of trees, but stimulating for all that — one could imagine seeing hunting parties crossing the slopes as they chased game. Later I hiked out of the ghost village, back through the road works and then on down the long winding road. Wutai finally loomed into view around lunchtime, and I stopped for a bite to eat at one of the village's restaurants on arrival. Some kind of tourist-driven commercial revival seemed to be taking place at Wutai; the hot air was filled with the reassuring noises of carpentry — but one wondered who and what it was all for. The sweltering day had by now taken its toll on me and I was looking to hitch a ride, which came along in the form of a group of Transportation Ministry officials. The officials were travelling in a ministry air-conditioned minibus and benevolently offered to take me back to Shueimen. It was they who told me it was possible to hike to Taidong along the old forestry road "in two days". I made a mental note of this for a possible future hike.

Before leaving the north-eastern corner of Pingdong County, which had proven to be yet another world within a world, I wanted to make one more trip into the mountains. I entered Majia District on the south side of the southern branch of the Ailiao River, and even though I was tired after walking from Aili to Wutai, I wasted no time in the village. Off I went up yet another mountain road, intending to hitchhike up this one to the Majia village. The uphill walk, coming on the heels of the morning's long hike, soon had me pooped. On a bend in the road, I stopped and waited for a vehicle to come by: hitching on the hoof was my usual style, but sometimes waiting passively for a ride under a shaded tree made better sense. Within ten minutes a local Paiwan couple who lived in Majia stopped, and I got in their roomy sports utility vehicle. The middle-aged couple were talkative and outgoing, unlike the Rukai people I had met, who tended to be reserved. Majia was six kilometres up the road. The route was subtly different from the other two roads I had travelled on in the area: its aspect encouraged more luxuriant flora, and it felt decidedly warmer on the south side of the valley. At Majia the cheerful Paiwan couple parked their vehicle and prepared to do some work in a stand of betel-nut trees. I thanked them for the ride, walked through the small village — which was lifeless in the early afternoon — and continued along the mountain road to Huawan on foot. Later I hitched another ride with a young couple who were going to a secluded waterfall for a swim.

But I could not find Huawan. The place where the couple dropped me off was essentially a crossroads. The village no doubt existed somewhere up one of the dirt tracks, but up which one was impossible to say. There were no signs or distance markers to indicate the way, and the couple who had given me a lift had not given me directions. Both of the dirt tracks I explored seemed to lead nowhere. Feeling a bit stupid, I thought it best to hold tight and wait for someone to come along, who could give me some directions. I moved back down the road, stopping at a small roadside hut that provided shelter from the sun, and here I sat all afternoon, waiting for someone to turn up. But no one came along. It was like being stuck in the middle of a Mexican desert, and there was absolutely nothing to do at the crossroads. To kill time, I pulled out my copy of the *Motorcycle Diaries* and ended up finishing it in one sitting.

Prompted by the publicity surrounding Hollywood's cinematic rendering of the book and by my own interest in travel writing, I thought it might be instructive to read the famous Che Guevara's travel diaries. In this book I think it is significant that Guevera dissociates himself from his early travels — or from the person that he was when starting out on his long journey through South America: "I'm not the person I once was", he remarks at the outset of his travelogue, acknowledging how he had been changed by the experience.

Guevara's ability to reflect in this self-conscious manner is one of his many attractive authorial traits. The narrative of the *Motorcycle Diaries* unfolds in a series of loosely connected episodes — some of which are very amusing, others prosaic, and yet others serious meditations on subjects such as education and indigenous culture. Guevera published the diaries many years after he wrote the travel notes on which they were based; and no doubt hindsight allowed him to fine-tune his ongoing reflections. Knowing his later revolutionary career, I paid particular attention to the narrator's explicit political commentary. I especially appreciated Guevara's anecdote concerning a discussion with an "Indian" teacher in Peru who rails against the injustice of colonial education: "Wasn't he in fact a typical product of an 'education' which damages the person receiving its favour…?" Guevera is here implying that it is not a case of indigenous people needing more or "better" education, but rather the fact that *everyone needs a different education*. Between the larking about and the travelling, Guevera starts to develop a political point of view informed by the social injustices he observes throughout neo-colonial America. By the end of the book, in a passage added perhaps much later, Guevara announces his conversion to the revolutionary cause declaring that he would "…take my bloodstained weapon and, consumed with fury, slaughter any enemy who falls into my hands". He had indeed travelled a long way.

The heat of the day had dropped off a few notches by the time I finished reading. There was not much to see in the immediate vicinity of the crossroads. But how was I going to cover the twelve kilometres back to Majia? In the end, the couple who had brought me to the crossroads gave me a ride back down the road. They looked refreshed after their swim. When they saw me stranded, they asked me why I had not joined them at the waterfall; a question to which I had no satisfactory answer other than fate had willed it otherwise. On the way back to Shueimen, the Paiwan man talked to me about travel. I explained that I was heading south and had got sidetracked by my desire to check out the Rukai people's home territory. When he learned that I liked mountain hiking, he recommended a hike up Mount Dawu, the most southerly 3,000-metre-plus peak in the Central Mountain Range. The mountain was sacred ground to the Rukai and Paiwan, much like Dapajianshan was for the Atayal. He assured me that the summer was a good time to do the hike and that it was a good walk. The couple dropped me off at Shueimen, where I planned to rest in a hotel for one night. But the only hotel in town was not great, so I took myself out onto the highway and started to walk slowly away from Sandimen southwards. Late in the afternoon I successfully hitchhiked along County Route 187 before switching to Route 185, which led directly south beside the foothills of the high mountains. Before dusk, I managed to reach Taiwu, gateway to Mount Dawu and 15 kilometres south of Sandimen. But the lack of suitable accommodation there forced me to tack over to Chaochou; a small city located southwest of Taiwu on the Pingdong plain.

THE CONTRAST between Taiwu and Chaochou City exemplified the differences between rural and urban, mountain and plain, and indigenous and mainstream cultures in Taiwan. The obvious difference between Taiwu and Chaochou was the disparity in their respective population densities. The traditional indigenous mode of production could never support a population like that found in Chaochou, and therein lies the explanation for the dominant culture's sense of superiority over indigenous cultures; not that they are completely mutually exclusive entities as such. The shocking thing, though, was how little the two worlds consciously interacted: the indigenous people came to the plains to work in agriculture and industry whilst the Taiwanese mainstream treated the mountains as their occasional playground getaway — the dominant mainstream culture had very little understanding of indigenous cultures. As Chaochou showed, the mainstream culture was materialistic: obsessed with money and selfabsorbed. Such was city life, right near the beautiful, open mountains that were an invitation to be free. If there was no money to be made in the mountains, then there was no need for money so long as you knew how to fish and recognized which wild plants were edible.

On my second day in Chaochou, I bought provisions for my upcoming hike; I then retired to the hotel and read Richard Harris's *Death of a Revolutionary*, subtitled *Che Guevara's Last Mission*. This book, sober and analytical but not detached — Harris, actually in Bolivia when the Bolivian army found and killed Guevara, immediately collected information on his subject — was another compelling read. After proving himself in the Cuban liberation struggle, Guevara could have had a cosy, for-life ministerial career in his adopted homeland beside Castro. But Che was a man of action, and he eventually tired of a bureaucratic life in Havana. He also had serious ideological misgivings about Cuba's increasing dependence on the Soviet Union, a country that had split with militant China and had dropped supporting world revolution in favour of protecting its own sphere of influence. Stung by his failure to foment a successful guerrilla *foco* in the Congo, the revolutionary turned his attention to Bolivia. It seems that Guevera sensed that his self-appointed task in Bolivia might not be successful. In a letter to his parents, before heading off on the doomed mission, he basically prophesies his own demise: "It could be that this may be the end. Not that I look for it, but it is within the logical calculus of probabilities". I think Guevera was being a little disingenuous here. I think he knew that pulling off a repeat of the Cuban revolution in Bolivia was very unlikely, something confirmed by his other final letters sent out to family and colleagues that read like suicide notes, albeit nicely considered ones. Of course, the mission failed. Guevera and his small band — badly informed, betrayed by the pro-Soviet clique in Bolivia, poorly prepared, and discovered almost from day one — found themselves on the defensive from the start; very much the wrong orientation for a guerrilla force. In the end, it is testament to Guevara's leadership qualities, strong will and sheer balls that he managed to keep at least a part of his outfit operational in the field for eleven months. He finally surrendered, but not without a fight; and when his captors executed him, he stood up and took it like a man – at which point the Che Guevera legend became sealed and enshrined for all time. Assessing this final mission objectively, after Harris, one wonders why an intelligent man like Ernesto Guevera should have thrown his life away on such an illconceived project as the Bolivian escapade — "At the outset, the essential task of the guerrilla fighter is to keep himself from being destroyed", Che had written in his manual on guerilla warfare. One can only surmise that he actually wanted to go down fighting; he wanted to slaughter or be slaughtered, to succeed or go out in a blaze of glory.

On a blazing hot blue-skied Monday morning, I left Chaochou City and embarked on my own mission to climb Mount Dawu. A rural bus got me up to the rural town of Neipu, and from there I hitched over to Taiwu. My sudden presence at the village's sleepy police outpost caused some momentary confusion, but eventually I filled out a form and was handed an A4 sketch map of the highway and of the trail up the mountain; this was all so much more straightforward than the rigmarole one had to go through at National Park offices. The map was not exactly detailed, but it did at least list a few landmarks together with their elevation and some places where fresh water was apparently available. But the trailhead for Dawu's North Peak was 22 kilometres away, so my next problem was to get there quickly so that I could start my hike in good time and reach the mountain hut named the Juniper Lodge before dark. After asking around the village, I took a ride with a Paiwan man who took me up the long road in his utility vehicle for a small fee.

We reached the trailhead nestled in a wide three-way point on the mountain fairly quickly. According to my Paiwan informant, it would take about three hours to walk to the lodge. I hit the trail at two o'clock in the afternoon basically feeling confident. An easy walk in the woods to start with, the trail rapidly deteriorated and I was soon clambering up steep slopes where the original path had been swept away by rain. Ropes and chains had recently been put in place wherever the path was particularly awkward or steep, and this was a great aid to me, struggling as I was with all my gear. A long section of the trail wound up through overgrown ferns, where I was obliged to don rain gear to prevent getting soaked on the wet foliage; my gumboots afforded pretty good traction on the wet stones and slippery mud runs. After an hour and 15 minutes of walking, I came to a trail marker that indicated I had hiked one and a half kilometres

— I had walked at about one kilometre per hour, a pace that I would keep all the way up and down the steep mountain. Further up, the path got a little brighter and drier as I passed out of the thick subtropical forest into mixed woodland, and I continued to climb steadily. After what seemed like a long time, but was probably only an hour, I got up to a high ridge, where the path evened out. Suddenly through a window-like break in the side of the escarpment, Dawu's distant angular peak came into view. It looked really magical sitting there like an emerald in the sun; I felt inspired to continue the walk in what were actually very reasonable conditions. I finally stumbled across a finger sign that pointed the way to the lodge — four hours after starting out from the trailhead.

The Juniper Lodge was nowhere near as exciting or exotic as its name suggested. A solid-enough hut, it looked a bit grubby and ramshackle, as communal dwellings often do. Outside the hut washbasins had been rigged up, but when I tried the faucets, no water emerged. Where was the water? Hunting around, I eventually found a mountain stream and filled my trusty three-litre plastic water container. Later I studied the sketch map of the trail I had been given, but it revealed very little. It did tell me that the lodge stood at an elevation of 2,145 metres, which usually means a cold night. It did indeed cool considerably as darkness fell over the forest but not to the extent that I had expected, the summer heat helping to keep the temperature up. I bedded down early in the manner of mountaineers. Several nocturnal creatures paid a visit to the hut during the night, one of which — a gem-faced civet cat — made a determined effort to get a free meal. The little critter had a nose like a bear and knew exactly where to find what it wanted; in the middle of the night I was obliged to get up and pack away my food bag to stop the audacious little mammal from helping itself to my provisions.

From the lodge I continued my hike up to the main ridge of the Central Mountain Range the next morning. For safety, I carried my tent and some food with me, even though, in theory, there was no need to. It was a warm morning and I changed into shorts, which was liberating. The lush vegetation, blooming begonias and summer warmth gave the mountain an intimate feel; there seemed to be no temperate zone, though the vegetation did thin out as I approached the high ridge. A slowly trickling waterfall constituted the last water point on the way up the summit, and I filled my three-litre container up to the brim before carrying on. A long and strenuous walk over rugged terrain finally got me to the ridge, where I dumped my tent, food and large water container, and then continued with only a small pack containing a camera and a litre of water. The final dash to the top of the mountain was a mini odyssey unto itself; in places the hike was very easy and the open panoramic views of the plain below impressive and uplifting; but in other parts the path proved to be steep, wet and full of false summits. I kept a close eye on my watch — midday being my turnaround time; I knew it might rain later in the afternoon and wanted to leave myself a generous margin for getting back to the hut before dark. I reached the 8.5 kilometre mark at 12.10 p.m., and ahead of me, there was still a steep walk up a forested slope covered in Chinese hemlocks to what might or might not have been the summit. It seemed like an incline too far, but I went for it anyway. Disappointed by the aborted hike on Nanhudashan, I was determined to get to the summit of Dawu, now that I was so close. The walk up the final stretch was not as bad as it had looked, and I reached the mountain's mistenshrouded, 3,092-metre-high peak 20 minutes later. After taking a souvenir photograph of myself by the summit marker, using my camera's self-timer, I immediately turned tail and hiked briskly back to base camp on the ridge, a surprisingly long walk. Gathering my things together, I then made the long descent back down to the hut, at my regular rate of about half a kilometre every half an hour. It did rain in the afternoon, and I got soaking wet on the way back down to the hut, but this did not matter as it was not really cold and I was on my way down.

The next day I enjoyed the hike down the mountain alone, accompanied only by the shrilling of mountain birds and the occasional monkey cry. It was one of my better descents and, although tricky in places, a very pleasant walk in the woods. Back at the trailhead I wondered how I would cover the 22 kilometres back to Taiwu. Something will turn up, I said to myself, like Mr Micawber, and stripped off to sunbathe a while by the bushes. An hour later a sightseer did turn up parking his van on the far side of the landslide. He came over and introduced himself to me. An intelligent man, he quizzed me carefully about the trail and we chatted a while about this and that. Unprompted, he then offered me a ride back down to the plain, a very felicitous happenstance.

MR CHEN FINISHED HIS CIGARETTE, got into the van, and drove us away from Dawu. I barely threw a glance back at the magic mountain, distracted as I was talking to my new pal. Chen was visiting a temple that was situated not far from Taiwu on the plain, and he invited me to stay there. I went along and ended up sleeping in one of the rooms at the large Western Way Buddhist Monastery. It was not a bad place to stay, and I was made most welcome.

The temple was quiet, spacious, and sort of relaxed. After arriving I took a bath in a private room and put my feet up as Mr Chen went about his idol worship. I walked around the monastery's ample gardens for a post-hike cool down and, through the groves of betel-nut trees, I watched, like King Kong, a calm sunset unfold in the west at the end of the day. In the evening I strolled around the veranda of the temple's residential block, admiring the symmetry of the building and the lines of yellow lanterns swaying in the cool breeze. Mr Chen, a former sea captain, tried to tell me something about Buddhism, but I had already seen everything there was to know and could not listen to another interpretation. A kilometre away from the temple across some dykes, Taiwu's population trickled home from work and school; the noise of motorbikes carried over to the calm monastery. But the world of the temple and the world of the indigenous village remained apart like two different visions of reality.

Drums, gongs and the smell of incense woke me up at a godly hour the next morning. As the monastery's resident nuns and some visitors performed their ritual worship, I busied myself packing and in the process threw away some worn clothing and equipment that I no longer needed. The previous evening I had paid for my room and said goodbye to Mr Chen, and having met these obligations, I now intended to slip away quickly. I duly left the residential block of the temple and walked over to County Route 185, which ran past nearby, a road that would convey me deep into the south of Pingdong County.

Mostly empty, straight, flat, and lined with telephone poles, Route 185 looked like the generic American state highway. Easily finding the road, I immediately started walking along it south. My intention was to hitchhike to Genting, which was located on the southern tip of Taiwan about 90 kilometres away. At first I was unable to get a ride and so hiked a few kilometres past over-grown fallow fields — ever diminishing mountains a constant reference point to my left. An occasional farmer wearing Taiwan's signature banana-leaf conical hat cycled by. One or two cars also flashed on their way to the coast, but they drove too fast to think about stopping for a hitchhiker, or to think about anything else, I supposed. Eventually a local Paiwan man did stop in his beat-up sedan and took me as far as his place of work, another Paiwan village at the foot of the Central Mountain Range. After buying a chilled can of peanut / milk congee in the village store, I continued hiking along the main highway. I passed many deserted sugar plantations — the economic boom years here were over and most of rural southern Pingdong was now quiet and somehow a little melancholy.

My next ride was with Mr Lin, a horticulturalist. He was delivering plant specimens to a government-run nursery and research centre in Genting and offered to take me all the way there in his spacious airconditioned combo van / car, a gift of a ride. Lin, a lean and friendly southerner, drove at a sensible cruising speed, stopping at one or two scenic spots by the road along the way for my benefit. Leaving the last of the mountains behind us, we joined the busier Provincial Route 26, which hugged Taiwan's far south-western tropical coastline. On one stretch of thin beach by this road, the Taiwan military had lined up some heavy artillery, the barrels of which pointed out into the Taiwan Strait — but the practice battery was inactive; it was simply too hot for training. "Those guns are out-of-date and only for show", was Lin's knowing assessment of the kit. Not having the time or the resources to explore the Genting National Park properly by myself, I was particularly grateful to Lin who took on the role of informal guide, pointing out a few landmarks within the park to me — a marina here, a nuclear power plant there, and lots of touristy hotels all over the place. We arrived at our destination mid-afternoon and Lin and I parted company at the gates of the government research centre.

Genting was wedged out with summer holidaymakers who paddled in the sea and played on the beach. At night throngs of visitors frequented local restaurants and bars, enjoying the balmy southern evenings. This holiday scene left me feeling a bit lonely and I felt like it was time to return to Taibei. After a hot and disturbed night in the tent I woke up wondering how best to end it. For the sake of form, I set off to find the very southern-most tip of Taiwan — a tiny peninsula and park known as Oluanpi. The park was easily accessible by bus from Genting. When I got there, I spent a couple of hours walking around the open grassy headland in the blazing sun, a choppy sea whipping up white crests in the wind. No trip to Oluanpi would be complete without a quick visit to the historic lighthouse built on the scenic coast by British engineers in 1882. I strolled over to the nicely preserved lighthouse, taking a few snaps of the white-washed structure. A small museum on the grounds of the light-house displayed some background information on boards, and I could not help having a chuckle when I read how Paiwan warriors used to raid the lighthouse on headhunting expeditions

— this no doubt explained why the lighthouse was built like a fort. Back in the park I made a picnic of it with my remaining provisions before taking a bus up the road to Hengchun. After a journey of over 1200 kilometres, Trip Four, the longest of my linear journeys in Taiwan, was all but over. From Hengchun I took a tour bus to Gaosyong, switching to a Taibei-bound coach in the big city. Mission accomplished.

6

TRIP FIVE: TAINAN AND PENGHU

IT RAINED IN TAIBEI, BUT ONLY IN SHORT BURSTS; THE SUSTAINED plum rains of the spring and early summer had given way to occasional thunderstorms. But summer in Taiwan is also the typhoon season, and during this summer season many tropical storms would blow in from the Pacific, some of which I would not even know about, as they did not really affect me. Typhoon Billis, which directly passed through Taibei whilst I was there between Trips Four and Five, did indirectly affect me. It caused relatively little damage in Taiwan; though it went on to wreak havoc in mainland China. The day after the storm, I visited the Beitou fields to inspect them with Alex, but to my surprise the crops were in pretty good shape. A small area of rice had been blown down, but the bulk of the green rice plants, papaya trees, squash, sweet potatoes, corn and water bamboo were not only still standing but thriving. A dirty little rivulet that joined the nearby Shuangsi River had been transformed into a healthy clear stream full of Wugu fish, colloquially known as "Mr Wugu", Alex told me — she used to fish in such streams in her child-hood. The passing of the storm signalled me to repack and get back on the road.

Trips Two and Four had involved making long linear journeys from the north to the southwest of Taiwan, but on this fifth trip I wanted a change of pace. I thus planned to make a leisurely circuit of a relatively small geographical area in the Tainan area, Taiwan's cultural heartland. I also wanted to visit the offshore islands of the Penghu Archipelago in the Taiwan Strait. Seeking to engage with my subject in a different way and having reduced the weight of my regular kit by a few kilograms by removing cold-weather gear, I decided to take a box of art materials, an easel, and a drawing board along so I could do a spot of watercolour painting en route. I had not touched my paints for a couple of years and thought Tainan would provide some good landscape subjects. Although I was quite correct in this latter assumption, I was probably wildly over-equipped for an amateur artist on the road. Instead of stripping my art gear down to a sketchbook, a small tin of paints and a pencil — which is what an experienced artist would have done — I bought a cheap shopping trolley and adapted it so as to carry what amounted to a portable field studio. With my two backpacks and now a trolley loaded up with an easel and paints, I would once more not be travelling light.

———

IT TOOK ABOUT five hours to get to Tainan City. The bus, a new tour model, was commodious, to my great relief. There was only one other passenger that got on in Taibei, but some more people embarked en route. During the tail end of the journey, sun-drenched temples, duck farms, flooded rice paddies and a certain amount of industrial detritus came into view through the bus window. Wearing banana-leaf conical hats to protect them from the overhead sun, several farmers were planting the year's second rice crop in flooded fields by the road, and it looked like exhausting work. Here and there a new expressway intersected the road, and one could clearly see that Tainan had not escaped Taiwan's ongoing frenzy of concrete construction. Neither had all the small backyard factories become inactive. From what I had seen and from what I remembered, Tainan managed to be preindustrial, industrial, and post-industrial all at the same time.

A hot blanket of humidity greeted me as I got off the bus at our destination. The Cuban ferns on Park Road were still there, a clear memory from my first arrival in Tainan many years ago, a poor but eager student. But the rest of the area was unrecognizable to me at a first glance. For one thing the buses no longer stopped along the road but now parked in a dedicated parking area that had been built in a vacant lot. The wall of the city's park had been knocked down, making the precious green space more open but less secluded. The other thing that threw me was a high-rise building on the horizon beyond the park. Back in the 1980s there had been no high-rise buildings in the city outside of a tiny area surrounding the railway station, and this new tall glass and concrete structure had completely changed the feel of the park area. After the momentary disorientation, I managed to get my bearings and the city gradually began to feel familiar again: the southern warmth, the smell of incense burning, the small street stores and tea shops invoked many memories. Times had changed though and the neighbourhood around the old colonial-era railway station was manically busy.

The city park, a place I had always liked for its tasteful replica Chinese pavilion set in a lake full of water lilies, was a natural choice for an opening attempt to paint something: I was determined to get right down to some work there. I thought the logistic challenge and mental exercise of doing a painting on a hot afternoon outdoors might take my mind away from nostalgia and help me to create new memories on the spot, and so it did. I stood in front of the lake and set up. First, I lightly sketched the scene before me on a large sheet of watercolour paper. After roughing out a simple composition, I used gauche paint, like water colour, and threw down some washes. My interest in the scene colour-wise was the way the bright orange of the pavilion's rooftop and the red of its pillars contrasted with the lush deep green of the park's trees; Cuban ferns poked up left of scene breaking up the skyscape nicely. In less than a couple of hours, I produced a picture. It was pretty bad, as first efforts invariably are: the lake looked like a slime bath, the temple roof was out of proportion to the pillars, and I had failed to render the white ornamented bridge balustrade surrounding the pavilion accurately. Some of this could be fixed later though, and at least I had done something in the park other than take a walk down memory lane. Exhausted, I packed up, left the park, and found a hotel.

From experience, I knew that Tainan night life was a non-starter for a single person, and quite possibly a non-starter, period. The Caucasian male in Tainan is associated, in the eyes of the local people, with American Man, i.e. with steak, test pilots and grotesque motorbikes; you sort of get pegged as a potential mate by local females desperate to escape into some version of the American Dream. Despite this foreknowledge, the first thing I did after checking into the hotel was to go out and seek a bar where I could have a couple of cold ones — the mid-summer session in the park had got me thirsty. I knew of a bar not far from the station, and it was still there when I went to look for it, an expatriate lighthouse shining in the midst of a Confucian sea. The American-themed "pub" was staffed by the usual young lovelies, who groped me with their eyes as I entered the establishment. I ordered a cold beer and sipped it at the counter whilst some visiting Germans at the bar kept up an inane chatter about business, a subject I find uninteresting. "Ja he is an asshole, he really wanted to cheat me..." whined one of the men. I wanted to talk about the good old days in Tainan, when one could get half a dozen well-paying English students just by walking down the road, but this subject would have bored the Germans even more than their business talk bored me. I ordered a meal, which took forever to be served, and quickly lost interest in it. Leaving half of the fatty sausage and cold fries, I finished my beer and left the bar vowing, a bit too late, never to go back.

I DECIDED — since my time in Tainan City would unavoidably be a nostalgia trip to some extent — to visit Chenggong University, one of my alma maters. By the time I left the hotel the next day, it was searing hot; the mid-morning temperature was already over 35 degrees Celsius. The university was only a short walk away, and I entered the campus along University Road adjacent to the school. The place had undergone a cosmetic facelift, but essentially it was still the same laidback, solid redbrick provincial school I had attended circa 1988. The sidewalk down University Road was crowded with more scooters than bicycles, but the same lovely trees graced the newly paved sidewalk. Trotting down this road, I took a peak over the recently lowered wall of the school at the running track and the dormitories beyond and saw that it was almost precisely as I remembered it, complete with weeds growing in the stands and banyan trees fringing the track.

I naturally gravitated towards the old language centre, a tasteful modern construction sitting discreetly next to a landscaped lake. But a huge new building dedicated to the liberal arts had been constructed next to it on a narrow strip of land that had once been a part of the lake area. Some effort had been made to blend this new college building in with the environment, but it was inordinately high and actually quite out of keeping with the rest of the colonial-era campus. The Banyan Garden, a marvellous green square dotted with enormous root-erupting tropical trees, was also still to be found within the campus grounds. It was here that a couple of Taiwanese friends brought me for a chat on my first day in Tainan all those years ago. I sat in the banyan garden one more time and made a quick watercolour sketch of an old tree, which did not work out too well, but what the hell was I doing here anyway? All my former friends had moved on, and so it was a case of goodbye to all that. I left the school and then went tramping around the old town in the western half of the city.

One or two new buildings had gone up since my last visit, but mostly it looked familiar. The capital of Taiwan for 200 years, Tainan is packed with temples and minor historical monuments dating back to the brief but influential Dutch colonial period. But actually it is the bits in between that are intriguing: the cottage industries, hole-in-the-wall restaurants, motorbike-repair workshops, pigeon coops, idols, calligraphy shops and other craft stores, which all go to make up this oasis of Chinese culture in the south. After making a long circuit of the atmospheric old town on foot, I arrived back at Park Road and checked into another hotel, where I would stay longer than planned due to an incoming typhoon. The storm took a little while to blow in and so in the meantime, I went sightseeing.

It made sense to visit the Chigan Tower first, the next day, as it was just a short walk away from the hotel. The present tower — a fairly simple three-storey, late-imperial-style structure — was built on the foundations of Fort Provintia, built by the Dutch in 1653. The Ming government in China had never regarded Taiwan as anything other than a barbarian-infested pestilent backwater, and therefore readily agreed to let the Dutch occupy the island in 1624. But Dutch rule ended in 1661 when the Ming loyalist prince Cheng Chenggong, also known as Koxinga, arrived in force and handed a crushing defeat to the Dutch garrison, who subsequently left the island for good. The Dutch interlude was important, however, for the pacification of some of the plains indigenous people — who adopted Christianity in droves — and for the disastrously exploitative trade in deer products that almost totally wiped out the native herds. With its Dutch foundations, Chinese and Japanese superstructure, and Cing Dynasty stone tablets, the Chigan Tower is a microcosm of Taiwan's modern history. In a pleasant landscaped garden, the first thing I noticed was a statue depicting the surrender of the Dutch governor to Cheng Chenggong. The symbolism of this statue is all the more powerful, given China's history of humiliation by the Western powers in the 19th century, and no doubt explains why Koxinga is still held in such high esteem by

Chinese people everywhere today. Some models of European ships, a bust of Cheng Chenggong and some cultural artefacts had been installed inside the tower; but actually it was the overall vibe of the place that impressed me, especially on a hot summer holidays' day when Taiwanese families walked about the tower and across the green lawn, taking snaps and sharing and building their Taiwanese identities.

The Official Guandi Temple is situated right across the road from the Chigan Tower, and I popped in to take a look around. The temple was fairly large and had a very elegant gabled roof; its solid walls were thick and freshly painted brown-red. Though some of the interior woodwork had no doubt been replaced a few times, the temple could not have changed much in almost 300 years. On the inside it was small and intimate, like a cottage, and worshippers stood about holding lit sticks of incense and praying. Some of these incense sticks looked like sprinklers whilst others resembled giant cigars. There were several special cauldrons in which one could place the smouldering sticks in the courtyard. At the back of the temple, a number of wooden idols sat in cases dressed in golden robes like puppets, one of which represented Guandi, the God of War, but also — by association in the Chinese mind — of Business. The temple was very active when I visited: the furnace for incinerating joss money burned like an ironsmith's forge. Without being overly solemn, the Taiwanese always behave their best when at a temple, and there was no self-conscious behaviour or embarrassment about their worship at all.

Through Koxinga, Tainan has a direct connection with the Ming Dynasty, China's last Han Chinese dynasty — the Manchurian Cing Dynasty was always considered foreign. But the Ming reign had already ended in China by the time Koxinga arrived in Taiwan, and the Ming prince died at age 38, one year after arriving on the island and before he was able to realize his dream of overthrowing the newly founded Cing Dynasty. Koxinga's son, Zeng Jing, kept the Ming banner flying on Taiwan for a further two decades, but in 1683 his fleet was routed by a Cing armada near Penghu, and Taiwan was formerly incorporated into the empire the following year. On learning of the defeat and realizing what the consequences of it were for him, Ning Jing, the last pretender to the Ming throne, committed suicide in Tainan. Rather than face the humiliation of having to humour the Cing court, Ning Jing's five concubines, Yuan Shih, Wang Shih, Sin Gu, Mei Cie and Hou Cie, all followed Ning Jing's example. The Temple of the Five Concubines, located in downtown Tainan, memorializes their virtuous tragic end.

I walked over to the small shrine and tomb erected in honour of Ning Jing's concubines, which was not far away over on the east side of town. The shrine was modest, but set in generous grounds that respectfully remain completely devoid of any kind of commercial development, something I found both touching and dignified. On the front of the shrine, painted murals of ladies-in-waiting peeled off the wooden doors. Above the doors the Chinese character for five had been inscribed on the lintel. The shrine was thus restrained but somehow perfectly appropriate — the Chinese always get these memorials just right, the mark of a highly civilized people. But what had actually happened? How did the five women meet their doom? Why had Hollywood not made a movie about them? In Taiwan, it seems a given that the women acted correctly, but I had my doubts. To question the women's judgement though would be tantamount to doubting the principles of Confucian culture; and is it right to try and question the historical actions of others from a contemporary perspective? On Bali, the royal house had committed suicide by rushing a line of Dutch soldiers, throwing money at the Europeans who ruthlessly cut them down — quite a statement when you think about it. The five women did what they thought they had to do to keep their dignity, and in the last analysis only they knew whether it was right or wrong to act in such a way.

On the way back into the centre of town, I dropped by Tainan's Confucius Temple. The Ming court in exile brought elite culture to Taiwan in the form of this academy, which was built in

1665 to encourage Confucian scholarship on the island. I had always liked this temple and its environs, which ooze a calm secular vibe. Set in a small park area, the temple is laid out in a regular and symmetrical pattern with small gates and gardens surrounding the main temple complex. The names of its rooms and gates — the Eastern Gate of Great Achievement, the Pool of Higher Learning, the Path of Propriety, the Shrine of the Great Officials, the Shrine of Local Worthies, the Shrine of Dedicated Filial Sons, and so on — are typically Confucian. The inner courtyard of the temple was not open to the public when I visited, it being reserved for upcoming ceremonies celebrating Confucius's birthday. These ceremonies have been taking place in Taiwan uninterrupted since imperial times, one reason why many Taiwanese people claim to be the inheritors of authentic Chinese culture. On this visit I took a walk around the gardens and peered into the courtyard, which reminded me in some ways of my old school in England; there was the same air of orthodoxy about the place, the same sense of oldfashioned elite values.

To the west Tainan City spreads out onto a delta area that continues to grow. On my third day in town, I visited this area, known as the Anping District, to see what was going on there and to revisit two old forts that I liked. I took a taxi out to the Lanan Bridge, and from there walked across the Anping Canal into the expansive district, which was full of vacant lots, supermarkets and factory-like karaoke venues. But bureaucracy was taking over. Grabbing the opportunity of open space, the Tainan city government had built itself a massive honeycomb office block in the neighbourhood. Passing by this office I popped in, curious to see what was happening. When I was resident in Tainan, the city's officials were housed in cosy colonial offices, and one would look forward to going there and having a friendly chat whilst handling a civil transaction. But the huge new Tainan city offices displayed features typical of what we might expect from bureaucracy in the future: suspicious security, endless corridors and desks, unwelcoming staff and zero information; in short a Kafkaesque nightmare. I left the place bemused by a display case in the middle of the foyer that housed a rare crossbred plant. What was that all about?

There were some other oddities in the Anping suburb, like a burlesque steak house — "Empire of Cattle" — which used a realistic depiction of a live cow on its signage. Meanwhile, the streets of Anping had sprouted generic high-rise residential blocks with names like "New Holland" and "Loyalty Mansions" around its edges and along its access roads. The local elementary school also caught my attention. The school had been designated "Creativity Central School of Tainan City" — this was a bit too good to be true, one felt. I walked into the school, which was closed for the summer vacation, after asking permission to walk around it from the gatekeeper. The school had no perimeter wall and was apparently quite open, though closedcircuit television cameras pointed inwards from every corner, just like they had at the Green Island Detention Centre. Sadly there was no evidence of creativity at the school at all. On the contrary, the whole place with its open plan design and cameras was firmly orientated towards social control. The only thing I saw hanging on the walls of the school were some road signs and some student profiles complete with identifying photographs. In sum, the arrangement confirmed my suspicion that most schools are really prisons for the young, often barely disguised ones. After walking around for five minutes, a female teacher who was showing some prospective parents around asked me, in her impeccable American English, my business, and when I informed her I was just having a stroll around, she charmingly ordered me off the campus.

The Erkunshen Artillery Fort, also out at Anping, was built in 1876 as part of the Cing Dynasty's efforts to bolster its military readiness; "Self-Strengthening". The fort overlooked the approach to Anping Harbour. The simple square fort, built according to a French design, but armed with British-made cannons, must have been a formidable fortification in its day, but evidently its relevance to modern warfare did not last for more than a couple of decades. The fort was tidied up on its centenary in 1975, and some mighty replica cannons were put in place at that time. These guns and the well-kept moat around the fort made Erkunshen actually feel like a fort; one could walk the grassy ramparts and enjoy unobstructed views of the surrounding area and feel like a general. After arriving at the site, I spent an hour or two doing just that and also did a couple of quick sketches of the place. The grass and trees that grew on the ramparts served to landscape the fort and large exercise square nicely. The slightly swampy park around the fort had been planted with some attractive subtropical plants and flowers, including a mass of red mussaenda and white and pink hibiscus. All in all, it was a very attractive and romantic setting and I wanted to do a watercolour there, but somehow could not make it happen. There were too many people inside the fort for me to work undisturbed, and the outside of the structure did not offer me the angle on the subject I was looking for.

Typhoon Kaemi hit Taiwan just one week after Billis. That night it rained heavily, and the downpour continued into the next day. It was only prudent to stay indoors until the storm blew itself out. I therefore set up my painting easel in the cramped hotel room and worked on a painting of the Five Concubines Temple, using a sketch I had made of it when visiting. My effort was clumsy to say the least. I sketched an outline of the temple and the tomb directly in black paint and then filled in the colours — a brand-new watercolour technique! The result was a building out of proportion to its surroundings, with black edges and a pink roof. My idea had been a good one, but it was beyond my ability to make an objective impression of the scene. Bollocks to it, I thought, throwing down the brushes and then diving out into the rain on a beer run. I talked to Alex on a public payphone outside the convenience store and told her I loved her, which was true, and that I was having a good time, which was not exactly true. The typhoon lingered around and the next day I was obliged to stay in my room again. The mood to paint had gone and instead, I cooked makeshift meals in the bathroom and read — I was now reading a collection of Leo

Tolstoy's short stories. It was tedious to be stuck indoors, but not nearly as bad as having a bomb drop on one's head.

Breaking my resolution not to watch television, I switched on the box in the afternoon only to witness another war exploding in the Middle East. The whole thing was very bizarre: correspondents who had spent months jawing endlessly on filler subjects like yachting and car racing were suddenly talking on camera as plumes of smoke from landing artillery shells rose behind them. You sort of felt the war had started as a reaction to boredom. Of course, the war in southern Lebanon was a deadly serious affair and a lot of people were getting hurt. I watched events unfold with a mixture of bemusement and horror, and then started to resent the intrusion into my life. But it was hard to get away from the conflict: about 30 screens in the local department store where I went shopping had tuned in, and the war was being played out non-stop on all the cable television news channels. When I got back to the hotel, I made it a point not to watch television, and read Tolstoy's brilliant *The Cossacks* instead. The story reminded me of how history repeats itself, not exactly but more violently each time: from skirmishing on the border to the carpet bombing of Grozny. What next? Mini wars, private wars, electronic wars, half wars and full wars — so much to look forward to.

The weather had still not fully cleared up but I was determined to go out and do a painting the following day regardless. My subject would be Fort Zeelandia. I went out to the Anping fort at midday optimistically taking my easel and paints with me. After a little walk around the fort's neighbourhood to take in the atmosphere, I entered the site. The only parts of Fort Zeelandia that date back to the Dutch era are its foundations and a wall fragment. The present redbrick superstructure was built by the Japanese who, in 1930, knocked down some offices and store rooms and replaced them with a Western-style villa and viewing tower. The fort therefore looks nothing like it used to, but it is still an interesting place. Before walking around the structure to scout a spot to paint, I took a quick look in the fort's museum, which had a surprisingly good collection of cultural artefacts, including 17th-century weaponry and some splendid artists' impressions of Tainan City. Most impressive of all were two huge busts of Cheng Chenggong and of Fredrik Coyet, the latter being the former governor of Taiwan. The busts had politely been given equal prominence, standing side by side like comrades-in-arms and not enemies. Of part Japanese ancestry, Koxinga always appears of rather severe mien, which might be expected from a man who had once ordered the execution of his own son on discovering that the prince had had an affair with a commoner. Fredrik Coyet looked more friendly, but not very martial. Perusal of the museum over, I looked for a subject to paint.

In one quiet far corner of the fort's grounds, I found a nice angle on the remaining banyan-covered Dutch-era wall, which included the fort's viewing tower in the background and a subtropical garden in the foreground. I set up, determined to capture this scene in watercolour. For the sake of quickness, I sketched directly in paint. I first painted in the diamond-headed top of the viewing tower, the main centre of interest, working it up to a high level of detail before putting in the foliage of the trees below it. Then I painted in the wall, the gardens and the foreground path that led the viewer's eye into the picture. Finally, I dashed in the clouds. Few people came to look at what I was doing, so I was able to work in peace. About half way through proceedings, however, it started to spit with rain. Undaunted, I rigged up some cover with my umbrella and got on with it. Painting a watercolour outdoors is like playing a game of speed chess: one wrong move and you could lose the game. I really concentrated for about three hours and the result was not a bad little daub, which succeeded, I felt, in capturing the mood of the place in some way. I had done a reasonable job drawing the tower, and the overall composition was pleasing; it was balanced anyway. One nice Taiwanese man came along and praised my effort: "beautiful!" he proclaimed, after some hesitation.

Although I spent a couple more days in Tainan City, I painted no more pictures and visited no more historical sites, though there were plenty of the latter worth seeing. Instead, I walked about the streets of the city getting a good look at the place one more time. Tainan remains my favourite city in Taiwan. But had I ever really known it? The concentric and exclusive nature of Taiwanese society subtly excludes the outsider, and there was in fact a great deal I did not know, and probably would not want to know, about Tainan. Instead, I am left with impressions of ancient temples and sprawling banyan tress, smells of smouldering incense and of southern Taiwanese cooking, and memories of a previous life partly spent in back alleyways, tea shops and old forts.

ON A HOT POST-TYPHOON DAY, I took a cab to the outskirts of town, where I got out and hiked across a new modern-arched bridge that spans the Lanshuei River. Thus I found myself in the city's huge northwest Annan District, a flooded water world of fish farms, salt fields and sultry lagoons. I used my umbrella as a sun shield, holding it up in one hand and pulled the trolley with the other hand. No one has done this, I said to myself, thinking how highly original I was, embarking on a tour of Tainan County, the island's eighth-largest county in terms of area, but number one in terms of available arable land. As I had anticipated, it proved difficult to hitch a ride once I got into the boondocks, and so I walked deeper into the empty and open district, oblivious to everything except my next step. A couple of drivers waved back to me cheerily, not realizing I was actually trying to get a ride by raising my hand. I wanted to get to the large Holy Mother Temple, which was located about a dozen kilometres down the road on the Zengwun Estuary. But there was only farmland between where I was and the temple — even though Annan was technically a city suburb — and there were no buses anywhere.

After walking beside an irrigation canal for a while, I finally got a ride with a young newly married couple who were out sightseeing. I just about managed to bundle my gear in the boot of their small car. But less than ten minutes later on the way out to the Holy Mother Temple, we stumbled across the Koxinga Memorial Park, and I got out of the car again. The couple spent less than five minutes in the park before leaving. I wanted to stay a bit longer and so we parted company. I picked up my gear and stashed it just inside the park under a tree and then went for a walkabout. The park, a fairly small place set in the middle of farmland, featured a small temple, a pond and a statue of Koxinga within its grounds. But the centrepiece of this odd park that appeared to be undergoing desertification was a tall concrete obelisk with the words *The People's Hero Cheng Chenggong Luermen Landing Memorial* chiselled in Chinese characters on it. Luermen was the general name for this part of Tainan, also the name of the former harbour where Cheng Chenggong disembarked his considerable army in 1661. Koxinga himself had a temple built at Luermen to memorialize the landing, and now there are a throng of such temples in the neighbourhood. The neglected park and the obelisk intrigued me, and I had a good look around for a place to camp, but there was no fresh water or shelter from the hot sun to be had. I therefore picked up my bags and trolley and walked the remaining kilometre into Tucheng, the nearest village.

Tucheng felt like a backwater even though it was situated close to Provincial Route 17 that runs north-south through the western coastal districts of the county. The village's branch library had been converted into a fish market. Outside the library, or market, some women sat huddled over baskets of oysters, cracking open the shells and disgorging the contents into plastic bowels. They tried to sell me some unopened oysters caked in mud, perhaps thinking I was a fish wholesaler. There were hairdressers and a few stores on the main village street, but no hotel or guesthouse. Walking around the village, I came across a dormitory-style residential block. A rent sign, together with a contact number, was spray-painted onto the side of the building, and a quick call brought the landlord to the premises. I explained to him that I wanted a short-term stay, maybe a couple of days, and he sympathetically agreed to let me a room on reasonable terms. If the dormitory room was a bit soulless, it at least had a refrigerator, an airconditioner and a large floor-to-ceiling, rear patio door that let in plenty of light. After walking around the village, I bought some mangos — this was the mango county, after all — and some fish at the local market to cook for dinner and then headed back to the dormitory for a quiet night in. There was no one living in the dormitory, but apparently students lived there during school time. At what school exactly, I had no idea, but every two-bit rural college had recently been upgraded to university status. In the dormitory I cooked up a meal on my stove alone like a disaster survivor and then went to bed dreaming of red lanterns.

The air-conditioning — which I had unwisely left on all night, having forgotten to set the timer — woke me up early in the morning. Shivering, I flipped the switch on the control and went back to sleep until the warmth of the day switched my nervous system on. After a leisurely morning I packed my painting gear and headed off purposefully to bag a painting. I succeeded in hitching a ride to the Koxinga Memorial Park just down the road. After getting there I immediately scouted for a spot to paint, looking at the park from various angles. The best position to paint a picture, it seemed to me, was on a path that led up to the centrepiece memorial obelisk. From this angle one could see the obelisk, the small temple and the statue of Cheng Chenggong — all telescoped into one frame. The obelisk naturally invited a portrait layout, and I set the board and paper up on my lightweight but sturdy aluminium easel accordingly. Once again, sketching directly in paint, I quickly drew the obelisk and then worked around it, finally painting in the characters on the stonework in red. It was another scorching hot day, and sweat dripped off me as I painted. Seemingly romantic, painting *plein air* actually demands a lot of concentration and much physical and psychic effort to get anything done. The act of painting allowed me to slow down and feel and observe what was going on around me, and it was this process, and not the final product, that really mattered to me. All the features of the park — the memorial obelisk, the temple, the statue, the pond, the trees, the birds singing in the trees, and the farmland beyond — were fascinating individually; but together, they made a powerful statement about Taiwanese identity. Though I had made a mess of some foreground details, my painting nonetheless pleased me because it succeeding in recording a vision of that neglected park. After completing the painting, I washed up and packed my gear away and then spent an hour resting in a small pond-side pavilion before walking back to Tucheng.

Back at the dormitory I took a cold shower and chilled out under the air-conditioning for a bit. The heat had really done it for me and I decided right there and then that any more painting would have to be done indoors. Before dusk I rallied and took a walk around the Shenmu, or Holy Mother, Temple. This temple has a long and venerable history dating back to the 17th century, when Luermen was a portal of trade between China and Taiwan. On a weekday evening the large temple was relatively quiet, and I took the chance to explore the building, strolling along its colonnades and onto the roofs, weaving in and out of the red pillars and ornate gild work. On the roof I peered down into the halls of worship — dungeons smeared black with incense smoke and guarded by a host of idols. In one of the halls, a huge golden Bodhisattva sat behind a glass screen; two worshippers kneeled before it in silent prayer. Outside, next to the temple, an old amusement park lay disused and derelict, a symbol of Taiwan's aging demographic profile. The canvas of the rides had been shorn away by high winds, and the woodwork of an old train ride rotted under the setting sun. In a vacant lot beside the temple a wooden dummy cannon and some other temple carnival paraphernalia burned in a bonfire, a mysterious sideshow. Thunder rolled across the plain, but no rain fell, and so the gaudy cannon burned on into oblivion.

For dinner that night, I ate stir-fried lamb noodles at a corner bistro in the village. As I waited for my order a few locals in the restaurant who had seen me murmured *Meiguoren* to one another. A television mounted up on the wall relayed pictures of pandemonium from a faraway country. Very sensibly no one paid any attention to the tube, and with my meal soon before me, neither did I. After eating I went back to the dormitory and read. Tolstoy's absorbing novella *The Cossacks* transported me to another era of internecine conflict, but one where the combatants seemed to have a certain amount of mutual respect. Or maybe that was just Tolstoy's romantic polish on events? It's hard to say. Certainly Tolstoy wrote this story with an impressive level of detail and obviously knew his subject well. The superb portrayal of "Daddy" Eroshka, the boozy old Cossack warrior and hunter, reminded me of Sokal of Hanshih: they had the same élan, the same disrespect for time and order, and the same obsessive love of hunting. How different a story it would have been, I thought, had Olenin remained in the Caucuses and married a Cossack girl, but Tolstoy eschews such a happy ending; the story's denouement is thus a conservative moral lesson.

The next morning, on the spur of the moment, I set off with my camera to photograph the countryside nearby Tucheng. The peopleless fields were fascinating in a peculiar sort of way. Many of them had been lined with plastic and functioned as fish pools. On the surface of these pools, homemade floating aerators pumped air into the pools like out of control paddle steamers; shoals of fish danced about feeding tubes at the corners of these fields. An assortment of improvised farm buildings were scattered about the plain, including a pigpen and some chicken coops. One farm had put its family cemetery plot in the front garden for safe keeps. Various beautiful subtropical trees helped to break up the monotony of the flat landscape that was otherwise crisscrossed with telephone poles. After walking for several hours through these flatlands and not finding a road, I bumped into a farmer who volunteered to give me a ride on his motorbike back to the temple. He went off to get the bike from his nearby house whilst I continued to stroll along. In no time he was back, and I was riding pillion on his motorbike. The main circular road leading back to the temple was not far away as it turned out. On the way there I asked the farmer to stop so I could climb a roadside embankment. The embankment was actually a levee protecting the plain from the Zengwun River, and the view on the other side, over fields of ripening rice, was actually quite stunning and the subject I had been looking for all morning. I photographed the scene before scrambling down the embankment and getting on the motorbike again. In less than ten minutes we arrived at Shenmu Temple. I thanked the farmer for the ride, got off the bike, and returned to the dormitory under a darkening sky.

A massive thunderstorm came and left the Tainan plain, clearing the air and providing me with an enforced pause on my trip around the county. Although I stayed in Tucheng for another full day, I never went out again except to buy drinks. I painted several pictures in the dorm based on the photographs I had taken. The scene of the fields next to the Zengwun River, simple and striking with nice angles and lines, had immediately suggested itself as a good subject — I liked the diamond shapes of the fields and the red roofs of the rustic dwellings on the horizon — and I painted a pleasing picture of it. I did some other paintings, but none of them were very brilliant; in the end I was eager to get back on the road.

MY LUCKY RIDE came along just as I was walking out of Tucheng. A local man who worked in a "materials factory" picked me up and drove me into the neighbouring district, which took me out of the Tainan City's jurisdiction for the first time; I was aiming to hitchhike up Route 17 towards Cigu. The man was very curious about me, but he could not quite figure out my mode of travel. "What is your transportation tool?" he asked me. I said "your car", not deliberately trying to be ironic. The man deposited me, of course, at a temple. This medium-sized temple, which had a couple of tour buses parked next to it, did not look uninteresting, but less than an hour into the day, I was not quite ready for another blast of incense. I therefore trudged back up to Route 17 and waited for another ride. On one of my maps, I noticed that I was in the Southwest Coast National Scenic Area. Among the tourist sites shown on the map within this area was the Taiwan Salt Museum, located near where I was hitching. I resolved to visit this museum and soon got there, after getting a ride at a gas station.

From a distance, the two giant white pyramids of the Taiwan Salt Museum looked like one of those modernistic buildings found in Paris. The pyramids symbolized salt mountains. But a real salt mountain stood just 100 metres to the west of the museum building, which made three pyramids. I entered the museum, left my bags at reception, and took a stroll through the pleasantly air-conditioned exhibition rooms. The museum, originally built by the Taiwan Salt Industrial Corporation but taken over by the county government in 2004, was actually very informative and interesting. The whole of coastal Tainan used to be covered in salt fields, and the industry boomed for decades before finally shutting down in 2002 due to global competition. The culture and history of this local industry was well represented at the museum, undoubtedly one of the best of its kind in Taiwan. The roomy first floor re-created a salt-field scene in a mock-up that included lifesize models and real salt. Lots of detailed diagrams explained the whole salt-production process, and photographs from the era were well annotated. Apparently, the salt business in southwest Taiwan was a major government revenue earner in the immediate post-war period. Indeed, salt, which had been produced in the area for 300 years, became a hot commodity — often targeted by thieves — and a Salt Field Patrol had to be set up to crack down on this theft. Some of the exhibits at the museum, like the one that posed the question — "Is salt necessary for our body?" — were obviously a bit behind the times, but the black-and-white photographs of workers toiling away in the hot fields were an useful reminder of the hard work that went into the making of modern Taiwan. After having had a good look around the museum, I collected my bags and walked over to the gigantic salt mountain. I climbed the salt staircase up the huge dirty mound of raw salt, along with a few local tourists. It was fun to do so, and I could just about make out Tainan City and the Cigu Lagoon from the top of it.

Later, I walked westwards, but the lack of an open road north left me stuck in a village, where absolutely nothing except dog barking was going on. I turned around and walked back towards the Salt Museum. Another thunderstorm was brewing, and so I hitched a ride to the nearest town, which was Cingkunshen Township. The small salt town had seen better days, but was far from dead. As in all of Tainan's small towns, the local temple stood at the centre of Cingkunshen's social life. As soon as I arrived, I was obliged to seek shelter in the temple's ground-floor car park. No one thought that this was unusual. I found a chair, sat myself down near a window, and read for an hour until the afternoon downpour eased. Walking outside into the village square later, I got my first frontal view of the temple: a three-hall Fujianese structure that had a typically exaggerated ornate roof — the pile with its curvatures looking like a samurai's helmet. The modest seafront harbour, just metres away, contained an assortment of fishing vessels, but the fish-seller in the market in front of the temple barely had a couple of kippers for sale. I left the low-key salt town two hours after arriving.

In a series of rides, including buses, I subsequently stopped at Jiali and Sywejia but, strangely, there were no cheap hotels in these bustling rural towns. From Sywejia I therefore went to Beimen, a town on Tainan's northwest coast. I made myself at home, and slept reasonably well, on a wooden bench in a temple, leaving early the next morning before anyone was about.

Having only got a few hours' sleep in the temple, I felt tired and disorientated the next day, but after breakfast — an uplifting egg-andbacon sandwich — I decided to visit another museum and walked out of town in the direction of the Wangye

Museum. I discovered that Beimen's whole economy was based on oyster cultivation. In numerous roadside shelters I saw women sat crouched on low backbreaking stools, shelling oysters. They wore gumboots, rubber gloves, and sun hats with cloth attachments that could be tied in front of the face like a veil if required. The women appeared to be local and not imported labourers. Shelling oysters was obviously hard work, and one wondered why a better sitting arrangement had not been devised. There was no reason, after all, why the shelling could not have been done standing up or sitting at a table. The work process looked lazy and unhealthy, but it was none of my business really, and so I passed by the oyster shacks, soon reaching open country again. The museum was about four kilometres to the south — ordinarily an easy walk, but a somewhat laborious one for me carrying so much gear, and so I hitched a ride there with a local man who spent the ten-minute ride railing against foreign-born brides. In Taiwan for every eight newly married couples, one bride is a foreigner, he told me. The man seemed to particularly dislike the women coming in from China, but actually this phenomenon was only the resumption of an historical trend.

Wangye is the plague god, one of the more important folk gods in Taiwan. Always depicted as a man with a black, distorted face and body, Wangye is the lord of all pestilences, and the Taiwanese custom is to burn his effigy in a wooden boat during important festivals to ward off disease. The origins of this custom go back to the early Chinese colonization of southern China and to the epidemics that frequently broke out among the settlers at that time. The plague god is therefore deeply embedded in the Taiwanese folk psyche, and Tainan County has a large number of temples where Wangye is the principal god. It was perhaps not surprising that the first thing I saw, after getting out of the car and waving goodbye to the die-hard Beimen patriot, was a plague-god boat. The wooden replica scale-model boat belonged to the Donglong Temple and rested on a stand inside a shelter. One day the painstakingly made scale-model replica boat and carved figures would be burnt like so many before.

As soon as it opened its doors, I bought a ticket and entered the three-storey district museum. The sleepy staff switched on the lights in each hall only after I entered them, a commendable energy-saving measure. The exhibits in the halls consisted of small scale models of plague boats and historical scenes from the Ming and Cing Dynasties that included numerous miniature carved figures. Some of these models and figures were very elaborate and worked up to a high level of detail, leaving me to wonder who all the demon modellers were. A map on the wall revealed that there were no fewer than 203 Wangye temples in Tainan County, far more than in any other part of Taiwan. Obviously for historical reasons, Tainan folk were obsessed with the plague. The models, maps and other bits of information usefully filled one floor of the museum; the rest of the floor space was underutilized. Maybe future plagues would provide the modellers with new subject matter, and a vast wooden container ship would have to be constructed and sacrificed to appease Wangye... On the completely empty sixth floor, I looked out of the window — as one does when there is nothing else to look at — over the burnt sienna roofs of the Donglong Temple, and towards Beimen Lagoon. The drowned world of the lagoon called out to me. It stretched a long way up the coast with lines of stakes in its calm waters marking out rows of oyster cultivation. The coast was only about a kilometre west of the museum, and I went there on the back of a truck.

A couple of orange-jumpsuit coast guards sat in a shack, keeping an eagle eye on all the comings and goings — smuggling and human trafficking being all too real problems in modern Taiwan — but mostly the lagoon was quiet. It was only nine o'clock, but already the day was stiflingly hot — the kind of day that melts roads. I left my bags in a derelict building near the harbour and went for a walk along a dyke that marked the landward edge of the lagoon. Empty oyster shells lay about all over the place, a mass of them even forming an area of landfill by the lagoon. White egrets pecked away at some of these shells by the water, extracting some leftover morsels. Using an umbrella to shield myself from the sun, I walked slowly past the slag heaps of shells and observed a series of lagoon events unfold. A tiny raft chugged out to a far corner of the still water, where a fishermen dropped a line in the stagnant water; in a larger raft, a small group of gumboot-clad workers drove out along the lagoons' highway next to the dyke, turned up a line of stakes, parked, and then began hauling in muddy piles of oysters, hosing them down before chucking them into baskets; another man descended the dyke and waded out to a row of stakes, where he began doing some impromptu repairs on submersed fishing nets — moments in the life of the lagoon. After venturing only half a kilometre or so along the dyke, I turned around and walked back to the harbour feeling as though I had made an extraordinary journey, a kind of moonwalk; such was the magic spell of the lagoon. I talked to two fisherpeople in the harbour area and they told me business was not what it used to be, and added that they struggled to make a living these days, the generic tale of woe. The numerous rafts lying about, idle in the harbour, seemed to confirm that the local economy had slowed down. On the other hand, the rafts' well-oiled outboard engines suggested that they were at least still in use. In typically Taiwanese fashion, every household in the village owned a boat; everyone wanted to be their own boss.

Getting back to Beimen involved more walking than I had planned to do — there was almost no traffic about in the early afternoon — and so I sweated some before getting a ride with a local postal worker who took me to the Beimen tourist office. The office was predictably hopeless at providing any useful information about anything. I already knew more about the Southwest Coast National Scenic Area than the young state apparatchiks there. The office had been converted from an older building — perhaps a former school or post office — and around the back of it stood a small bust of Sun Yat-Sen, the famous Chinese revolutionary and "Father of the Nation". Sun was the originator of the "Three Principals of the People", a blended philosophy that went on to become the official political doctrine of the Chinese Nationalist Party. The three principles — nationalism, democracy and socialism — were a bit contradictory, but that never bothered Sun. Incredibly, the Three Principals doctrine is still taught in Taiwan's schools today, though its meanings have obviously been adapted to suit current political exigencies. The socialist element of the Three Principals, for example, is very much downplayed these days. But once upon a time, it really meant something, and the Chinese nationalists were serious about engendering equality in society. Emblazoned on the bust was Sun's slogan, *Tian Sia Wei Gong*, which literally means "all under heaven for the public good". The slogan, which chimes in with traditional Chinese values, remains potent, and one feels the busts of Sun Yat-sen will be among the last symbols of the Chinese nationalist era to disappear from sight in Taiwan. There was absolutely nothing else of interest to hold me at the tourist office, or in town.

From Beimen I travelled to Nankunshen, a large temple and monastic retreat located on the far northwest coast of Tainan County. The large, atmospheric temple is particularly popular among Taiwan's common people, who go there to pray for good luck and to reaffirm their connection to the Ming Dynasty and their ancestors. It was the weekend and so sure enough, there were plenty of people around when I reached the main temple on the back of a fish truck. I enquired at the temple office about accommodation. Yes, they had rooms available in the temple's swish Kang Lang Villas. When I explained that I actually wanted to stay in the free dormitory, I got a few sharp looks and the clerk struggled to deal with the request, but eventually it was arranged. I headed over to the old dormitory, where I was met by an officious caretaker who asked, as he inspected me with his eyes, how long I would be staying. He then informed me I would have to leave the next day as a group were coming to stay. I signed in and selected my room.

The temple had a lot of annex buildings, gardens, pavilions

and such, and I wandered about the place with an eye on the lookout for a possible subject to paint, preferably something easy to do with simple lines. But the architectural detail was complex and challenging to draw, so I contented myself with just a stroll through the temple's courtyards in the late afternoon. Here couples sat on wooden benches negotiating life issues, families brought their children to throw coins at the Lucky Bell, and adults burned incense and prayed by the temple's smokeblackened altars. As the sun went down, I walked up to a deserted palace under construction on a hill overlooking Nankunshen. A lot of work and money had gone into the building of this annex but it was still not complete. Dedicated to the gods, it had been built in a modest style which reflected the design of traditional Taiwanese residences. The perfectly proportioned rock garden, however, was clearly a Japanese influence. From the top of the hill, I could see the Bajhang River to the north and the opulent roofs of Nankunshen and flooded farmland to the south. It was my intention to leave this coastal plain now and head inland, the next day most probably.

In the evening, while looking for oysters, I walked to a nearby village and found a restaurant where I was able to get an oyster omelette. The juicy omelette was very good — southern Taiwanese cooking was several notches above Taibei's. Later I sat in a chair outside the restaurant and studied the night sky. The waxing moon was almost full and looked massive when magnified ten times. I thought I saw rabbits on its surface, or maybe they were just dried oceans and mountains. One or two revellers from the restaurant said hello to me, but I declined an invitation to join their drunken party, an endless round of drinking games. Instead I made my way back to the empty dormitory at Nankunshen, where I wrote up my journal before falling into an anxious sleep. That night I dreamt I walked to the top of the hill and met Alex there; both of us were chased away by a group of angry acolytes who had debouched from Nankunshen. I guess this dream meant that I wanted to leave the temple before I overstayed my welcome and that I wanted to be with Alex, or some combination thereof.

The caretaker rudely barged into the dormitory early the next morning, an "accident", but I was already up and stretching. I soon left the temple and began hiking beside the Bajhang River. The estuary of this river was a wide muddy expanse at low tide. Hardy Kandeliacandel mangrove grew here in the rich brown alluvium as it did by the Jilong River near Taibei. Crabs scurried about in the mud flats between the tufts of mangrove. A father and son fished in the river, relaxed and at ease with each other and the world. In the receding distance a modern bridge carried the main traffic flow northwards into Jiayi County. I headed inland. Within a few hundred metres, the river's levee obscured the view out over the river and my attention was thereby diverted to the farmland behind Nankunshen. Some of this land had been left fallow and teemed with bird life. Other fields had been converted into fish pools, and the paddle aerators whirled tirelessly on them. This summer scene was engaging, but the cool start to the day belied the later heat. As I walked down the road, the sun rose in the sky and the temperature soared. It was time to hitch a ride, but few cars came by. For almost the whole morning, I hiked along the riverside in what became something of an ordeal. Eventually a small truck picked me, and at last I got well clear of the coast.

TAINAN THROWS UP SOME SURPRISES, like the huge aluminium smelting works a couple of kilometres inland from Nankunshen. One would not normally associate such heavy industry with duck farms and fish ponds, but there it was, big and bold as brass tacks on the horizon and evidently operational. Viewed from the road, it looked like another temple of some kind. The driver who picked me up repeated the Chinese word for *aluminium* several times, but I had to look it up because I could not guess what he meant. At first I assumed he was talking about ducks; but no, it was aluminium. The farmer took me as far as his farm about ten kilometres down the road. He apologized for not taking me any further, but I assured him I did not mind walking to the nearest main road, which was not far away. Another local man who hailed from Tainan County's central Liujia District picked me up at the main road. The egg-delivery worker was surprised to see a foreigner with so much baggage wandering about on a Tainan county road alone, and he was even more surprised when I told him where I had come from. "You are so bold!" he ventured, but I felt this remark did not actually reflect his thoughts. He took me as far as Yanshuei Town, where we said our farewells on the outskirts of town.

Yanshuei is famous in Taiwan for the annual exorcism rite that celebrates the ending of a serious cholera epidemic. The climax of the rite, held every March and much reported on by Taiwan's media these days, involves spectators swaddling up and then running into a "beehive firework" bonfire. My interest in Yanshuei was in finding a place to stay, but a couple of phone calls drew a blank on accommodation. It was a shame because there were one or two interesting temples in Yanshuei, and the surrounding countryside was quite picturesque. Also, my eyes had got singed during the arduous walk I had done that morning, and I wanted to avoid the sun again for the rest of the day. But it was not to be; and after a whirlwind tour of town's main street, I got back on the road. My goal now was to get over to Sinying City, the capital of Tainan County.

Sinying was six kilometres southeast of Yanshuei along County Route 172, which more or less directly joins the two urban centres. Whereas Yanshuei prospered in the 19th century because of its proximity to the Bajhang River, an important transportation artery at the time, Sinying prospers today because of its political function and its proximity to Taiwan's major north-south expressway. I thought getting there would be a cinch: there was bound to be a lot of traffic on Route 172. I had forgotten that hitching a ride out of a town or city is almost never easy and due to the peculiar characteristics of traffic flow on this section of county highway, I ended up having to hike all the way to the county capital. Between the two urban centres, large motels and a number of national franchise outlets created a corridor of concrete down which cars swarmed in a strange way, the drivers hypnotized; and so I slogged it all the way. I reached Sinying totally exhausted as the sun started to go down. Within 20 minutes I was ensconced in a cheap hotel, luxuriating in a shower.

Tainan's county capital set new standards in dullness. The place was a mass of soulless box-like concrete edifices with a few high-rise buildings thrown into the mix at random. I took a stroll around town that evening; the fact that everything except houses of ill-repute shut at nine o'clock proved that Sinying was more pokey country town than sophisticated city. But because not one but three typhoons were homing in on Taiwan, I was obliged to consider staying in this dreary town for a few days. Maybe I could use the hotel room as a temporary studio? The next day the news informed me that a typhoon was about to make a direct hit. I mentally prepared for a longish stay at the hotel. Bored out of my mind, I then decided to tour the town before the storm hit. Lacking alternative sightseeing options, I headed over to the city's cultural centre.

Sinying Cultural Centre was a weird bureaucratic white elephant. The odd multi-storey building looked something like a provincial hospital; there was almost no sign of life at the centre, as though its entire staff had gone on permanent furlough. Outside in some parkland, a post-modern "ecological park" had been decorated with life-size, multicolour plastic reindeer. An as-yet unused, empty ultramodern glass and steel service centre, which would cost a fortune to keep airconditioned in the summer, stood in the park. If solar panels had been included in its glass-house design, then that would have perhaps justified it in some way; but there were none so far as I could see, sheer criminal negligence. By a tiny pond in the park, a sign intoned "Danger — deep water. For your protection, do not swim, shower, or release and catch animals in this area without prior consent". Shower? Giving up on my desultory sightseeing, I went back to the hotel and watched the weather reports on television. Two typhoons were apparently headed in our direction. I sighed, picked up the telephone in my room, and booked a flight to Penghu, an archipelago of islands in the Taiwan Strait. I was not going to fly there immediately, but I needed something to look forward to.

The next day it had not even started to rain. The two typhoons were repelling each other, pushing the main action north and south of the island. Seeing my chance, I quickly packed and almost ran out of the hotel. The woman at reception was surprised to see me leave as I had told her I would stay a couple of days, but I was out the door before she could finish saying "ten percent off". I took a bus from Sinying railway station to Baihe District in the northeast corner of Tainan County. The ride out to Baihe took about 45 minutes. Most of the other passengers on the bus were high-school kids returning home from school, nearly all of whom alighted from the bus before we arrived at the final stop. Baihe Station was tiny and the town turned out to be very small as well. I checked out the local hotels in case I needed a bolt hole in the event of heavy rain. After finding one that would suffice in an emergency, I walked down the main street, where at an ironmonger's store, I took the opportunity to weigh my kit on some weighing scales — thus went the tally: backpack (large), 15 kilograms; backpack (small), 6 kilograms; binoculars, 1.4 kilograms; camera, 500 grams; total, excluding trolley, 23 kilograms. It was a lot to be dragging around, but then again, I was almost totally self-sufficient. I walked on out of Baihe in a northwards direction. My map indicated there was an Industry and Cultural Centre in the northern part of the district, and not having a better idea, I thought I would go there — if only for the ride. On the outskirts, a man driving a flashy sport-utility vehicle stopped. He had done a U-turn in the middle of the road to pick me up, then did another one, assuming I wanted to get back to Baihe, and finally did a third when I told him that in fact wanted to go north and not back to Baihe. Off we sped into the water-lily wilds of the rural district.

The cultural centre turned out to be some kind of rural handicrafts and painting school. The wooden buildings had obviously been converted from an old farm property. Downstairs, a classroom was cluttered in the manner of a working studio; Chinese ink-wash paintings of water-lily flowers hung from the walls of the room, some of them very accomplished. Upon arriving, the driver who had given me a ride there took it upon himself to arrange an interview with one of the centre's staff members before disappearing. I had not asked for an interview, but I suppose one had to have a reason to be there, and so I pretended to be a journalist to save them from any embarrassment. I was kept waiting a decent interval before the "interview", and used this time to take a little stroll around the old farm. The garden around the back of the building had a neglected charm to it — slightly weedy and overgrown, an effect beloved by Chinese romantics. A little distance from the building, however, and the dense subtropical woodland was quite impassable. Called back from my walkabout, I finally got to meet the PR lady, who took me upstairs. Suddenly all was revealed: this centre was the brainchild of Wen-yue Lin, a noted local ceramicist and painter. Mr Lin's ink paintings, calligraphy and ceramics — displayed on the second floor — were outstanding exemplars of the genres. It takes much practice and a calm, cultivated temperament to produce such exquisite works. As I walked around the small exhibition area, admiring the master's art works, a group of young teenagers surfaced from a classroom. One girl said hello to me, but the PR lady kept talking and the girls retired in shyness. I declined to be shown the garden and classrooms. My brief tour of the centre thus over, I thanked the woman who had shown me around and made a quick exit.

Relieved to get away from the stifling virtue of the cultural centre, I struggled to find my bearings outside. Just as I reached what appeared to be a main road, an ear-splitting boom shattered Baihe's rural calm and left my ears ringing for several long seconds. There must have been a military base in the district, and at that very moment, they had decided to fire their heaviest weapon, probably a self-propelled gun or a giant howitzer. Rattled by the massive report, I waited for a couple of minutes to see if there would be another one, but there was no more firing. They had probably used their ammunition quota with that one shot. At the main road I checked the road signs and my map and then started to walk southwards away from the direction the humongous big bang had come. The back road was so quiet; I wondered how I might get a ride. Suddenly along came a car, which stopped. The driver, a man, had been out on a fishing trip and was now returning to the Guan Zi Ling area southwest of Baihe ten kilometres away, which, as it happened, was exactly where I wanted to go.

Guan Zi Ling's modest claim to fame is its geothermal hot springs. Perhaps it would be my lost Shangri-la, where I could stay and paint to my heart's content for a week or more. But it quickly became apparent to me that the mountain resort was in fact a tourist trap. The hotels, which had been squeezed onto the sides of the slopes in the most exploitative fashion, were both expensive and tatty, and my three attempts to negotiate a lower room rate left me amazed at the sheer cheek of people who would not budge on price despite the fact that it was midweek and their hotels were empty. Because of the hoteliers' intransigence, or perhaps because of my own intransigence, I soon found myself undertaking yet another arduous rural hike in the sun, and this time I was actually hiking uphill. County Route 175, which I would travel the length of in the coming days, began in Guan Zi Ling and cranked high above the town before it flowed southwards. The walk uphill was taxing, but at least the views over the Tainan plain were rewarding and I got another excellent cardiovascular workout that day. Cloud cover provided relief from the sun later, but only a trickle of vehicles passed by, mostly tourists with little room in their car for an overloaded hitchhiker.

A conical-hatted farmer picked me up a few kilometres

outside Guan Zi Ling, although he only took me a short distance down the road: due to a misunderstanding, I got off the back of the farmer's truck at a fork in the road in the middle of nowhere. Cursing my luck, I started to walk along what was a totally isolated mountain road. If there was a moment when I regretted the whole idea of this quixotic tour, this was it. What on earth was I doing walking about the hilly byways of rural Taiwan at the height of summer carrying 23 kilograms of kit and pulling a trolley full of art materials behind me? Tainan County was pretty and sort of interesting, but not quite the paradise I had envisaged. Getting around the county was proving to be difficult, especially as my trolley was now starting to fall apart. It all seemed insane and I dreamt of doing a nine-to-five job, as one is apt to do on such occasions.

South 175 km, read a roadside sign, the meaning of which was not really clear. I struggled up the other side of a dip in the road and arrived at a village named Pingding. It was lunchtime but the village was mousey quiet. I pulled past a bus stop that promised more than it could deliver. Beyond a small roadside shrine, the road started to climb again, this time quite gently in between acres of densely packed betelnut trees that in aggregate looked like a miniature pine forest. Just as I was getting tired of this hike, another local farmer came by and offered me a ride. He could only take me a kilometre up the road, but I accepted the ride to break the jinx. I then continued on foot like a war refugee. The stop-go pattern was repeated one or two times and allowed me to make some progress through Tainan's backwater foothills. I eventually crossed over into Dongshan, the next county district to the south of Baihe. My final ride was with a man who recommended I stay in one of the local temples for the night, and he later took me to the Dongshan Monastery, which lay just off Route 175 — one of the typhoons out in the Pacific was now closing in on us. As I got out of the car at the monastery, it started to rain hard. Waving goodbye to my lucky ride, I dived into the main temple, where an attendant met me.

I WAS NOW ABOUT HALF the way around the county and safely ensconced in a monastery as a storm blew across the plain. Things could have been a lot worse; I could have been out walking in the rain, for example. After settling in to a crummy room, I went for a walk around the concrete monastery, which had many rooms, auxiliary altars, and even a huge canteen on its first floor. There were a few monks and nuns about and one or two families hanging out around the hallways and staircases. As the rain kicked in, most of the families drove off in their cars, and the monastery fell quiet. I booked in for dinner and went to the cavernous canteen at the appointed early hour. The communal vegetarian meal was perfectly acceptable if a bit bland. Two families who had elected to stay at the temple for the night joined me. A father and son sat, both of them sporting shaved heads, and ate in front of a wall mural depicting Chinese children playing with a spinning top. The children in the mural also had shaved heads, and the cultural continuity represented at the dinner table that evening was quite striking. "Eat!" said the father to his son, which is the rough equivalent of saying "I love you" in Chinese. After dinner I stretched my legs on the staircases before retiring to my room. It howled with wind and rain during the night, the typhoon reaching maximum intensity at about three o'clock in the morning, and this made the accommodation feel much cosier.

Breakfast was announced with the clanging of a gong, but I decided to skip it. It was still raining outside, and so a rest day was in order. After reading in bed for an hour or so, I cooked some pasta on my small camp stove and warmed up a ready-made curry for brunch. It was late morning by the time I went for a little stroll along the balcony and up to the main temple. The storm had moved on and the rain eased considerably; the atmosphere was cool and refreshing and the view out over the plain was clear of any haze for a change. I stood at the edge of the temple's viewing platform and surveyed the landscape through binoculars. From this angle Tainan County looked verdant and wellwatered with green hills stretching far into the distance. It would have been possible to have travelled on such a day; on the other hand, it would have been risky since typhoons have tails, which can bring intense rain.

As I was standing there, and out of the blue, two busloads of visitors arrived at the temple. No sooner had the visitors alighted from their transport than loud firecrackers started to explode. The bubbling group then gathered at the bottom of the elevated access road behind some kind of idol that was being carried on poles. They slowly walked up to the main temple, all the while letting off more firecrackers as they went. The effect was like an infantry attack. The group seemed to be divided into two halves: dedicated acolytes and followers. The acolytes had their hands all over the cradle in which the idol sat; the followers brought up the rear, carrying sticks of lit incense. The point seemed to be to bring the god to a suitable resting place whilst warding off evil spirits. The show came to an end when the idol was finally placed inside the temple, after which everyone relaxed and dispersed to the monastery's walkways and rest rooms. This was the day's main event and nothing much happened after that. I sat in my room and read.

Tolstoy's *The Death of Ivan Ilych* is one of the Russian master's most poignant stories. The story idea is simple: a person falls ill and dies. What is interesting about the story is the way Tolstoy uses it to make a profound philosophical statement about life: he intimates that a life not lived right is a tragedy. But what does it mean to live right? The answer can only be found only within oneself and not from without. Ivan Ilych leads the perfect bourgeois life. He makes all the right moves and slowly edges his way up the social ladder by marrying respectably and gaining a position in government. His career is not spectacular, but he does not debase himself by engaging in corrupt practices. By sheer dint of industry and orthodoxy he finally gets the dream job and salary. But his marriage is unhappy. Consumed with work, he never seems to be able to please his wife except on an occasional basis, and the malaise extends to overspending on his new house. Then the protagonist falls sick. Tolstoy never mentions the word *cancer*, but most modern readers will recognize the symptoms, and we feel Ivan's pain and suffering as he tries to put a brave face on things. The end is inevitable, and it is at the very end of his life that the man who had always done the "right thing" suddenly realizes that somehow it had all been wrong. An intensely sad and depressing story on the surface, Tolstoy is in fact telling us an enlightening truth, and by doing so, he invites readers to ruminate seriously on their life and its assignations. This wonderful short story prompted me to reflect on my own odd career in Taiwan and on whether I had done the right thing, embarking on a lengthy grand tour of the island at my own expense. One of the interesting things about Ivan Ilych's personality is that until the very end of his life — until judgement day — he never had any self-doubts.

A light mist enveloped the western foothills early the next morning; the rain had completely vanished. After a rice-gruel breakfast in the monastery's canteen, I gathered my things together and left the concrete temple after putting a little money in a donation box. I was soon down on the highway marching along, no self-doubts intruding — if only life could always be like an early morning walk in the countryside. The monastery receded from view as I hiked up and along the road that cut through betel-nut-tree-carpeted hills. I continued climbing the gently ascending road until the monastery disappeared from view behind mountains.

———

THERE WAS VERY little traffic out on the highway and I walked many kilometres in the fresh post-storm air. After what seemed like a long time, but in fact had only been one hour and 50 minutes, a man driving a four-wheeler came down the highway and picked me up. He was headed to Tainan City via a south-eastern route and offered me a ride into Nansi. My interlocutor had stayed at the Dongshan Monastery too, and this helped to facilitate an immediate good rapport between us. The man asked me about my travels and where I usually stayed and so forth. A mention of camping brought us around to the topic of venomous snakes. My perhaps naïve view was that snakes in Taiwan were not really a problem for campers as long as they observed sensible precautions and zipped up their tent at night. But the Tainan man, who had done a lot of outdoor work in his time, was afraid of snakes such as the Taiwan banded krait, or "umbrella snake", as it is known colloquially. The neuron toxin from this snake has been the subject of an impressive amount of academic research, but my friend did not need to read all that stuff to know just how potent it could be. Clearing out some brushwood one day, a small umbrella snake nicked his leg. At first he felt nothing, but later in the day he struggled to stay awake. Realizing this sudden tiredness was the effect of the snakebite he slapped himself to stay conscious and managed to get to a hospital before it was too late: if he had fallen asleep, he would never have woken up again. Such was the fate of a neighbour's child, the man informed me, who collapsed and died after getting a full bite from a branded krait; "We knew it was an umbrella snake because her bones had turned black".

As we drove along, I noticed a nasty rash had broken out on my arm, something I had picked up in the unclean and unventilated monastery room. The driver was sympathetic when he saw my ailment, a very common one among Tainan country folk, and recommended rubbing mint leaves into the rash. After reaching Nansi District, we stopped at a Chinese medicinal store to get some leaves, and I tried the remedy. The mint-leaf juice did not provide any immediate relief, so I then slathered on some iodine and followed this up with a layer of antifungal cream for good measure. The itchiness of the rash eventually wore off, but which application did the trick, I have no idea. Not long afterwards we arrived in Yucing, just north of Nanhua. The Tainan man dropped me off here as he was headed westwards back to the city, whereas I wanted to go to Nanhua.

So there I was walking around another one-horse town in the searing midday heat with a gammy arm. Painting was about the last thing on my mind, but I had not completely given up on the idea of finding an idyllic rural retreat where I might kick back and put my portable studio to some use. I therefore aimed for Nanhua, ten kilometres distant, getting there in one hitched ride. Nanhua District stretched north-eastwards into a river valley that had been dammed to create a reservoir — there were a number of such small reservoirs in the county, which needed the water for agricultural use. Judging by what I could see of Nanhua on the way to the local administrative centre, it was basically all over for me in Tainan County. The town was quite small, and there was no place to stay other than the local temple. I asked around about accommodation, but there was nothing available in town; one had to go out to the reservoir to find any guesthouses, and I could just imagine how overpriced and boring those places would be. After eating I decided to close my circuit of Tainan County by moving westwards towards Tainan City. I bought some provisions and then walked out of town in the direction of Sinhua, the next township to the west.

A couple of hundred metres out of town, near a row of residences, I noticed a sign for a country guesthouse. Intrigued, I walked down the lane indicated by the sign. The countryside by the lane was pleasant; a mix of fallow fields and gentrified farmsteads with some mango orchards sprinkled in between — the romantic element was present in spades. The guesthouse, set in a couple of acres of lush subtropical land next to a small river, looked like just the ticket. Here, perhaps, I could work. The guesthouse was made up of an odd mix of old-style country houses, wooden chalets, and modern concrete apartments. I trundled down a driveway and through the wrought iron gates of the property. At reception I was met by a Vietnamese girl who spoke a little Mandarin Chinese, and she called her boss over to speak to me. Mr Lu, the owner of the guesthouse, invited me into his office, and there we sat and chatted over tea. As I put it to Lu, I was travelling and doing a bit of painting here and there and would like to stay if he could arrange a discount. Having made my purpose known, I sat back, sipped the tea, and changed the topic of the conversation in the Chinese manner. The affable owner — who had made his fortune exporting household items to America back in the 1980s — was a savvy businessperson, and it took me a while to knock his room rate down.

Over the next three days, I made myself at home at the lodge. My room was neat, clean, well-furnished and comfortable. The lodge's greatest asset, though, was its secluded location, and the delightful grounds. I would take a little walk around the gardens every morning and marvel at the sheer vitality and luminance of the trees' foliage before going back to my room to draw and paint. I produced half a dozen completed watercolours during my stay — one of the lagoon at Beimen, based on a sketch, and several of the lodge's garden painted *plein air*. The lagoon scene came out the best because I did it indoors, where I could better control my environment. The subtropical countryside, however, was less easy to interpret, and working outdoors always introduced problems and distractions — painting *plein air* requires a lot of practice and fortitude, I discovered. On my last day in Nanhua, I borrowed a motorcycle and went for a drive into the nearby mountains, which appeared to be densely settled. There were innumerable residences, guesthouses and small temples up in the green hills, and one wondered how the land could support so many people and so many businesses. I sketched a little from various vantage points, but then ran out of steam.

As though he were trying to impress someone with his generalship, Mr Lu was in the garden, supervising his female employees when I left the lodge. I stopped and chatted with him for a short while. To be fair, he had invited me over to tea a couple of times during my stay, but I was too busy painting or thinking about painting to take him up on these offers. Too bad — maybe I could have learned the secret of success from this aging entrepreneur; but after saying goodbye to him and the Vietnamese girls, I walked down the country lane without looking back. Provincial Route 20 was empty and I waited quite a while for a ride, but eventually a car stopped and I was soon headed back to Tainan City with a cold beer in my hands, kindly proffered to me by the driver.

———

PENGHU — "THE PESCADORES" in Portuguese — is a destination that conjures up images of romance and history in the minds of most Taiwanese people. The islands have variously hosted pioneer farmers, pirates, colonisers and soldiers. The Ming Dynasty's last stand was made at Penghu, where the Cing armada met and crushed what was left of Cheng Chenggong's old fleet — Penghu had long been stripped of trees in order to build war junks. The group of islands remain strategically important and the Taiwan government keeps a strong garrison on them. In modern times, the fishing industry provided the basis for Penghu's economic growth, and more recently tourism has brought further prosperity. But Penghu was a place I knew nothing about first-hand; before going there it was hard for me to imagine what the islands really looked like or how economically developed they were. At Tainan Airport, I studied maps and reread some pages I had photocopied from a guide book, but they were not very detailed. Some blown-up photographs of coastal, columnar basalt cliffs in the small departure lounge hinted at Penghu's scenic appeal; but other than that, it was hard to get a handle on the place, and this lack of foreknowledge made me anticipate going there all the more.

The small propeller-driven passenger plane arrived on time but came nowhere near the airport terminal. Along with two dozen other Penghu-bound passengers, I stepped onto a wide-bodied shuttle bus that took us out to the midday plane. Tainan Airport is heavily militarized, and we passed many bunkers filled with the latest USmade fighter jets as we crossed the tarmac. Once on the small propeller plane, it was simply a case of buckling up, sitting back, and waiting for takeoff. As we lifted off and got underway, I observed Tainan City and, as the plane banked, Annan's fish pools for the last time.

Makong airport is a military base; please do not take photos, draw a picture of the airport, or make an observation with a telescope, read a sign in English on the wall of the airport building. Walking towards the entrance for arrivals, I went past four copies of this sign. The repeated exhortation seemed completely pointless: satellites can take very detailed photographs of airports; and what satellites miss, the resident spy worker at the airport will look at, memorize, and sketch later. In fact, I had taken half a dozen photographs of jets in their bunkers at Tainan Airport before someone politely pointed out to me that this was against regulations. At arrivals in Makong I collected my bags, which appeared very promptly on the small baggage carousel, and walked out into the bright, air-conditioned steel and chrome glint of the terminal's foyer. The passengers who had arrived with me quickly dispersed into waiting private vehicles, talking cheerfully as they went. Some small groups of young sunburned people sat and giggled, and took photographs of each other as they waited for their departing flights. These scenes left me feeling lonely, and for a moment I, too, felt like I wanted to belong to a group of happy tourists. Were there no other independent travellers in the whole of Penghu? I wanted someone to talk to on an equal footing. But the dreary tourist desk at the airport and the crap map of Penghu they provided left me feeling more depressed. The next bus departure for Makong would not leave for over an hour. I could not wait that long and so simply walked out of the airport into the heat of a sizzling hot day.

At the main road my instincts told me to move in the opposite direction to the tourists. Aimen, a village opposite the airport, had a beach nearby, and that seemed like a good start, so I crossed the main road and made for the settlement. A line of brand-new scooters sat parked outside a rental outlet by the road, an ominous sign; but as I would find out, Penghu was quite a large place. At the village, which I soon arrived at, all of

Penghu's charms suddenly became apparent: there was almost no traffic about, the air was noticeably clean, the houses in the village were surrounded by small garden plots enclosed by coral walls; the light had a fantastic clear quality to it and served to enhance the colours of the land and its plants; and the village temple was immaculate both inside and out and fitted in perfectly with the environment, its interior decorated with baroque-like murals of scenes from Chinese folklore. I watched a child climb over the temple's high door frame, momentarily disappear, and then jump back over and run down the street. Beyond this temple, I followed a lane that led down to Aimen beach, a ten-minute walk away. To my surprise the coarse coral sand beach, covered with purple morning glory at its landward edge, was totally deserted. A couple of kilometres along the coast eastwards stood three enormous garbage-incinerator chimney stacks. In the foreground a beached rowing boat sat in the sand like one of Van Gogh's empty chairs.

I continued walking eastwards into Penghu's Hushih District and arrived at the village of Lintou. Like all of the settlements in Penghu, Lintou remained unspoilt by tourism: most of the houses were twostorey concrete structures with flat roofs. The Lintou villagers were house proud: there was not so much as a cigarette butt on the streets, and the houses were neat and tidy without being fussily decorated. These houses had replaced the more traditional residences made of brick, stone and coral. One or two of these old coral homes could be found in every village, usually in an advanced stage of disrepair. I looked closely at one of these houses in Lintou, fascinated by its coral walls; apparently coral is a good building material as it is light, strong and wind-resistant. Nearby at a pavilion in the middle of the village, a group of senior citizens played Chinese chess whilst waiting for a pile of groundnuts to dry.

Back on the coast road, I hiked along contentedly beside the coral walls of Penghu. These dividing walls were generally about five feet in height, constructed something in the manner of the stone walls to be found in the north and west of the United

Kingdom. The walls were built close together because the plots of land were small and the winter winds strong. In addition to the ubiquitous squash, groundnuts and taro, bitter melon grew in the small market gardens between the walls. On one plot of land, I saw a woman labouring outside. Her head was almost entirely swathed in a sun hat and veil, and she worked under a parasol for further protection from the sun. Behind her stood a modern three-storey house, the fruit of her patient industry.

Longmen, further along the coast, had a large but inactive harbour. By the harbourside I heard the light-hearted banter of Vietnamese women workers, winding down after another hard day slaving away in the heat — they worked in a fish processing factory on the quayside. Not far away stood a fairly large hotel that looked promising, but it was expensive, and so after getting some directions from the local coast guard, I left Longmen and carried on hiking up the road. I was looking for Lijhangjiao, a tiny settlement at the south-eastern extremity of Penghu. All being well, I thought, I might camp out there somewhere. By now it was late afternoon and starting to cool down a little. A platoon of young male soldiers came jogging along the road, obviously taking their daily exercise. The typical Taiwanese conscript is not a fitness fanatic, but jogging was probably the highlight of the day for these young men. I snapped some photographs of the group as they passed, and they sportingly waved and smiled at me as I did so.

Not long after the soldiers went by, I came to a lane beside the road. A finger sign indicated Lijhangjiao, and following it, I arrived at a shrine next to the shoreline.

The walk over to Lijhangjiao, barely six kilometres from the airport, had exhausted me. I hung my sweat-drenched clothes out to dry on the walls of a small pavilion and enjoyed the evening's cool sea breeze. On a small offshore island out in the ocean, a lighthouse had been painted white and black, making it look like an upright umbrella snake. The rocky shoreline of the main island was basically empty. After sunset I read in my tent for a while before dozing off into a fitful sleep. Later in the evening a young couple came to the shrine to make an offering of fruit and, trust my luck, to burn some ghost money in the shrine's furnace. Good citizens that they were, they also reported my presence to the local police, and two military police officers soon dropped by to interrogate me. The police were nice enough, even a tad deferential, but still wanted to know what I was doing there. My explanations satisfied them, but evidently not their senior officer, who also came by later wanting to see the crazy foreigner personally. I repeated my explanations, and finally he was satisfied; but instead of leaving, the officers stood around talking to each other in the way that Taiwanese people who want attention do sometimes. Then the couple reappeared, all smiles, and offered me a plate of fruit.

Guoye, a larger village three kilometres up the coast from Lijhangjiao, had become the early morning venue of choice for tourists to watch sunrise. As I got up and walked about in a daze early the next day, it occurred to me that my present location was almost as good as being at Guoye, the sun rising at just a slight northerly angle to the shrine. I grabbed my binoculars and sat in the pavilion to watch the day dawn, yawning all the while. The sun appeared, a small orange dwarf spreading a belt of yellow and purple along the horizon, making it look like a sponge cake. The back lit rocks on the tidal-sea platform stood out in silhouette, a plate of crumbs. A few terns glided across the early morning sky, turning and wheeling almost like eagles. Then the rising sun climbed quickly in the sky, erasing the sponge cake and sending a strong glaring light into the pavilion. Every contour of the grassy banks next to the shrine that only half an hour before had been lost in a black mass now stood out clear and defined. The shrine itself suddenly appeared very small and my own presence there very obvious. Sunrise over, I packed and left.

The lane I had walked along the previous day was in fact a bicycle track of some kind. There were no cyclists riding along it early in the morning, and it made a superb path to walk on. On its landward side the path had been planted with dwarf trees to help prevent wind erosion — the sapling trees themselves protected from the wind by emplaced black mesh netting. Wind erosion on flat-as-a-pancake Penghu was clearly a problem, and in places the path almost disappeared under sand that had been blown up from the shore. At one point the low shoreline developed into a low cliff. A disused pillbox stood on top of this cliff, one of many I would see scattered at strategic points along the coastline. Beyond the cliff top the path forked, and I followed a lane inland, thinking to walk cross-country to Guoye. The landscape in this south-eastern corner of Penghu was grassy with only a few dairy cows on it — although in one tiny hamlet, a pigpen was being mucked out. A pitchfork, stuck into a pile of grass fodder on the back of a small truck, added to the sense of rusticity. But it was the ornately roofed temple — which appeared between some green ferns as I walked over to what I thought was Guoye — that identified the scene as Penghu. The temple was actually in Longmen Village, and I suddenly realized I had doubled back on myself.

In Longmen I got on a bus that was going to nearby Hushih and reached the district centre within five minutes. I was now in a position to do a little exploration of Penghu's north-eastern coast, but first I looked for a place to stay. The disturbances of the night before, and the morning's walk in the hot sun had combined to motivate me to seek out a hotel or guesthouse. I found a nice little homestay on the outskirts of Hushih, which had rooms with high ceilings and no televisions; in fact I would not camp out again during the rest of my time on Penghu.

No longer carrying heavy bags, the walk to Beiliao — a small harbour town on the eastern side of Hushih Bay —was a great pleasure, even though it was still hot. The open, desolate and flat landscape of Beiliao was a relief to my eyes after the closed-in density of Tainan's countryside. The shallow bay was a kilometre or two across and almost completely drained out at low tide, making it look like a gigantic empty swimming pool. On the way to Beiliao, I passed by the village temple, a regular Fujian-style structure with the usual ornately carved roofs. The temple's orange roof tiles complemented the blue sky. Perhaps an imaginative stretch, but the temple as a whole seemed to look like a figure, maybe a farmer or a soldier — an impression suggested by the top-heavy construction.

Some fisherpeople were untangling long fishing lines in a small pavilion as I entered Beimen's harbour area, and I went over and chatted with them for a while. There were two women and two men in the group. One of the men had a badly swollen leg, perhaps caused by elephantitis or some similar affliction. The fisherpeople were curious about me and asked me many questions. I asked one of the women about the fishing industry, and she told me that although it was generally in decline, it was still possible to make quite a good income from fishing; and the work was more varied and interesting than many working-class jobs — though of course it wasn't without risks. The long-line fishing technique involved dragging a long row of hooks attached to a line through the ocean, a method that caused far less collateral damage to the environment than nets, but the lines had to be tidied up after use, a fiddly time-consuming job.

Leaving the fisher folk to it, I walked back from the harbour and over to the east side of the village, which faced out onto some islands. Apparently one could walk over to the islands at low tide — but why bother? Four young people arrived on scooters and actually did walk over to the nearest of these islands, which was quite energetic of them, considering the monstrous mid-afternoon heat. I dived into a beachside shelter to get out of the sun, and lazed about for a couple of hours, occasionally observing the sea and the horizon through my binoculars. Nearby, some kids were knocking about on bicycles, and it struck me that Penghu — with its ocean vistas, clean air and open spaces — was a fine place to grow up; a hunch perhaps confirmed by the fact that none of the children wore spectacles. The sea, as always, had a calming effect on me and it was never boring to look at. I watched the tide come in and envelop the outer islands before hiking back to Hushih.

The next day the friendly couple who owned the guesthouse

kept asking me how I would travel to Baisha — a bus had come by earlier in the morning, but I was too busy eating breakfast to catch it and the next bus was not for a while. I said something would turn up. Packed and ready to go, I stood outside the old-style wooden storefront of the guesthouse for a few minutes, after which a local woman who happened to be travelling up the road stopped in her truck and offered me a ride up the road — that was how I was going to get to Baisha.

The Hushih woman drove across the countryside and then headed north along Route 203, which joined up Hushih with Baisha and Siyu. An ornate gateway — one of several on Penghu — marked the beginning of the approach to the Jhongjheng Bridge. Just before the bridge I temporarily took leave of Mrs Lin in order to take a look around the Anlong wind farm situated on a low headland overlooking the Penghu Sea. I walked up a grassy knoll towards the tall turbines. The unmoving blades of the generators made them look like hunched sleeping giants, and I associated them in my mind with the electricity pylons of Tainan County. Although providing only a small proportion of Taiwan's overall power needs, the turbines seemed benevolent enough. There were about 16 turbines on the farm, but there are plans to put many more offshore in the future, which really would create a farm effect. A few tourists arrived at the wind farm when I was walking about there. The gaiety of the tour group, and in particular the sight of women carrying sun umbrellas, harked back to an earlier era in Taiwan when everyone took their holidays together with friends and associates. Many of the visitors said hello to me cheerily. One could not imagine this scene taking place outside a nuclear power plant, but who knows what the future will bring.

It proved difficult to hitchhike across the bridge, so I walked it instead. The open seascapes by the way were expansive; rich coral flats flanged them all around, forming a black and brown crust. Cars passed at high speed across the two-kilometre long bridge, and it seemed unlikely any tourists would even notice these impressive tidal flats. From a greater distance the Anlong turbines looked like oversized lampposts. But carrying all my luggage around in the heat of another sunny summer's day was quickly becoming a drag. At a village just beyond the bridge, relief came in the form of a small restaurant, where I sat and ate a bowl of milk-fish-rice gruel. I was now on Baisha Island. The Penghu aquarium, located about five kilometres up the road, was my next planned stop, and after paying for the snack, I resumed hitching. I soon got a ride up the road.

It was at the aquarium that I picked up some basic data about Penghu: it was 126 kilometres square in total, had a coastline 320 kilometres long and its highest point — on Cat Island — was 79 meters in elevation. In other words, Penghu, which would fit into Canada's Vancouver Island about 257 times, was pretty small. Small, but oozing with character, from what I had seen. The aquarium, built next to the ocean in a small park, was stocked full of colourful specimens of fish, which included groupers, lionfish, starfish, small sharks and even a stingray. The exhibits were quite modest overall, in keeping with the setting; one was not overwhelmed or overawed by the spectacle of seeing a giant sea creature, such as a whale, in captivity. Taiwanese families at the aquarium seemed to be enjoying their time together.

Mrs Lin, who originally hailed from Gaosyong, came along the road on her way north. She had been on business in Makong but also needed to go to Siyu — the West Island — and we had arranged to rendezvous near the aquarium. Lin told me that she had been living in Penghu since she got married. She seemed to have a need to talk to someone, which is always handy for hitch-hikers; and after I got into her truck again, she immediately launched into an invective about one of her neighbours who would not sell land to her on anything other than cash terms. "It's too much. Who can pay that amount of money up front...?" Such were Mrs Lin's concerns that morning. She noticed my artists' gear and showed an interest in my idea of painting some landscapes in Penghu. Up to now of course I had not painted anything on the island. She said, "I am interested in painting. I loved it at school. But I have no time to do it". She would get a teacher and have lessons after she had retired, she promised. People are often like this: dreaming of doing what they really want to do after doing what they think they must do. It was the Ivan Ilych syndrome. At Cigang, I thanked Lin, got out of the car and went over to the passenger terminal.

The boat ticket for Jibei Island cost US$4. The fast boat was scheduled to depart an hour later, and this left me some time to put my feet up and watch the trickle of passengers arriving at Cigang's small terminal. They came in twos and threes, and there was not another single independent traveller to be seen anywhere; a number of chartered excursions left from Cigang, which catered to the tourist market, and some small groups of people later added to the numbers in the terminal. About a dozen people finally lined up to have their tickets checked by the coast guard before getting onboard the Jibei-bound vessel. The powerful boat finally got underway, and it took only 30 minutes to reach our destination.

I LIKED JIBEI IMMEDIATELY: an almost completely treeless, flat, uncluttered, pear-shaped island — it was just big enough to give everyone who went there the space they needed, but small enough to feel neighbourly. On the way over I saw a long sandy spit on which a handful of people were frolicking about, a couple of them on sand buggies, and several driving through the sea on surf skis. I made a mental note to avoid this sand spit until the end of my stay on the island. After arriving on the boat, I checked into a hotel near the harbour and then set out to explore the island on foot.

The narrow main street of the village opposite the harbour was quiet in the midday heat. I followed a path that led away from the village and around the low, rocky northeast coast of the island. Out to sea next to an islet, an old, wrecked cargo ship lay tilted on its side, presumably the victim of a storm. Nearer the shoreline, disused stone weirs drew semicircles in the half-submerged tidal shelf. The piled basalt walls of these weirs — there were 88 of them in the intertidal zone around Jibei's northern shore alone — looked immaculate despite not being used anymore; the windswept northern coast of Jibei was almost completely devoid of settlement. On a calm, hot sunny day, the scene out to sea was a sublime, an endless blue ocean in all directions, broken only by another lighthouse out on a tiny islet. Landward, the bricks and concrete of tombstones lay busted up among piles of sand and hardy vegetation. The place looked a little like a desert. During a five-kilometre walk, I only met a handful of people, who chose to traverse the island by scooter, but they drove slowly and acknowledged me. Jibei had that kind of intimacy; one could see almost all parts of the island from any one spot without any high-rise buildings getting in the way, and everyone seemed to be friendly.

The next day I walked the whole way around the island, a tenkilometre hike. I first repeated the walk of the previous day. Not far from the northern tip of the island, which I reached around midday, I came across a beach station that had been set up to receive a tour group. A handful of swarthy male beach lifeguards cum attendants lounged about like lizards under parasols as the afternoon heat kicked in. They occasionally got up to brew a tea or check how a barbecuing sausage was doing. I introduced myself and then found a suitable spot to sit and read during the siesta hour. An hour or so later, the tour group arrived on a slightly worn-looking bus. The group of about 40 people, mostly families, quickly debouched, fussing like ducks as they did. On a signal they then kitted up in life jackets, helmets and snorkels. The beach boys stirred and helped the guests with their life jackets and other bits of equipment before towing them out to sea on a diving raft. The raft looked like a doomed ship about to be scuttled, but the tourists presently jumped into the sea for a bit of snorkelling and looked as though they were enjoying themselves. Before leaving the beach, I slipped into the sea for a quick swim, but retreated when the beach attendants started to drive surf skis around like demented bikers.

Later I hiked directly across some balding grassland towards the south-western sector of the island. From there it was possible to view the coral sand spit a little further around the coast. The collection of dilapidated wooden chalets and marquees on the elongated spit resembled a shanty town or perhaps a temporary military encampment, but there were quite a few people on the beach dressed in bright swimsuits. To my astonishment, a couple were flying in the air above the beach in a Chitty Chitty Bang Bang-like winged dinghy; a risky activity, considering Taiwan's unfortunate aviation safety record. From the south-western hummocks, I walked down past the fun-time sand spit and then joined up with the coast road that led back to the harbour. At a harbour restaurant I ate seafood noodles and drank cold draught beer, a perfect ending to the walk.

At almost five kilometres long, the Penghu Great Bridge used to be the longest bridge in East Asia, and it still cuts a dash. Back on the Penghu mainland the next day, I started to hitchhike westwards across Baisha towards Siyu. Travelling on the back of a truck with the wind blowing through my hair was possibly the best way to enjoy the fiveminute drive across the bridge. The workers who gave me this ride took me as far as Siaomen, a small satellite island that was joined to Baisha at the waist. In the small Siaomen village, I left my bags at a store and went off for a quick walk. It only took half an hour or so to cover half the circumference of the volcanic outcrop, after which the path disappeared. From the northern tip of the Siaomen, one could see the Great Penghu Bridge, about two kilometres distant in all its afternoon glory. Most of the tourists who arrived at Siaomen headed down to the shoreline not far from the village to look at a sea cave, but actually, Siaomen's whole shoreline with its black basalt columns, boulder fields and stone weirs was very visually engaging. All-black birds, which resembled crows, blended in well with the environment. Before picking up my bags and leaving Siaomen, I dropped by the local geological museum. The small museum was excellent because its subject matter related one hundred percent to its immediate context; and it was there that I learned that the mysterious all-black birds were in fact eastern reef egrets.

The two-kilometre walk from the small island over to Route 203 was not really a problem, except for the sweltering heat. By now I was regularly using my umbrella as a sun shield, but the sun here seemed to bounce off the tarmac road and gather about my head. As I walked across to the main road, a military helicopter circled above me like a vulture. By the time I got to the highway, I was about ready to hitch a ride. But the road was extremely wide, almost an expressway, and this invited fast driving, by vehicles of every type. I ended up walking eight kilometres down the road in blazing sunshine, my last long walk for several weeks as it turned out. I had wanted to spend most of Trip Five taking leisurely strolls in the countryside and painting watercolours — not doing these long tiring hikes. When eventually a garbage truck came along, I made a determined effort to flag it down; and it duly stopped. The public-hygiene officer took me down to the end of the island.

At Waian, a vital fishing port, I dived into a convenience store and bought a clutch of cold beers, then spent a couple of hours sitting in the shade of the harbour wall, drinking them. I admired the small, slim white fishing craft moored in the inner marina and watched their comings and goings as I celebrated the end of my summer walks. The boats, with names like *New Sea*, *Shining Star of Tomorrow* and *Happy Fish*, seemed to come and go at will, and one romanticized about the fishing way of life, which was in fact a tough and dangerous job. On the quayside, racks of in-season pinkish squid had been laid out to dry in the hot sun, and I made a mental note to try some the next time I visited a restaurant. But although Waian was lively, it was not an especially accommodating town, and it proved impossible to find a place to stay. I thus got on a Makong-bound bus early that evening and made it to Penghu's major tourist centre in about an hour; the journey being a kind of fast rewind of the previous few days' travelling.

MAKONG HAD ALL the hallmarks of a small Taiwanese city: convenience stores galore, scooters and motorbikes all over the place, and a high population density. Down by the harbour a large mock-up ship served as a shopping arcade. Inside the ship, and all about town, shops sold dried-fish products, which visitors bought to give their families back on mainland Taiwan. Seafood restaurants catered to groups and families. Makong Harbour, itself a small bay within a bay, hosted an active fishing fleet plus a small ferry terminal serving the Penghu South Sea. Other parts of the harbour were dedicated to fish processing and the importing of supplies, such as building materials and natural gas. In an attempt to beautify them, the gas-storage tanks had been painted with seaside murals. After arriving in Makong and conducting a long search for a suitable place to stay — during which I got the measure of the town — I finally found a suitable hotel down by the harbour. Leaving some of my luggage in my room, I then departed for Wangan Island with a few clothes and my battered trolley.

The boat to Wangan Island — a smallish island some 30 kilometres south of Makong — left at nine o'clock in the morning. At a first glance the *Number 1 Heng An* looked like an old tramp steamer, but on closer inspection I could see that it was not a bad boat and probably represented the state of the art in small passenger ferries circa 1975. Quite a few people got on the boat, maybe 50 in total. On the way out to Wangan, the boat passed a series of low-lying basalt islands and then ploughed over to our destination harbour. A third-finished bridge jutted out from the side of the island — a bridge that will in future link Wangan to Jiangjun Island, its smaller neighbour only one kilometre distant. At Wangan I disembarked and walked over to the Wangan Green Turtle Conservation Centre.

A good amount of information about turtles was on display at the Wangan centre, most of which I took the trouble to read — essentially green turtles are an endangered species; there are perhaps only 200,000 of them left in the world, and their nesting habitats are disappearing at an alarming rate. Apparently, the turtles mate and nest every two to nine years, always returning to the same nesting site, and produce between one and nine nests each mating season. Typically, a nesting turtle will lay about 110 eggs in a single nest, but only about one in a 1,000 hatchlings survives to full adulthood. As if these odds were not bad enough, the green turtle is a fantastically fussy nester that will lay eggs only where the sand grains are the right size, the moisture content is appropriate, and where there are not too many pebbles or other impurities in the sand. Basically, turtles need clean sandy beaches to nest on. Taiwan used to have many such beaches, but development and pollution steadily reduced their number, and now there are only a few suitable nesting sites left, found mostly on the outlying islands. Wangan Island had a couple of turtle-friendly beaches; and after years, when the turtles were caught and slaughtered for food by local people, the authorities finally put in place a serious conservation programme. The centre — large, airy and air-conditioned — also exhibited photographs and information about local ecology, birdlife and folk culture. Given that Wangan Island was evidently a pristine offshore environment it slightly disappointed me to see a group of young people drive up to the centre on rented scooters. It occurred to me that in treasuring one part of the island's ecology, a problem was being set up elsewhere.

I walked back past the harbour, which had no fewer than six tour buses parked in its car park. Where did these buses come from? They had arrived on a roll-on roll-off ferry from Makong and would leave the same day. The tourists were making their way to the Turtle Centre, which no longer seemed overly large, considering this flush of visitors. Between the centre and the harbour, I walked past small roadside dwellings. In the front yard of one house, sliced bitter melon had been laid out on a sheet to dry in the hot sun, a scene reminiscent of traditional Penghu life. Agave plants, fern bushes and morning glories, and a lovely yellow and a white sandy bay greeted me around the corner away from the harbour. The village of Wangankou was only a short distance away.

At first it seemed unlikely I would remain in Wangankou any length of time. It was almost by accident that I stumbled across an old courtyard-style house that served breakfast and doubled as a small guesthouse. The owners, an old but healthy and active local couple, gave me a good deal for five nights. My tiny room had a low ceiling and small windows but it did not feel in the least bit claustrophobic for the simple reason that it adjoined a communal courtyard. In the winter, it would be a cosy place to shelter from the cold north easterlies; and in summer, the high roof and thick walls of the house painted blue left the rooms feeling cool.

Over the next few days, I got into a routine. In the morning, during the breakfast rush hour, I would pop out across the road and take a dip in the ocean. The Blue House was only a two-minute walk from a clean beach, which was always deserted in the mornings. I swam for half an hour before settling down to painting in my room. From sketches, I painted the Beiliao village temple and the Jibei village high street, among other subjects. None of these efforts came out especially well, but whenever I got fed up with it, I would go out and have a wander round the island. Wangan was not very large and I probably could have walked around its circumference in a day. My chosen mode of transportation on the island though was electric scooter, which could be rented down by the harbour. The bikes were comfortable and silent, and the batteries held just about enough juice in them to get me fully around the island once.

There were three villages on Wangan: Wangankou on the south coast, Jhongshe on the west coast, and Shueian on the northern shore. The east coast was where the modern harbour and new infrastructure was located, and this development had no doubt absorbed a small village. Jhongshe consisted of a street of traditional houses that had effectively become an outdoor museum, since few people lived there and many more visited. The coral and stone traditional residences were intact exemplars of the Penghu house. They had sloping gables that rounded attractively where they met the supporting roof beam; the gable walls were decorated and included embedded green ceramic tiles that let daylight into the interior rooms; coral had been used extensively in the house walls, making them tactile-looking. At the top of the island, the remote Shueian remained dedicated to a rustic lifestyle. The northern village featured a small stark temple that faced south, away from the wind. Either side of Shueian, two small peninsulas jutted out northwards into the sea, like crabs' claws — the western peninsula affording some spectacular views of Wangan's rugged western coastline. On one trip out to this spot, I watched a fisherman sail a boat near the bottom of the cliff, drop anchor, and then dive into the water with a net to pluck shellfish from the reef.

The crowded-looking shore of Jiangjun Island was clearly visible from Wangan's east coast, and I made an excursion there one day. The smaller island's harbour village, basically a slum of tenement buildings, had an altogether different character from its counterpart on Wangan. After arriving early in the morning, I walked about the village and looked for signs of life, but most residents were still sleeping, like in a city. Outside the crowded harbour, Jiangjun proved to be a typical treeless Penghu island, dotted with coral-walled farmsteads, small village shrines and the occasional grave. I attempted to walk around the circumference of the island, getting maybe halfway before losing my orientation and prematurely walking back to the harbour. Nevertheless, I found the absence of tourism refreshing; and the island's basalt rock coastline was as pretty as any that could be found in the Penghu archipelago.

Chihmei, one of Penghu's larger outlying islands located 46 kilometres south of Makong, was also accessible from Wangan and I went there too. The bulk of the passengers on the boat out were locals, including schoolchildren, who evidently plied the waters between Chihmei and Makong daily to attend school. The short 17-kilometre voyage from Wangan across a silver sea took just over an hour to complete. On the way we passed one or two of the smaller South Sea satellite islands that were home to various species of migratory terns — one of these islets, "Cat Island", peaked at the highest ground in Penghu. On arriving at Chihmei, I rented a scooter, intending to make a quick preliminary reconnaissance of the island. Much of Chihmei was open, treeless and windswept. There were some small, picturesque settlements dotted about, full of traditional stone and coral houses. I stopped in one village to ask about accommodation, but it was expensive for what it was, so I decided not to stay the night. Instead, I completed my quick circuit around the coast road, returned the bike, and got on the same passenger boat that I had arrived on one and a half hours before. I dozed on the boat as it made its sluggish way back to Wangan.

NOT WANTING to go back to the cauldron of Taibei in summer, I stayed on in Makong for a couple of weeks. I spent some time painting at the hotel down by the harbour. The painting was really a cover for my idleness — which is what long-term travel tends to lapse into eventually. Plein-air painting had not really worked out for me; it had been a struggle to do any kind of painting, and I was disabused of my conceit that conjuring up impressionist-like masterpieces on the spot could be done by anyone. The weather in Penghu remained hot — too hot to go to the beach. I made one or two side trips to various locales near Makong in the late afternoon though and watched boats weaving in and out of the harbours. Towards the end of my stay in Penghu, Alex flew over to join me for a few days. I took her on an abridged tour of the three main islands and also out to Wangan on a daytrip. She loved Penghu, as I did, and on arrival immediately set about taking pictures of the coral walls and picturesque traditional residences. We tried the in-season squid at a local restaurant and it was good; we spied the ROC navy docked in harbour; we went to Jibei and played on the sand spit; and we drove past the Anlong wind farm, seeing the floodlit sweeping blades of the turbines swishing through the air like aeroplane propellers in slow motion.

7

TRIP SIX: MATSU, KINMEN AND THE NORTHWEST

"SLEEP WITH YOUR SWORD AT THE READY", SHOUTED THE CHINESE couplets that adorned the face of a giant concrete tower overlooking Nankan's harbour. Chirpy music playing over the ship's public-address system awoke me at 6.30 from an uneasy slumber, marking the end of a slow 273-kilometre overnight cruise on the aging *Tamalun*, a 1960s car ferry. I stumbled out of my bunk and onto deck. That's when I saw the propaganda. Closer to shore, the seven-storey-high structure looked even more impressive, as a minibus passed along the road below it — a tiny bug compared to the Great Wall-like tower. The ideograms on the building — literally meaning "pillow the head on a spear and await the dawn" — were a reminder to visitors that here was not just a sleepy island off China's coast, but a garrisoned outpost of the Republic of China, a beacon of "Free China" standing against "Red China", a place Taiwanese conscripts may have to put up the fight of their lives to defend. The cooler October temperatures at Nankan compared to Keelung — where I had embarked on the old tub of a ferry the night before — and the gaggles of smart and reasonably fitlooking young soldiers also preparing to disembark added a further note of Cold War frisson to my arrival in Matsu.

Put together, Matsu, a small group of islands standing cheekbyjowl with China's Fujian Province, would be able to fit into any one of the latter's larger peninsulas, and it really is a wonder how the Chinese communists failed to grab them in 1949. The Chinese nationalists, however, dug in on these remnant bits of territory after losing the civil war in China and, with the help of the Americans, turned the islands into impregnable fortresses. Sensibly, China has left the islands alone since its failed attempt to bombard Kinmen — a larger island group to the south of Matsu — into submission back in the 1950s, when the Cold War became decidedly hot in this region. American forces withdrew from Matsu and Kinmen after the US switched diplomatic recognition from the Republic of China to the People's Republic of China in the 1970s, which left the defence of the islands to the scraggy but determined Taiwanese conscript army. I was curious to see Matsu and Kinmen for myself having known their names and historical significance for a long time. Matsu could be reached by sea, and being furthest away from Taibei psychologically speaking, it made a natural first-choice destination to open Trip Six.

Nankan's Fuao Harbour was huge, considering the relatively small size of the island. On the expansive quayside three military engineers stopped work and watched as the ferry nosed itself up against the dockside. I got off the ferry along with about 100 other people, mostly soldiers. Also on the quayside a marine, dressed in nothing but red swimming trunks and a snorkel, stood at attention as an officer ordered him about, like a scene from the theatre of the absurd. But at one time, underwater inspections of the quayside for mines were routine. Next to the harbour a school sports meet was taking place on an all-weather running track. ROC flags and large red balloons had been placed next to the track for decoration. As a schoolgirl jogged around the track to claim her modest placing, I noted the time: 7.30. There was something touching about watching school kids running their socks off at that time in the morning, regardless of any military menace that may have been lurking underwater, in the sky, or around the corner.

I set off to walk around Nankan Island in an anticlockwise direction. After passing by the concrete propaganda tower and an abandoned army barracks, I stopped at a convenience store to rest and do some map study. The map I had brought with me, however, was next to useless, so it was impossible to get a sense of how best to approach exploring the island. The road ahead looked rather isolated, which ordinarily would have attracted me, but with limited water supplies, I doubled back to the harbour instead. From the harbour, I climbed up a steep road onto the island's backbone ridgeline before heading west towards the furthermost village of Siwei. By now the day was really quite warm, as October days often are in Taiwan. The walk up the road from the harbour was blessedly short, and from the high point, I then walked an undulating five kilometres through beefwoods, lush grasses, subtropical plants and blooming flowers to reach Siwei, a nondescript hamlet tucked away on the side of Nankan facing China, where I turned around and hiked down into the village of Matsu.

Matsu took its name from Taiwan's most revered folk god — also namesake of the whole ROC-occupied island group. The local temple was a popular draw with Taiwanese tourists, a few dozen of whom had arrived on Nankan by air that day and were wandering about the seafront. Next to the temple five World War II-era landing craft sat parked on a small beach. The most sophisticated-looking of the craft lay half in the water with its loading door down, so it was obviously in use. But what use exactly remained a bit of a mystery. I surreptitiously took some photographs of the landing craft before moving on. The quiet and scenic south-coast road would eventually get me back to the harbour, I calculated. At Cinsha, another small fishing village, I stopped a while. This village had found itself on the frontline during the artillery duelling of the 1950s, and some tourists were milling about disused beach bunkers near the village when I arrived. The village itself consisted of attractive stone-wall gabled houses and was neatly kept — someone had clearly been making an effort for the benefit of visitors. I made a sketch of one of the traditional houses and then left.

There was no doubt in my mind, as I traipsed past more dug-in bunkers and barracks that may or may not have been abandoned, that on this particular day, I was getting a lot more exercise than any member of Nankan's military garrison. According to my casual observations this garrison may have numbered 500 young men — a fraction of the number who would have been stationed here in the 1950s, when Cinsha took several direct hits from long-range Chinabased heavy artillery. Whatever the actual number, the lack of sentries at various strategic points along the road suggested a low state of readiness. As I walked past small mountain-enclosed bays and around rocky promontories, I mentally surveyed the landscape from the point of view of a military commander, picking out places of tactical vulnerability and making my dispositions. It then occurred to me that the hard igneous rocks of Matsu afforded excellent protection from air attack, so keeping underground and out of sight was probably not a bad idea.

After a long uphill slog, I rejoined the mountain road and then headed back towards the populated end of the island. On the way I passed a kaoliang distillery. Just the smell of this spirit — the Chinese equivalent of rum — wafting in the air made me feel like I wanted to vomit. The distillery, which was celebrating its fiftieth birthday, produced the "Tunnel 88" brand, named after a nearby former tank tunnel that had been used by the distillery since 1988 to store their wicked brew — "yesterday the smell of gunpowder, today the aroma of wine", some tourist-board poet had penned. From the road junction at the distillery, I turned down a lane and popped down into Nioujiao Village. From this small settlement one could get a clear view of Beikan Island to the north. Nankan's twin island was sufficiently far away to make mutual support between the islands in the event of a military conflict difficult if not impossible. Jieshou, Nankan's main village, was just a ten-minute walk down the other side of the ridge from the distillery. Far larger and livelier than the other five villages on Nankan, the place was nevertheless a bit of a dump and an expensive tourist trap to boot. I returned to Fuao Harbour, where I ended up pitching my tent between two old fishing boats in the marina's car park.

The bad news was that the *Tamalun* was not due back for a couple of days: what would I do on Nankan? At the harbour the next day, I tried to get a boat out to one of the nearby islands, but it was already too late to go, so instead, I spent a day exploring Jieshou — a waste of time. Later I booked into a hostel above the inter-island boat booking office. Camping in the harbour was fine, but I wanted to be ready to go at short notice in the morning. It was in the hostel later that evening that I met Meili, a local resident. After enquiring as to what I was up to, she started to tell me her life story in the way strangers do sometimes: she had planned to study in the US as a child, but her father was finally dissuaded from allowing her to go when jealous neighbours told him that America was a wicked and promiscuous country of outrageous sexual equality. Meili never went. But she went on to raise a big family, and so had achieved a lot we agreed.

It was Meili who encouraged me to visit Siguang and Dongguang, half an hour away by boat from Nankan. The small motor launch left Fuao the next day at 7.00, and I got on it along with a dozen or so other sleepy heads. We got to Dongguang before the small island had awoken. The harbour at Dongguang consisted of a modest wharf, a neat little coast guard's building and a helipad; but the coast guard were nowhere to be seen and the helipad landing area was not guarded — a dawn attack against it any day of the week would almost certainly be successful. After getting off the boat, I walked up a steep hill to Dongguang's main village, passing a couple of defunct light tanks by the roadside along the way.

Dongguang, effectively shielded from China by Siguang, was a delightful little backwater. I walked down the island's tail on a newly asphalted road that ran dead centre through the 2.63-square-kilometre granite outcrop. Of the dozen or so arrivals on the island that morning, I was the only one to make this short journey on foot. The scrubby landscape included some gorgeous flowering tree groves, a few old concrete sentry boxes overgrown with agave plants, and a number of disused tank bunkers. One or two more derelict tanks lay scattered in the grass off road, their rusting turrets missing hatches. Recently retouched camouflage paintwork on a parade ground building indicated an active garrison was out there somewhere though. The island's spine road eventually led up to a lighthouse that stood on a small expanse of grassy land atop high granite cliffs. Near the lighthouse immediately above the cliffs, an army barracks lay abandoned and in an advanced state of decay. At one time a whole company must have been stationed here, their mission to keep an eye on the seas around the cliffs. I stood in a sentry box and scanned the waves for commando dinghies, but time and the ocean had swallowed the threat whole and only the hard, immutable black cliffs remained.

At Fucheng, a village nearby the lighthouse on the northern coast of Dongguang, I finally came across the island's small garrison, a detachment of ROC marines. The small base came complete with dummy tanks and a heliport, but I only saw two soldiers. The tanks had just been given a lick of paint — not to fool the enemy, surely, but to give the soldiers something to do. On the shoreline below the military blockhouse, a wrecked fishing vessel laid on its side stuck in the sands, a useful bit of cover for a night landing, I noted. But nothing had ever happened here, and it looked like nothing ever would. I returned to the harbour via a shoreline track. By now the sun was shining and the clear blue waters of the ocean looked quite inviting, but swimming in the probably mined sea somehow seemed like a nonstarter.

Nearer the main village I was amazed to stumble across the base of a mechanized company that appeared to be battle sharp. Nine brandspanking-new armoured personnel carriers sat parked together in a neat row outside a tidy army barracks. They were not especially well concealed. As I observed the building through binoculars from a distance, an officer dressed in crisp combat fatigues marched out and started to bark orders at two subordinates. And get some camouflage netting up, I thought. On the forecourt outside the barracks, personal and heavy weapons had been placed in neat piles, perhaps for lifting into the carriers at short notice. Continuing my walk back to the harbour, I passed the two young soldiers I had spied earlier as they walked in the opposite direction on some errand. They were in their early twenties and looked like school boys in fancy dress. Their heavy semiautomatic rifles, however, were entirely real.

Catching the midday round-Matsu boat, I managed to get over to Siguang — Dongguang's twin a couple of nautical miles to the west — by midday. Almost the same size in area as Dong-guang, the vibe at Siguang was less sleepy. For one thing, the harbour was much bigger than the one at Dongguang, and it was guarded by a large gun that was being cleaned and oiled when I arrived on the launch. The cliff emplacement that housed the anti-aircraft piece was even covered by a camouflage net, albeit a rather tatty one. Siguang obviously served as the administrative base of the army for both islands, and its military was thus more substantive and active. Wasting no time after arriving, I set off to explore the island. The walk up the second steep hill of the day got me up to a military base, where a non-commissioned officer wrestling with an improbably large machine gun said hello to me. The sight of the gun made me feel sick. Why would anybody ever volunteer to join any army given the frightening assignments one was supposed to carry out? But of course most of the soldiers at this base were conscripts — not by choice, but by legal obligation. From the base I proceeded to hike rapidly around Siguang's lovely isolated coast road, which took me past a ghostly military hospital and a heavily fortified but oddly deserted heliport. Having completed the circuit, a three-hour walk, I hopped on the last boat of the day and got over to Beikan before dark.

Beikan was to Nankan what Siguang was to Dongguang: the senior and more military-orientated half of a small neighbourhood. Not that I was able to judge this immediately upon arrival, but the density of soldiers hanging about at the harbour was an early indicator. By now I had a much better map of the island group, courtesy of the Matsu tourist centre at Nankan — strangely, given the militarized nature of the islands, this was by far the best and most detailed map I would come across in Taiwan. According to this map there was a beach about a kilometre up the road from the harbour. I started to walk there, thinking to camp on it that night. But on arrival I found the beach was guarded by a company of soldiers. An officer raced out of the military camp on a motorbike to catch up with me. The young man was quite friendly if a bit anxious; he wanted to practice his English. He asked me my business and I explained. He was surprised that anyone would consider travelling alone for such an extended period — this was an unthinkable indulgence to the average Taiwanese male; indeed, career suicide. The officer told me that he had volunteered for eight years and was in his fifth year of service — his third on Beikan, a posting he found "boring". He earned about US$1500 a month, which is not bad money in Taiwan. Did he think a fight with China was likely any time soon? "No. We won't fight the Chinese. We are all Chinese, and we know each other", was his unscripted reply. Those were nice sentiments to hear, but of course historically Chinese have fought each other, and sadly they will again in the future. After saying goodbye to the officer, I walked back to a temple located next to the sea and made camp nearby.

The next morning two of the Matsu landing craft chugged across the sea in front of the temple, a scene out of so many war movies, it seemed like. They were heading in a northwards direction, perhaps on a supply run to a satellite islet. I stared at the boats in amazement for a minute and then returned to my chores. Knowing full well the temple would have visitors later in the morning I prepared to leave as soon as possible. It was then that I noticed a scruffily dressed stray soldier loitering on the beach near the temple. He affected to not have seen me as he stooped down to splash some seawater on his face, an odd thing to do. The soldier may have been sent to check on me, or he could have been on a routine early-morning inspection of the area, so I made a point of saying hello to him when I left, only to have him silently follow me down the road. The dull soldier eventually gave up the pursuit after we reached Pilan Beach, where I had met his commanding officer the day before. I then took a local bus up onto the island's ridge, a five-minute hop.

My walk along Beikan's ridgeline road took me past yet more military infrastructure, and for the first time I was able to view at close quarters a whole battery of artillery dug in by the roadside. The bunkered and concealed guns had been left unattended, but they were in good condition and looked very formidable. A round from one of these guns would make a real mess of any landing craft, assuming a direct hit. But would any of these guns be able to hit a moving target in the bay below? It was hypothetical military-science questions such as these that exercised my mind as I walked on past the carefully concealed guns. A pleasant four-kilometre hike finally brought me to a hilltop fort and bunker complex built at the island's highest point. The base commanded a spectacular view over Beikan's main airstrip, which had been built on reclaimed land. The fort was quiet with only the occasional sentry drifting in and out of the concrete labyrinth; one of its outer walls had the sleeping-with-one's-sword-at-the-ready slogan stencilled in yellow. By a viewing platform I gazed out over the ocean and observed terns twisting in the sky over the small islets next to the airport — this was my summer holiday moment. I later walked all the way the down to the airport, caught the bus back to Beikan harbour, and then got on the last boat for Nankan.

Whilst waiting for the orange and white-liveried *Tamalun* to turn up, I rested in the sunshine at Fuao Harbour. Fisherpeople and military personnel went in and out of the area, and a few village residents came out to exercise on the running track in the evening, but mostly it was quiet on the island until the ferry turned up. The arrival of the *Tamalun* on a bright morning was quite a heartening sight. A few days on Matsu had altered my perception of the vessel, which now looked like a sleek destroyer to my island-adjusted eyes. The ferry terminal, normally devoid of people, was busy before embarkation; a number of troops were returning home for the mid-autumn festival holiday, and an endof-the-school-year spirit pervaded the hall. But I was not going back to Taibei with all the other passengers, but up to Dongyin, the most northerly and exposed territory under ROC jurisdiction.

Dongyin oozed grittiness; the light that deflected off bare granite was harsh and unforgiving. The parts of the island I could see from the ship were treeless and crawling with military bunkers, pillboxes and gun emplacements. One could just imagine how bitterly cold it got here in winter, even though it was rather hot when I arrived. After getting off the ferry, I imme-diately started to explore the island on foot. Bunkered in on all sides, the military garrison on Dongyin apparently meant busi-ness — but apart from the odd sentry there were not many soldiers on view. The rocky spit joining the western and eastern halves of the island had been developed and a big road had been built across it. Halfway across, a huge statue of former president Chiang Chingkuo, housed in a pavilion, sat gazing out to sea. The former president looked rather melancholy there — a colossus staring out to the Chinese mainland he never did return to. Skipping past the monument, I crossed over to Dongyin's smaller half and spent a couple of hours walking around its barren hills. There was not much to see except for military posts of varying sizes and function. Dongyin was certainly more heavily garrisoned than any of the other islands in the Matsu archipelago, but the soldiers kept a low profile. Fearing stum-bling into a minefield, I returned to Dongyin's sole village by the harbour later in the day, finding a discreet spot to camp nearby.

The bigger half of the island, which I set out to explore the next day, had a running track and fuel dump located in the middle of a depression. Near to this running track, I came across an operational barracks, one at which some soldiers were under-going weapons training. The detachment at the barracks went by the moniker "Invincible Tigers", or something similar, but most of the soldiers were school boys in reality. The barracks' parade ground had been decorated with light antitank guns from a former period, but the boys were being trained to use the very latest heavy machine guns. On what was another warm day, I pushed on to the eastern extremity of the island, where I ended up visiting an early twentieth-century Britishbuilt iron lighthouse, one of the island's few tourist attractions. To reach the lighthouse, it was necessary to walk a half-kilometre hike along an obscure cliff path. About a dozen tourists had made it out to the lighthouse, and they all looked at me as though I were a descendant of one of the British engineers who had built it. The locale was really impressive — stunning cliffs rose out of the sea like a battleship, the sun glancing off the steel-like granite — but going there was the beginning and the end of my sightseeing on the island.

I left Dongyin the next day, boarding the faithful and tireless *Tamalun*, which had been back to Taibei and out to Nankan once more whilst I had been on Dongyin. The ship's purser upgraded me to a business-class cabin shortly after embarkation, perhaps mistaking me for a secret military advisor of some sort.

ALEX and I headed out to Taibei's domestic airport together and took an early-morning flight to Kinmen, Taiwan's most famous offshore possession located 227 kilometres west of the main island, but only ten kilometres from Siamen, a major port on China's coastline. I had only got a few hours sleep after arriving back in Taibei from Matsu, but was soon ready to go again. We made the flight and about an hour later entered the arrivals hall in Kinmen's small, neat and tidy civilian airport. Given that Kinmen had been under direct ROC military rule for more than three decades, the tidiness was perhaps to be expected. The large number of passengers flying to the island first thing on a Monday morning, however, came as a bit of a surprise.

The idea was to walk as much as possible, but Kinmen was far larger than I imagined — shaped like a dumbbell, it measured about 20 kilometres east to west and around 15 kilometres north to south at the ends. Alex suggested we take a bus, but stubborn old me insisted we hike so as to take in the scenery and to get the measure of the island. Walking along we stumbled across the Kinmen National Park Headquarters, where we stopped to take a rest and look around.

Inside the light, airy post-modern visitor centre the official story of Kinmen unfolded in a series of text and image displays: in 317 CE, six clans moved to the island to escape political instability in China; another twelve clans came across in 803, after which, development of the island took off; a salt mine was established in 1297; in 1387, the island was fortified; the island was claimed by Cheng Chenggong in the 1640s and became a major battlefield for the first time; the island witnessed major emigration in the 19th century as Fujianese used Kinmen as a transit hub for travel from Siamen, a treaty port, to Southeast Asia; the island was occupied by Japan in 1937; it became a battlefield again in 1949; most recently, in 1958, it was shelled by communist forces; and Kinmen National Park was established on 18 October 1995. There was an anthropological subtext to this historical narrative: each village on the island was basically occupied by one family clan, a close-knit bunch of people who renewed their ties every year. They lived in traditional Fujianese-style houses and also in some Western-style houses that had been built on the island in the early twentieth century.

Finally leaving the centre, and giving up on a pointless walk, Alex and I hitched a ride into Cincheng. In town we found a family-run hotel and based ourselves there for the duration. As Kinmen was evidently so big and because Alex was with me, I relented and rented a scooter to get around. We visited one or two tourist places that evening, like the Kinmen Liquor Factory and the Deyue Tower — the latter a Chinese nationalist-era nostalgia museum. At Shuitou, a small harbour and boat terminal, we spied a tour boat arrive from China packed full of

Fujianese day-trippers coming over to Kinmen apparently for sightseeing and shopping. Here was a great irony: for decades Kinmen represented the first line of defence against communist China, and China-Taiwan relations remain very frosty today; but here were crowds of Chinese mainlanders being welcomed, coveted even, by Kinmen's authorities. After making enquiries about the boat to Lieyu, or Little Kinmen, Alex and I returned to Cincheng for the night, buying a takeaway Peking duck for dinner.

The 823 War Museum, located on the eastern half of the island, seemed like an essential place to visit. The next day we drove out to the museum along Kinmen's southern coast road, which took us past numerous traditional dwellings spared from demolition and development by years of martial-law rule. On a nearby beach we came face to face with defunct tanks and anti-tank obstacles. During the 1958 crisis, the beach had been used as a landing zone for supplies shipped over from Taiwan; it had been a highly dangerous mission to haul boxes of shells up the beach during that battle. Alex jokingly saluted as we passed the defunct tanks, but a large military transport that flew overhead as we traversed the coast road confirmed the presence of an active military garrison, again very low-profile. We found the 823 museum a short while later, it being located a little further inland.

On 23 August 1958, all hell broke loose over Kinmen. That evening the People's Liberation Army (PLA) of China started a heavy artillery bombardment, firing at Kinmen from all available angles. Several hundred shells landed on the island before the night was out; a total of almost half a million would hit the island in just one month, making the action one of the most intense and sustained artillery bombardments in history. China's purpose was to stir things up and provoke Taiwan and its close ally the US. America stayed out of the local battle but did sail its fleet through the Taiwan Strait as a warning to China not to expand the offensive. The Americans also helped supply the Kinmen garrison with some guns and ammunition. Although the communist forces had many advantages — including higher ground, more space and more artillery pieces — the nationalist forces were quite well dug in and were able to mount a well-targeted counter-bombardment. Meanwhile, communist attacks in the air and on the sea against nationalist forces failed abysmally — they were no match for the better equipped and more motivated nationalist forces. The huge bombardment did tremendous damage to Kinmen's civilian infrastructure, especially on Lieyu, which was within relatively close range of the communist guns. The 823 Museum memorialized the battle very well without being too one-sided in its explanations or vitriolic about the enemy. Although the Americans did not get directly involved in the fighting, US support for the nationalists was vital in tipping the balance of the battle their way and forcing a stalemate, a point well-made and well-illustrated inside the small but comprehensive museum. According to one very detailed map showing where all the shells had landed on Kinmen, no fewer than 50,000 shells landed on Liaoluo Beach alone during the battle — the sands of which Alex and I had just visited — and one tiny islet just to the north of Kinmen received a staggering total of 82,000 incoming rounds.

Preceding the 1958 bombardment by a decade, the PLA had in fact made an attempt to occupy Kinmen physically. On the night of 25 October 1949, the communists landed a substantial force numbering around 10,000 men in a stealthy night attack. It was a daring move and the communists made some initial gains before being beaten off by an effective and determined nationalist counterattack. Those communist forces not killed in the heavy fighting surrendered in short order. Their mission had been doomed, one surmised, by the failure to reinforce their beachhead promptly. It should be remembered that at this point in time, the PLA was on something of a roll and had been used to beating the nationalist forces easily. But Kinmen's nationalist garrison fought back tenaciously. Alex and I visited the Guningtou War Museum after driving right across Kinmen to the place where the invasion force had landed. Among the period artefacts on display at the museum there were old rifles, faded battle pennants and the battle records of the ROC armed forces. The battle orders were not hurriedly scribbled orders, but beautifully brushed notes made in a fine calligraphic hand. It seemed incredible someone should have taken so much care writing them when dealing with something as practically-orientated and situationist as battle deployments, but the nationalists were a little bit old-fashioned in that respect. The museum also had an impressive series of oil paintings depicting the battle, pictures that naturally emphasized the victorious counterattack. In a bunker-like corner of the building, it was possible to view the city of Siaomen on the mainland in the distance through binoculars. On the far shore before the city stood the inevitable propaganda billboard, this one reading *One Country Two Systems Unite China*. I repeated the slogan to myself, and yawned.

We spent our second day in Kinmen on Lieyu Island. The old military tunnels hewn out of solid granite and measuring some 790 metres in length were now a tourist attraction of sorts, but few people seemed to want to visit them mid-week. Backtracking from the far side of one tunnel, we set out to explore the rest of Lieyu, driving ever so slowly on the bike. With its mined beaches, aging blockhouses and pretty countryside, the island indeed proved to be a smaller version of Kinmen, but it was quieter than the main island and something of a refuge for birdlife. "The General's Fort" had once been a strongpoint on Lieyu's highly exposed coast facing China, but it now lies empty and disarmed, a rambling deserted bunker camouflaged on the outside for the benefit of tourists. Interestingly, we never saw one soldier at this fort or all the way around Lieyu. Taiwan's military has relied heavily on minefields to keep intruders out of these areas. But the government of Taiwan currently has a plan in place to remove all the mines on Kinmen and Matsu, a project that will take seven years to complete at a cost of US$127 million. The chance to take in the local bird sanctuary seemed all the more urgent considering this threat. The lagoon-like wetlands further along the coast were idyllic, though tiny; but the birds, sensing our presence, flew away as we went by.

Our time in Kinmen ended in Cincheng, where we spent a day wandering its streets in search of the unusual or exotic. But this provincial and laid-back town was much like any other in rural Taiwan: it had a couple of markets, a couple of karaoke bars, a bunch of standard retail outlets and a sprinkling of convenience stores. It was noticeable how tame the military garrison on Kinmen was: they kept a very low profile, as on Penghu: the only soldiers we saw sat transfixed in Internet cafés, playing simulated-violence computer games, oblivious to the rich ecology and history around them. Domestic tourists and visitors from China hardly bothered to look around the town. When the time came to get on a plane and leave Kinmen, we took a taxi back to the airport. But instead of returning to Taibei directly, we flew to Jiayi.

———

JIAYI, terminus point of my third trip earlier in the year, was very hot when we arrived, and a jaunt out to the mountains naturally suggested itself. I wanted to take Alex up to Laiji, the magical valley in the shadow of mysterious Tashan Mountain. On arrival in Jiayi, I went to a supermarket and bought some provisions: I purchased lamb, beef, pork, some processed fish products, cheese, pasta, pumpkin, green peppers, bananas and satsumas plus a bottle of wine and a small bottle of whisky for the trip. Thus victualled, we got on a Fencihu-bound bus. The small bus only went as far as Shihjhou, halfway to the scenic mountain resort, before turning left along the transverse mountain road that led to Fencihu. The road was as lovely in autumn as it had been in spring, when I had last hiked along it. We arrived at Fencihu at four in the afternoon. The former logging village was cool and wet; the planted pines by the road breathed out delicious air.

But things appeared to be not promising hitchhiking-wise at

Fencihu. It had started to drizzle, and tourists were in full retreat down the mountain. My guess was that if we were patient, we would get a ride across the mountains, maybe all the way to Laiji; and so in a reversal of the usual scenario, Alex kept an eye on our bags whilst I tried to canvass a ride. It was an hour or so before a truck picked us up. The friendly Tsou man who stopped actually lived at the edge of Laiji; our transportation all the way to the village was thereby guaranteed. The 45-minute drive took us up and over the sides of valleys covered in fecund tea plantations and past Tashan, a miniature Table Mountain. Alex was impressed. The Laiji driver eventually got us to the Tashan Lodge.

In the warm autumnal sunshine, the valley presented a veritable Eden landscape. Close to the guesthouse a plethora of marvellous flowers — including azaleas, bell-shaped Indian mallows, morning glory-like purple ruellia, marigolds, cantana and poinsettias — bloomed prettily; trees alive with nesting birds swayed in a cool mountain breeze; a gentle mist sat over the upper half of the valley blunting the outlines of the sharp valley spurs and diffusing light over cultivated terraces. In short, the valley was a classic Chinese waterand-mountain scene. Delighted to be there, Alex and I threw an impromptu barbecue party for Aaron and his family upon arrival at the lodge before enjoying a restful sleep in a simple but well-appointed room.

The next day the two of us set off to explore the valley. Laiji seemed to reach its peak of perfection at about nine o'clock in the morning, when the sweet bird melodies lifted to an almost deafening crescendo. After half an hour we reached the turning for Titanic Rock, a huge cliff behind the village, where we switched onto a steep mountain road. Alex complained of the heat and of the strenuous nature of the walk. I knew it would soon get cooler and that we might be able to hitch a ride anyway, so I urged her to dig in, which she sportingly did. Umbrellas kept the sun off our heads as we plodded up the road, which followed the course of a small mountain creek. On and up we went. The valley became ever more lush and green as we gained altitude, and later we found ourselves walking through a cooling mountain mist among tall Formosan alder trees and creeping fig plants. We refilled our water bottles from an obliging feeder stream by the roadside before carrying on with the mystery tour, gravity pushing against us all the way. A young couple on an outing wheezed by on a scooter, but the bike would be no use to them up on the cliff trail. Just as we were getting a bit tired, a small truck came along and piggybacked us the rest of the way up to a station on top of the mountain.

Planks of wood had been laid on the path for the benefit of hikers, and it was a simple matter to find the approach to the cliff; a staircase made out of tree trunks lashed together guided walkers up the side of a steep, almost bare slope. The edge of the precipice was indicated by a substantial railing, a barrier that must have prevented innumerable deadly accidents; for on the far side of the slope we had just climbed up lay a sheer drop of at least 200 metres. Part of this cliff had been formed in recent times by the "921" earthquake and it was an extraordinary creation. The horizon was dominated by 2,000-metrehigh mountain peaks, the valleys between filled by misty impenetrable forest. Below, a fast-flowing river, a tributary of the Alishan, cut a deep valley. As we clambered around the thrilling path, literally stepping on a former seabed, the Titanic's railing was most reassuring, though to my horror Alex started climbing on it at one point. "Get off that right now!" I yelled at her, but she would not get down off the railing until I had taken a photo of her posing insouciantly. The path eventually took us back to our starting point. The subtropical forest hummed louder, a sign it was time to be getting back down the mountain. The little tourist station was deserted when we passed it, and so we hiked all the way back down the road. The forest, with its lush trees and sprawling broadleaf plants looked more enchanting than ever in the gathering afternoon mist. We arrived back at the guesthouse satisfactorily wearied at a time that seemed quite early considering the wide range of our walk.

Laiji, I reflected later, represents a dying human culture, but maybe that culture would revive in the fullness of time; indigenous cultures are truly sustainable, unlike modern civilization, which is obviously going to become a victim of its own 'success'. Once unlearned though, how will anyone ever know what to look for in the forest or how to hunt? Aaron knew, but the next generation cares not to learn, and the indigenous economy actually no longer exists. The only hope is to maintain indigenous languages, because if the Tsou language, and others like it, can survive, then the knowledge of generations may be passed on. Sadly, Aaron's mother spoke to her daughter in Mandarin Chinese, and her beautiful girl would be stigmatized at senior school for being a "mountain person" anyway — by inference, socially inferior to her ethnically Han peers — and this will make her all the more eager to fit into the dominant culture. Aaron, a robust and principled man struggling to maintain his own identity in the world was, perhaps, among the last of the Tsou.

Our generous host gave us a ride to the main road the following morning, and Alex and I hitchhiked all the way back from there to Shihjhou. We continued to hitch down the Alishan highway in spurts, leaving the Tsou, who lived in the shadow of Alishan. A bus got us back to Jiayi City, where Alex hooked up with a Taibei-bound train; I booked into a hotel.

TWO WEEKS of rain-free travel had set things up nicely for the final leg of my travels in Taiwan. I wanted to return to Taibei overland, taking in as much of what there was to see in the north-western corner of the island as time allowed. There was no rush and the weather, I knew, would remain dry in the coming weeks. It was with some confidence then that I jump-started this final push by taking a bus the next day out to Meishan, a rural district 15 kilometres northeast of Jiayi.

Getting off the bus, I wandered around a village trying to get my bearings. County Route 149 crossed from Meishan into

Nantou County, and eventually joined up with Provincial Route 3, according to my map, and so I started to hitch along this road. A road sign indicated that the settlement of Jhanghu was 20 kilometres away; I aimed to get there by nightfall. Getting a ride up to Huashan, a small coffee plantation in the hills, was easy enough. I ignored the small rustic coffee houses there though and immediately started to walk along the picturesque mountain road. Soon I was lost in my own thoughts, walking through a rural idyll of lemon trees, palm plants and long grass on my first serious hike since the summer meltdown on Penghu's West Island. Few cars passed by, and those that stopped were only travelling short distances to their homes, so getting another ride proved difficult. I trudged on for more than 15 kilometres along the isolated road finally making it to the small settlement of Jhanghu. No one was about: the place was a depopulated village. By now my legs and back were aching painfully and I stopped to unload and take a break. The market town of Jhushan was at least another 20 kilometres along the mountain road but the boredom of Jhanghu was too much to face. When another pickup truck stopped, I gratefully jumped on. Due to a misunderstanding, however, the friendly driver, a local farmer, ended up taking me back down onto the plain and not to Jhushan. To my chagrin, he dropped me off in the middle of Touliou City — the farmer naturally thought I needed to get to a railway station, not imagining I might want to stay in the mountains.

In Touliou a Taiwanese folk-religious street parade was in full swing, trumpets blaring, cymbals crashing and drums beating. I was totally exhausted and thus totally uninterested. A meal purchased at a convenience store provided me with enough energy to start looking for a hotel, a dreary task. It was while wandering about half-heartedly looking for a place to stay that a new benefactor appeared out of nowhere and approached me with the offer of a ride. Still annoyed with the result of my last lift, I responded coolly to this unsolicited offer, but the man was headed north and here was my chance to get out of the city, so I finally accepted. We got into his small car. "Where are you going?" asked Rack Liu, a schoolteacher hailing from Ershuei, a rural township 25 kilometres to the north in Changhua County. "Anywhere up the road", I replied slumping morosely onto the back passenger seat of the car.

Rack was about my age and he seemed delighted to have a chat with me, a chance to practice his English, but ironically we ended up speaking in Chinese for smoother communication. His genuine enthusiasm made me forget my bad mood that he had not even noticed. When Rack realized I had no definite plan as to where to stay the night, he immediately suggested putting me up at his family's home at Ershuei. I told him that was kind of him without actually accepting the offer, leaving my options open. But Rack was likeable. "You're from England? Green belt!" In Rack's mind a number of associations like this one popped out, some of them, like "English gentleman", being rather stereotypical. I liked the fact that he mentioned green belts before English gentleman though. Rack was a secondary-school citizenship teacher; his wife taught Chinese language at the same school. They had been to the religious festival in Touliou that day to pray for good luck. His wife, an attractive woman, sat in the front passenger seat quietly as Rack nattered on.

Rack told me he had served as an officer in the artillery during his mandatory military service, spending a year and half blasting shells up the Silou River in Baihe. He expertly identified the big booming gun I had heard there as a 190 millimetre self-propelled gun. Our wideranging conversation drifted onto the subject of war and strategy and we both agreed that relations between China and Taiwan were a game of patience and it was important for Taiwan not to allow itself to be provoked. "Declaring independence means war", I intoned solemnly, sounding like a Chinese communist apparatchik. "But Taiwan is in fact independent already", Rack reminded me. He had a point, and as long as you don't care what other people think, then that is a perfectly tenable position. Unfortunately, Taiwan does care about being ignored diplomatically. "Ignore them back: problem solved", I proposed as a strategy for dealing with diplomatic isolation, but of course it is not quite as simple as that. The China-Taiwan Great Game continues. Rack and I concluded that any war between Big Brother and Little Brother would be a tragedy and very bad for business. Time flew by as we talked, and soon we arrived in Ershuei.

In the space of one day, I had jumped out of Jiayi County, walked across a chunk of Yunlin, and now found myself in Changhua. All of these counties had a quite distinct feel to them; Changhua was perhaps a bit more developed and settled than its more frontier-like neighbours to the south. And here in Taiwan's Midwest, I suddenly found myself in the modest but nice living room of a family of Changhua teachers; though they had retired, Rack's parents also belonged to the pedagogic profession. Gigi, Rack's wife, maintained a low profile in her motherin-law's house whilst Rack's younger brother, a returnee overseas student who went by the English name Edward, regaled me in his American idiom. "Don't worry, we not bad people", he assured me, wearing a deadpan Confucian facial expression. I said, "No, *I'm* the bad one". At this Edward declared: "Gairay, you funny man!" I liked Edward. He was a quick learner and immediately applied some advice I gave him regarding his sitting posture. Rack's father, a benevolent presence, sat at a desk in the living room, nodding approvingly at my instruction: when you meet teachers, teach them something. And in this house I slept peacefully on a hard bed, inhaling the autumn scent of ripening pomelos, buzzed by the occasional mosquito.

Rack had to take Gigi to work the next day, so we left the house early. The private high school where Rack and Gigi taught was all abuzz as we approached it. Gigi joined the masses on their way to class as Rack and I slipped away, like two naughty school boys truanting. "Have you heard of the eight-coloured bird", asked Rack. I had not, I confessed. Five colours, yes, but eight? Rack took me to a rural area nearby that had been set up as a sanctuary for this endangered bird, a kind of woodpecker with rainbow-like markings: white, two shades of brown, green, yellow, black, red on the belly and shiny blue on its wings —

extraordinary really. We looked in vain for the protected bird, however; and in the end had to content ourselves with viewing a painted wooden mock-up. Later Rack dropped me off in Checheng, not far from the Sun Moon Lake area, a once bustling logging town. As Rack drove off, I waved goodbye before collapsing under a shaded tree to take a nap; the day was surprisingly warm, and I was surprisingly tired.

LIKE ALL SMALL TOWNS, Checheng's secrets remained concealed from the casual visitor, and the local all-wooden railway station was not much compensation for the lack of action. I checked my maps and then hit the road after the sun had passed its zenith. The mountain road north out of Checheng was where I tried my luck, and a ride soon came along: a kindly betel-nut and banana merchant picked me up, and off we went at a steady clip in his beat jalopy. The barefoot merchant puffed on a cigarette, chewed a limed betel nut and pushed his car hard around the bends of the road as he cursed his competition. Taking me for a tourist, he recommended a visit to Fenjiou Ershan, a local valley that had been attracting visitors from afar since the 921 quake. The valley was en route, so I thought I might as well go there. The merchant dropped me off at an access road, where we parted company. I then walked up a steep side road to a high point overlooking Ershan, where I saw a wrecked house that sat at a 45 degree angle on a slope.

The 921 earthquake was a shaker, the likes of which are only experienced on the island once in a lifetime. When it happened, I was living in an apartment in Taibei and was awoken by the seismic shock early in the morning. My apartment block swayed like a blob of jelly, and a radio fell off a shelf in my room, but no major damage was done. Somewhat rattled by the quake and its aftershocks, I knew that we had escaped a major disaster. One apartment block in Taibei had collapsed, killing dozens of people. But most of the 2,000-plus deaths caused in an instant by that earthquake occurred in Jiayi and Nantou counties near the massive quake's epicentre. The buildings in this area of Taiwan actually held up pretty well to the shock, but still there were collapses and therefore many casualties. Because of the nature of Taiwan's topography, a great many landslides in mountainous areas occurred, reducing the island's forest coverage by many thousands of acres. One group of 15 experienced hikers out on a walk disappeared without trace, presumably buried by one of these land slips. They were not the only ones. The power unleashed by the 40-second megaton eruption shifted the ground in the Fenjiou Valley, causing the movement of three and half million tons of rock and earth that filled the valley floor, raising it up by 100 metres at its lowest point; 39 people that lived there were confirmed killed; the remains of another 18 missing people have not been recovered.

The Fenjiou Valley is quiet now and will probably remain a rural backwater for some time to come, but a steady trickle of curious visitors help support a few tea stalls and a mountain-lodge restaurant. I hiked over to the restaurant along a recently built road. The immediate landscape with its crumpled and exposed rock layers, sliced up slabs of concrete and flattened houses clinging to the sides of slopes looked odd and apocalyptic. A few cars drove past as I walked about on a still warm day, enjoying the fresh air but sensing latent energy and negative vibes about me. At the lodge a couple of tourists from Mainland China sat and lorded about like imperial officials visiting a provincial tavern. I sipped a tea at the lodge and smiled at the Chinese folk, who ignored me and soon left in their minivan, hurrying off to some pressing appointment. I left the restaurant and made my way back past the food stalls that were operating next to the first wrecked house I had noticed. The valley had mildly spooked me — perhaps that was the whole thrill — but it also felt depressing, and I quickly made tracks after buying a bottle of water at one of the stalls.

I HEADED NORTH-EASTWARDS, hitching rides through Guosing Township before crossing over into the Beijiang river valley. Out of curiosity, I decided to pursue this Nantou river system upcountry. The journey, made on foot, took me up into the hills, and the scenery quickly became mountainous and rustic. The Beijiang valley, one of so many of its kind in Taiwan, was captivating. A vigorous swirling river flowed downwards between lush embankments teaming with greenery that included betelnut trees and innumerable species of palm plants. White cranes swooped over the watercourse, apparently headed downstream for the night. Mountains stretched up behind the river, covered in a light mist that thickened as the evening cooled. I watched as the light drained away over the horizon, leaving the forest crickets chirping in the darkness. A roadside sign that read *Atayal Summer Resort Village* looked intriguing. As far as I knew, Nantou was traditionally Bunun territory, but actually the Atayal had also originally migrated upstream along Nantou's rivers before turning northwards. Meiyuan, a small village halfway up the valley was an Atayal settlement, also populated by Hoklo Taiwanese who owned stores and one or two hotels in the area. After walking quite some distance, I started to look for a place to camp near Meiyuan. The rear veranda of a disused hotel overlooking the river provided me with just the spot I was looking for, complete with outdoor washrooms and running water.

The next day I slipped away from the ghost hotel early, before anyone in Meiyuan had stirred. The so-called Atayal resort village two kilometres up the road turned out to be a dreary holiday camp of some sort and nothing much to do with Atayal people. I decided to continue up the road to visit Hueisun, a forest camp run by Taiwan's Forestry Bureau. An Atayal man on his way home, which happened to be near Hueisun, came along and gave me a ride up the mountain in his minivan. Courteous to a fault, he immediately agreed to take me all the way up the road, briefly stopping to buy us drinks. The man introduced himself; his name was Bazek. The middle-aged

Atayal man was wellbuilt and still strong. He invited me to go hunting, which by now I realized was another courtesy and not necessarily a serious offer, and so I said I would call him later and we left it at that. Bazek got me in past the gate of the forestry centre without me having to pay an entry fee. Hueisun overlooked the Beijiang river valley, which at this higher location was in effect a narrow gorge. Getting out of the van at a vantage point, Bazek pointed to the impenetrable forest plateau on the far side of the valley. He talked about hunting, his passion: "That's where we hunt. But it's hard walking to get there. We start in the afternoon and then hunt at night". He explained the Atayal's laboursaving ambush technique: "We find a place where the animals drink, and lie in wait. That is the easiest way to hunt". When I asked Bazek what he hunted, he mentioned the flying white squirrel, hardly big game but a popular meat among Taiwan's indigenous peoples. Any wild boars slain at watering holes were usually sold to merchants for cash, as I had witnessed at Hanshih. A large deer would bring in US$250 on the black market, Bazek informed me.

Gathering my things from the van, I said goodbye to Bazek and then explored the forestry centre alone, hiking around a walkway overlooking the gorge. The Azalea Trail meandered a short way down the valley through a delightful mixed forest. The day was warm, but a cool mountain breeze kept things nice. On the other side of the valley, the rugged terrain looked Triassic-like and would clearly have presented many challenges to an experienced hunter, let alone a casual hiker. The thought of going hunting, which had once so excited me, now seemed a lot less attractive. Having travelled so many kilometres, including hiking along the ludicrously rugged path out to Old Haocha, I was in no mood to go out exploring. Getting down the mountain in one piece after a stress-free walk around the landscaped trail would do me just fine. And that's pretty much what I accomplished at Hueishan.

After eating a modest but decent meal in the camp's canteen, I walked back down the mountain road in a leisurely manner.

The forest was lovely and made the ten-kilometre walk a great pleasure.

At Meiyuan the village's children were just arriving back from school as I trotted through. I pushed on down the road, resolved to head over into Taijhong County before nightfall. But hitching a ride down the road was not easy, and it took me all evening to get down as far as Guosing, where I was obliged to rough it for the night — beside the township's main road, I camped in a disused building. Exhausted after many hours of walking, I collapsed in my tent with a macaroni quick meal purchased at the local convenience store. It was day 177 of my travels.

DAY 178 STARTED SLOWLY as I nursed aching leg muscles. From Guosing I hiked over onto Provincial Route 21, which headed northwards directly into Taijhong County. My goal for this day was to reach the defunct Central Cross-Island Highway, the other end of which I had passed by at Lishan. At its western extremity this highway was open up to a certain point, and I was curious to see how far I could go up it. Later in the morning a man on his way to work in Tianleng, a small town where the Central Cross-Island Highway began, picked me up. The 39-year-old man worked for a franchise dentist and was posted at Tianleng, even though he lived in Guosing 25 kilometres away. We talked about his job as the dentist drove along the picturesque and lightly settled mountain road that eventually led into elongated Taijhong County. The kindly dentist dropped me off at the beginning of the fabled highway.

Like the Taroko Gorge Road, the building of the Central CrossIsland Highway amounted to a major engineering achievement. But the engineers had defied nature, and it wasn't long before the latter reasserted itself: the 921 earthquake damaged the road beyond safe use in most places, and a series of severe typhoon-related floods further damaged many portions of the road and villages located at lower elevations. After eight years of repairs, setbacks and yet more repairs, public-road access was restored as far as Kuguan, a hot-spring resort near the Dajia Dam, but the rest of the highway — which I actually drove across on a scooter in 1991 — will never be reopened. I started walking up the road at Tianleng, vaguely aiming for Kuguan. The road gained elevation gradually at first, but the warm day was making it hard going, and it was a relief when an engineer driving a small truck stopped for me. The driver, a Hakka Chinese man, told me to get in and, furthermore, took it upon himself to act as my guide to the highway.

Zen Lan worked for Taipower, the state energy agency responsible for supplying electricity to all of Taiwan, and he was very knowledgeable about what was going on in the area. He drove slowly and deliberately and spoke in a similar manner. After just a couple of kilometres, the valley narrowed considerably and we passed the first of a number of extensive road works. So far as I could see, a large amount of rock debris was in the process of being removed from the access roads to small riverside settlements. Zen gave me the timelines on the various projects, which he had watched unfold with his engineer's eye. Meanwhile, electricity pylons crammed the slopes of the steep valley ahead, some of them Zen's own handiwork. And it was no mean achievement to put one of these pylons up on a steep mountain side, as all the building materials had to be brought in by hand. Once again I was impressed by the ingenuity of Taiwan's engineers and the sheer guts of its workers. We had a bite to eat at Kuguan, a much-reduced tourist centre, and then Zen took me up the road to the dam, which was still in one piece after the earthquake. Indeed, the Japanese-era hydroelectric system in the Dajia River basin was something of a marvel in its complexity and durability; Zen tried to explain it all to me, but the only bit I understood is that a mass of water disappears down a huge hole in the lake, driving electrical turbines. The road itself, closed to the public from Kuguan onwards, was threatened by overhanging rocks that looked like primed booby traps. We drove up this restricted road. On the other side of the valley, exposed rock strata and a lack of vegetation told a story of catastrophic collapse. At the dam, which we soon reached, Zen showed me an electrical supply line he had put in with his team next to the hydroelectric management office, and it looked like a fine job all round. We had tea with the bored staff at the dam offices, where one worker told me that travel any further up the valley was completely out of the question, and I had no reason to disbelieve him: the road beyond the dam ended in the lake.

Having seen what I came to see, it seemed like a good idea to return down the road with Zen. He had some business to take care of in Kuguan that afternoon, which included watering his vegetable garden at the company dormitory. I watched him with admiration as he lovingly caressed his plot of vegetables at the dorm with spray from a hose. Meanwhile, I lovingly sank a cold beer taken from a supply in the refrigerator. The dorm would be Zen's weekday home for the next year and a half whilst he helped organize the relocation of the local power plant. Later we jumped back into the truck and drove down to Tianleng and then headed north all the way to Dongsi, the small provincial city where the engineer lived. During this ride Zen had explained to me how the Hakka Chinese, though highly capable, were discriminated against in Hoklo Taiwanese society and were not promoted within the engineering field above a certain level. This kind of discrimination was something I had heard about before, but not directly from a Hakka person, and the remarks made in passing left me feeling sad. From what I had seen of Zen's handiwork and demeanour, he would have made an excellent senior manager, and it was regrettable that he felt he had been held back in his career. At Dongsi I said a fond farewell to Zen and boarded a bus for Taijhong.

TAIWAN'S third-largest city was located about an hour's drive from Dongsi in a south-westerly direction. I needed to go there to get a new pair of boots. Magic can be found in every city if you choose to look for it, but Taijhong seemed like a hellish place to me: a mass of random urban development and choking traffic. The high-rise buildings and never-ending planes of concrete got on my nerves. On arrival I went out and bought some boots and then hid in a hotel for the duration, which was not very long.

I left Taijhong by bus the next day, which took me as far as Choulan on the north side of the Taijhong-Miaoli border, a boundary that followed the course of the Daan River. Having entered Miaoli, one of Taiwan's least industrialized counties, I stopped briefly in a village to eat something and then got a ride with a group of middle-aged daytrippers in a minivan — they had been visiting hot springs in Taijhong. As we rapidly travelled north, the countryside got greener and more densely foliated, and the air outside cooled. The vehicle swept past the Syueba National Park headquarters, where I had gone to get my climbing permits in the spring. Taibei was now a mere 90 kilometres away via Route 3, a distance that could easily be covered in a minibus in less than two hours. Tack inland a bit, however, and the mountains opened up a whole different world. It was at the village of Shihtan in Miaoli County that I asked the day-trippers to drop me off.

County Route 124, which swept through forested hills, initially headed east in a loop towards the Snow Mountain Range. With no particular destination in mind, I walked up this road, enjoying the isolation, the cool temperature and the presence of the mysterious forest. A couple who were out cruising picked me up later and gave me a ride as far as Sianshan, a Hakka Chinese settlement ten kilometres down the road. It was whilst browsing in the local tourist office at Sianshan that I noticed a reference to the Saisiat indigenous nation for the first time: a poster had been edged with the abstract patterning found on Saisiat weaving. It was one of my goals on this final leg of the grand tour to try and make contact with the Saisiat, whose ancestral lands lay somewhere in the vicinity. The Miaoli hills, green triangles dotted with blooming mountain flowers, looked really lovely, and in fact I ended up walking many kilometres through this forest wonderland northwards towards Penglai, a Saisiat village.

When I finally got to Penglai, rather exhausted, I stopped to rest. A posse of children emerged from the dwellings and gathered around me, curious to know who this odd stranger might be. Their good looks, lack of anxiety and open body language gave them away as Saisiat children. "Are you from America?" asked one young boy whose cropped hair and fine bone structure made him look like an overgrown baby. "No sir", I replied, "I am from Taibei". That flummoxed him. The questioning soon gave way to play. I surrendered my binoculars, camera and walking pole to the children, who were eager to try them out. Three young pretty girls took photos of one another, delighted by the instant feedback of a digital camera. The walking pole was soon in two halves, something only a child could have achieved. Worried, I reclaimed my possessions. The pole was repairable, and after fixing it, I left the kids and continued down the road to look for a spot to camp. I discovered a residential farm that even had a dedicated campsite, but upon enquiring, the owner told me they were fully booked. At first I thought this an unlikely story, but then I remembered the weekend had just begun. Frustrated at not being able to find somewhere to set up camp in paradise, I decided to hitch into Nanchuang, the nearest major town. It was my good fortune at that moment to bump into Sewzai, a Penglai elementary-school teacher who happened to come by in his van and offer me a ride. He was headed to the Saisiat Association offices in Nanchuang on business, and thus I got my lift into town and an introduction to the Saisiat community at the same time.

———

SEWZAI INSISTED I stay at the association offices, which doubled as a kind of drop-in for delinquent Saisiat teenagers and stray hitchhikers — "you come, you stay". After parking the van in the middle of Nanchuang, we entered an old two-storey brick building. The front room was filled with desks covered with lengths of the predominately red-coloured, abstract-patterned Saisiat woven cloth. This room was used for formal business and was lightly cluttered with trophies, books and piles of papers. A personal computer sat in the corner of the room, unobtrusively, like a sewing machine. We went through into the back office, an untidy room with a sofa and large desk. Sewzai sat at the desk and fielded some phone calls whilst I settled onto the sofa. My new friend had to go out to pick up some youngsters but called his intellectual pal, John Shawan, who came over to see me.

John, a dignified and lean middle-aged Saisiat man, introduced himself to me. He lived in Taibei with his wife — ironically, *Sai* means "location"; *Sai-siat* means "people who live in this place" — but was visiting his ancestral home in Penglai as the Pas-taai, or dwarf ceremony, would be held the following month, and he was helping with the preparations for this event. John questioned me closely about my travels. The indigenous people of Taiwan were never overly surprised by my wandering about, for they are wanderers themselves, and even today it is not unusual for the men to disappear into the mountains on long walkabouts. John, a former broadcaster and sometimes cultural worker, was quite well-travelled himself and had recently spent time in China doing research on indigenous nations there. We discovered we had both visited some of the same places in south-western China, and talking about our shared experiences helped us quickly forge a personal bond. John explained to me that in former times the Saisiat Nation inhabited a large area in Taiwan, stretching from the Dagan River in the north to the Daan River far to the south, but in due course it was driven back into the Miaoli hills by the expanding cultivation of the uplands by Hakka Chinese — Nanchuang is principally known as a Hakka settlement. The Saisiat had also long been threatened by the Atayal — their more powerful neighbours to the northeast — and influenced by the plains Chinese to the west, but remained a distinctive and proud ethnic group. In effect, said John, there

322

were two major Saisiat tribes left in modern Taiwan, one based around Nanchuang and the other one in nearby Wufong, Sinjhu County.

By and by, Sewzai returned with a couple of young people in tow. Raki, an errant teenage boy, was being raised by an uncle. He sat and took some interest in all that was said between John, Sewzai and me before slipping off to read some pornographic magazines stashed under his bed. A pretty teenage girl also sat with us, and others came in and out during a pleasant social evening. Later Raki and I played chess, and he beat me, which pleased him. The girl refused to play chess and instead sat demurely by herself in a typical division of the sexes. The young people worked in low-paid jobs in a city on the plain, and Sewzai, who was a community leader, picked them up every day and brought them back to the association, where they were lodging temporarily.

Not long after Sewzai returned with his young friends, John took me to a Pass-taii Saisiat Cultural Association conference. The conference was held on tribal grounds about ten kilometres away in the hills. We drove there through the darkness in John's car. A few lights below us indicated that we were climbing a mountain. The cultural village we arrived at half an hour later was known as Namuran to the Saisiat. In the dark I could not make out very much, but the sweetness of the air suggested a forested area. We entered a long hut to find the conference already in progress. The association's committee sat at a long table in front of a small gathering. About 30 people, mostly men, sat in rows listening to the speakers give speeches in the bureaucratic manner, a number of drunks occasionally interrupting with witticisms to stop the whole thing becoming too pompous. But the interesting thing, from my point of view, was that such a meeting was taking place at all and that the Saisiat language was spoken in about equal measure to Mandarin Chinese, Taiwan's lingua franca. When I asked John about the linguistic code switching, he informed me that the association's members spoke Saisiat when they did not want outsiders to know what they were talking about. I tried to follow the proceedings. One man, obviously an elder and a cultured man, made a long speech — more a plea actually — to ask people to stop criticizing his Atayal wife's weaving. "She is an Atayal, but her weaving is excellent", intoned the man, noting that the woman had been living among the Nanchuang Saisiat for more than 20 years. There was long discussion about money, the exact details of which eluded me, and some talk about responsibilities within the association. The upcoming Pas-taai ceremony and matters concerning dancing seemed to invigorate the conference's participants. "No one can dance anymore!" muttered one. "But Nanchuang is better than Wufong", claimed another, hinting at a local rivalry. The general consensus reached was that the Pas-taai should be carried out with due solemnity and seriousness and that all the traditional rituals must be observed. The conference ended with a simple communal meal of noodles and boiled pork taken in another hut. After dinner John and I returned to Nanchuang. On the way back my host complained about the drunks at the conference — he was a teetotaller — but actually their behaviour had not been that bad. I said, "You should go to England", alluding to the educational experience awaiting foreign visitors to that country.

Sewzai tried to wake me up early the next day, but I couldn't move. My body ached all over from the previous day's long hike and it refused to get up. People were in and out of the offices from nine o'clock onwards. I hid under the covers in the back room, refusing to budge. Eventually John turned up and that was my cue to get out of bed; there was no denying his authority. John wanted to take me back up to Namuran to visit the museum there and attend a wedding banquet. It seemed like a good plan and we were soon off. Under warm autumnal sunshine the Nanchuang Valley glowed with vitality: wild flowers bloomed, fantastic transparent rice paper butterflies alighting on them; bamboo leaves glittered in the bright sunshine like bayonets on parade; elegant aging trees splayed out in all directions, avian life flittering in and out of their extended limbs. This rich and varied flora belied the lateness of the year — here was the magic of Formosa. After a half-hour drive through the valley and up the mountain, we arrived once more at Namuran, known to most Taiwanese by its Chinese name of Siangtianhu, or Facing Heaven Lake. The location was higher in the hills than I had thought, the power of the car taking all the strain. The communal Saisiat wood and bamboo huts at Namuran formed a wide semicircle around an expanse of flat ground. Beyond this ground a small mountain lake glistened in the middle of mixed forest. We drove into the grounds of the village, passing cooks and other assorted workers who were busy preparing for the wedding banquet. John parked his car next to the Saisiat museum, a modern multi-storey structure erected right next to the lake.

It was Saturday and the cultural village was full of visitors who had come up from the plains for a day out. At the museum, John, a cultural spokesperson for the Saisiat, found himself pulled away by some visiting media hounds, leaving me to wander around the exhibits by myself. All good museums — and this was a good one — are modest and focused. Saisiat culture, as reinterpreted through the prism of modern culture, was the subject matter of this local museum, and there was just enough there to give one a flavour of traditional Saisiat customs, social structure and economic activity without the whole thing becoming an overwhelming onslaught or an exercise in superficiality. In one large room on the first floor of the museum, a number of artefacts were displayed together with an array of information boards explaining various aspects of indigenous hunting culture. Tellingly, the information was presented through the medium of the Chinese and English languages — the native language, the very heart of the culture, was missing. One comparative statistical table grabbed my attention. According to this table, those officially registered as ethnic Saisiat in Taiwan numbered 5,425 persons — a small population, but about the same number as the more dispersed Tsou of the Alishan area. As John explained when he rejoined me after doing a television interview, only about three out of every 10,000 Taiwanese persons were classified Saisiat, and meeting so many in one place as I had done the night before was quite rare. The other bit of information on display that intrigued me was a brief explanation of the mysterious Pas-taai rites, colloquially known as the dwarf ceremony:

> *The Pas-taai is the most famous known dwarf ceremony. This festival is the most important ceremony among all Saisiat. Pas-taai continues celebrate for few days. It is the most influential and spiritual rite the Saisiat holds. In fact, the rite itself holds a complicated rites and structure. Pas-taai is an extensively difficult and large scale ceremony. It is also the most famous known culture for the Saisiat.*

The explanation then went on to discuss in detail when the Pas-taai was held, which essentially was once every two years, a full-size rite being held once every ten years. But there was no mention of the obscure origins of this rite, which I knew involved ethnic genocide.

Once upon a time, so the legend goes, a small band of dwarf-like people migrated into Saisiat territory. The new people were more technologically advanced and fleet of foot than the Saisiat, and were welcomed by the north-westerners. The pygmies taught the Saisiat how to grow crops, among other things. Relations soured, however, due to the dwarf men's predilection for Saisiat women. At first, the Saisiat men shrugged it off with admirable magnanimity — who could blame the little men for chasing their beautiful wives and daughters? But the serial philandering eventually tried the Saisiat warriors' patience. One day the Saisiat council decided to put a stop to the miscreants' bad behaviour once and for all by enacting some very rough justice. At the appointed time the Saisiat braves gathered and set an ambush for the randy dwarfs, unfortunately making quick work of massacring them all when the latter appeared from their caves by the river. The lone surviving person of this murderous attack cast a damning spell on the Saisiat before committing suicide by jumping off a cliff. The Pas-taai is therefore an elaborate act of sincere atonement for the massacre of a group of people; a long lament to ward off bad luck and to appease the spirits of the dwarf people. I had arrived in Nanchuang one month before the once-in-ten-years ritual would take place.

On the village's communal land, a marquee started to fill with people. Before long John called me over and took me up to the wedding reception. A Taiwanese wedding banquet is generally a very informal affair, though guests are normally expected to give a gift of money in a red envelope to the bride and groom. Foreigners who turn up unexpectedly are waived this obligation and are welcomed for their exotica value. On this occasion I found myself seated next to a Hakka Chinese couple from Nanchuang. After sitting down at the table, I did my best to engage the taciturn couple in small talk. The sumptuous meal included fried shrimps, pork knuckle cooked to tender perfection, sashimi, sweet rice, and pork balls wrapped in cabbage. The bride and groom swanned about the round tables, toasting the guests, and everyone took the whole event in stride. Then came speeches made from a small stage assembled in front of the tables. This was followed by the inevitable karaoke singing; the groom crooned one of his favourite tunes as everyone ignored him and carried on with the business of eating and drinking. Just as I was getting tipsy, John the teetotaller informed me that the wedding party was over for us, thus saving me from any alcohol-related disgrace. Both grateful and resentful of his intervention, I hobbled back to the museum, half-cut and flushing like a bloated puffer fish.

Later, the usual suspects gathered at the tumbledown association offices. That evening I had a long and engrossing talk with Raki about travelling, knives and hunting. The boy turned out to be a fount of knowledge on survival techniques and had evidently made several extended trips into the mountains, carrying nothing more than a knife, a little salt, some rice, some garlic and a small bottle of liquor; everything else could be provided by the forest if one knew where to look. Raki actually had first-hand experience of building fires from fallen logs, sleeping in makeshift shelters, and damming mountain streams to catch fish, and he spoke about these activities with great enthusiasm. I truly admired the lad for having travelled in such style; I was a rank amateur by comparison. But this knowledge was no longer valued in the education system Raki was being put through, and he had ironically been labelled a person with "learning difficulties"— but who was really having the difficulties here?

My time in Nanchuang on this occasion came to an end the following day. After a leisurely morning in town, John drove me over the hills into the Wufong District, Sinjhu County. John talked about the Pas-taai and he invited me to take part in the ceremony in a month's time, an invitation I would be only too happy to take up. At Wufong I got out of the car at the top of a hill overlooking the village. I thanked my friend for his kind hospitality and then left the cocoon of his car for an absorbing walk through another fabulous landscape full of flossflowers, ferns, bamboo and flowering silvergrass. The walk helped clear my mind and prepare me for a change of pace: I was leaving Saisiat territory and would soon be entering the realm of the Atayal once more.

THE VIBE AT CINGCYUAN, a hot-spring resort and major Atayal settlement near Wufong, was quite different from Nanchuang. The Saisiat, early slash-and-burn agriculturalists and Cing Dynasty mercenaries, had clearly been highly influenced by Chinese culture, though of course to some extent the reverse was also true. The Atayal, on the other hand, remained rugged individualists and unabashed outsiders; they kept up a strong hunting ethos. The Atayal tribes around Cingcyuan were less affected by Chinese culture than their neighbours, and one *imagined* them to be quite wild, which of course they were not

328

allowed to be anymore. The Atayal, like all indigenous nations and despite their reputation as fierce raiders, had a rich culture and their spirit lived on in this mountain valley; they were a race quite apart from the Hoklo Chinese. Staring up the valley, I could see many majestic peaks in the distance, and this inspiring sight alone seemed to breathe freedom. As I approached the village, a column of smoke from a cooking fire floated high into the windless blue sky.

Sauntering into the village by the Dagan River, I stumbled upon a lively Sunday afternoon scene: families and children walked up and down the narrow street on their way to friends' houses; a large women with a bunch of noisy young kids in tow shyly said hello to me, adding "God bless you". The body language and mannerisms of the local people were startling in their total lack of Confucian reserve; they could have been Californians. At the only store in town I bought some extra provisions, thinking I might need them in the mountains, before decamping via the river just beyond the village. The river was shallow and harmless-looking at Cingcyuan, but the huge piles of debris and large rock boulders that filled the valley floor told a different story. In full flood, this river could be absolutely deadly, as indeed it was in 2003, when a typhoon washed away riverside homes and killed 14 Atayal villagers.

In a car park by the river, I cooked a meal whilst watching the comings and goings of people who came to visit the local hot springs. To get to the healing waters, one had to walk across the river on a suspended footbridge. The bridge had evidently been built after the typhoon disaster and was quite a tidy bit of construction. I liked the statues of Atayal men, which had been placed so as to hold the ends of the bridge's suspended wires, as though they were holding it up by their own strength. The bridge was one of several in the area spanning the valley. The whole place was beguiling and made a great place to explore, I thought. After lunch I headed back to the highway. By now it was the middle of the afternoon. I decided to try to get up to Guanwu, a mountain station 30 kilometres distant, and began hiking up the mountain road, intending to stop at the first mountain stream that intersected the highway. Just as I had settled all this in my mind and started walking, a man came hurtling down the opposite side of the dusty road in a pickup truck.

"Yaroii!" he yelled in greeting. Where was I going? Guanwu. Okay, no problem; he would take me there. Guanwu was many kilometres away, it was true, and so I got in the pickup. Tasa, a lean and young-looking middle-aged man, had obviously had a drink, but he was not yet drunk. I had to make a quick calculation as to whether he could be trusted to get me to Guanwu. I reasoned that if he couldn't get me up the mountain that afternoon no one could. Tasa first took me back to the village and introduced me to his friends and neighbours. Outside one house we stopped at, I was amazed to see a man butchering a mountain serow on the back of a sofa frame he had adapted for the purpose. With one deft chop he cleaved the skull of the slaughtered beast into two, chucking half the dissected head into a bucket containing other bits of the animal. He sliced a little of the exposed stomach off and handed it to Tasa, who gobbled it down. I was offered some of the raw game meat, but declined it. I agreed to buy some gas for the pickup and further bought wine and cigarettes for Tasa; if he got me to Guanwu, I would of course pay him a fee for the ride. He agreed to this deal and with a wave of his arm drove us out of Cingcyuan, honking and revving the engine of his truck as we went.

The game meat in the bowl on the dashboard gave off a potent aroma. Tasa urged me to try some: "sushi!" he shouted, trying to get me interested in the liver-like cuts of stomach. As we trundled up the road, he sipped from the bottle of rice wine, which was not a part of the plan: the more he drank, the lower the odds of getting to Guanwu would become. Tasa's attempts to speak to me in English, though a bit garbled, were full of endearments: "I love you" was a phrase he repeated often, which he usually followed with "you want to fight me?" Somehow he managed to be drunk and sober at the same time, talking nonsense and leaning all over the cabin, but actually manoeuvring the truck with the skill of a rally-car driver. Would we ever get to Guanwu? By now the highway had become a steep dirt track covered by a thick mountain mist, which together with the oncoming darkness blotted out the panoramic views. Tasa started to complain that there was not enough fuel in the truck to get us to Guanwu, at which point I realized we were not going to make it. After about 15 kilometres, the road levelled out for a stretch. Here we arrived at an Atayal house, the last settlement of any kind before Guanwu. The evening was cool, but not cold, and it was refreshing to get out of the truck to stretch our legs. Unfortunately, Tasa seemed to have become really drunk. I put any notion that would we would get any further in the direction of Guanwu out of my head. Before going anywhere, Tasa barged into the Atayal house — everyone knew each other in these parts — and demanded I arm-wrestle with him in the living room. He did this in front of a woman and child who were trying to sleep. Apologizing for the interruption, I made quick work of twisting Tasa's arm down. The crop-haired tough could not accept being beaten by a city softie like me and demanded a rematch. I won the rematch. "You're strong", he stated, sourly. I said "No, you're just drunk". Eventually we got back in the truck, did a U-turn, and left the poor people at the isolated homestead in peace. As we drove back down the road, Tasa asked me if I was frightened of him and whether I wanted to fight him in the way that drunks do. He stopped the truck and tried to wrestle with me again. This was all getting rather tiresome and it was a great relief when another truck came by. Not missing a beat, I waved the truck down and quickly transferred to it after explaining to the driver that I needed to get away from Tasa. In the hurry to transfer, I left my binoculars behind in the pickup, something I would curse Tasa for later, though the loss was entirely my own fault.

Back at the village I camped out. The next day I tried to track Tasa down to get my binoculars back but couldn't find him. The binoculars were heavy, but I did miss them and made a concerted effort to recover my property. In fact, I spent two days at Cingcyuan searching for Tasa in between walks. I figured I would bump into him eventually, but he had disappeared. A couple of cold nights reminded me that winter was now well on its way. On the morning of the third day at Cingcyuan, I packed and, after glancing back one more time at the magnificent high peaks of the Snow Mountain Range, walked back up to the highway and then hitchhiked down to Wufong. From the Saisiat village, I caught a bus to Jhudong, the nearest city, and from there returned to Taibei by train.

———

IN THE DARKNESS a long line of people danced in a circle. Most were dressed in distinctive red rectangular smocks and wore red headbands. The dancers swayed in a steady two-step, arms linked and bouncing belts of hip-bells as they went. The steady percussive chink of small bells was accompanied by a dull baritone lament sung by the tribe in unison. Occasionally the colourful line would break as new dancers joined in or as others broke away to take a break. Stewards pushed the line back in when it went astray. The dancing had been going on all afternoon and it would go on all night until dawn, and then continue into the next day and night. Around the field on which the dancing was taking place, crowds of visitors and well-wishers mingled. Only Saisiat people, however, were admitted to the main communal hut to take part in an informal ritual involving sipping wine and repeating some set phrases, something like a communion. Everyone wore a twisted grass stem tied to their arm, a symbol of the Pas-taai ceremony.

After a one-month interval, I was back on the road and attending the enlarged dwarf ceremony of the Saisiat people in northwest Taiwan. I had made the journey back to Nanchuang by bus, first travelling to Jhunan in Sinjhu County, and then on to Nanchuang via County Route 124. The intensely developed northern corridor of the national expressway stood in stark contrast to the rusticity of the Miaoli hills — two completely different worlds right next to one another. At Nanchuang I stayed once more at the Saisiat Cultural Association offices before setting up camp by the museum at Namuran. John, whom I had called beforehand, gave me the exclusive use of a secluded space at the back of the museum, which was close to the lake and the all the goings-on at the cultural village. Winter had kicked in and the night was cold enough to warrant building fires. Alex joined me at Namuran, travelling up by public transport a couple of days later.

The whole of the Nanchuang Saisiat population had turned out for the Pas-taai, but there were about an equal number of outsiders at Namuran, mainly curious onlookers from town, but also a hefty contingent of cultural workers, including media hounds and photographers. The Japanese colonial authorities had tried to ban the Pas-taai ceremony. It is hard to say why, since it was an altogether peaceful and restrained ceremony — though it may not have always been that way. There is no doubt that the ceremony plays an important bonding function in Saisiat society, and it is perhaps those bonds that the Japanese were attempting to break — that was very much the colonial pattern. But the Pas-taai ceremony has revived in recent years, and the get-together is clearly a source of cultural pride.

On day two of the ceremony, Alex and I roamed about the Namuran cultural village. More Taiwanese people from the plains arrived to take part in the festive celebrations. Most people came by car, though a group of touring cyclists dressed in racing clothes and riding excellent bicycles — made in Taiwan — appeared around midday on a cool, cloudy day. John had his work cut out dealing with the press, all of whom wanted to know the inside story of the Pas-taai. But who really knew what it was all about? The tradition is clearly linked to a historical event, but the forms of the ceremony have obviously changed over time, and many questions will always remain unanswered. The Pas-taai today is simply an echo of earlier ceremonies, and it had also evidently become something of a tourist attraction, which is fine — the money brought into the village by visitors benefited the Saisiat in a relatively non-exploitative way.

On the second night of the Pas-taai, the number of people dancing seemed to increase. At any one time there more than 100 in the line, and often many more. Non-Saisiat people were welcome to join in the dancing. Plenty of wine was consumed but there was a total absence of loutish behaviour; all who drank held their drink. Everyone except perhaps Raki. I bumped into the Saisiat teenager fairly early on in the evening. He was walking around with cut glass sticking out of his hands and trying to find someone to help him out. When I asked him what was up, he told me he had been on a drinking spree and had cut his hands on a broken glass, a common-enough youth scenario. After grabbing my first-aid kit, I took him aside, plucked the shards of glass out of his hands with tweezers, and dressed the cuts. The poor boy then had a good puke, which seemed to relieve his discomfort. It was noticeable how no one took an interest in Raki, which was a shame, because he was a bright boy. Later during the night as the casual visitors drifted away from the village, Alex and I danced in the line. Most of the adults had flopped down, so the night dance belonged to the young and the young at heart. Shortly before dawn, the stalwarts reappeared and the circle's rhythm once more gained intensity until the first shafts of sunlight marked the end of the Nanchuang ceremony.

Over the weekend the focus of the Pas-taai festivities shifted to Wufong District, so Alex and I packed our bags and left the village. On the way out of Namuran, we said goodbye to John and the other people we had made friends with, including Raki and Sewzai. We then started to walk along the mountain road to Wufong, but in no time a truck stopped and gave us a lift across the silvergrass-covered mountains to our destination. The truck formed part of a small convoy on its way to the Wufong Pas-taai and we quickly made friends with a new group of people. At a vantage point along the highway, the three vehicles of the convoy stopped and sweet millet wine was passed around; two cups was enough to make me feel woozy. During the final leg of the journey over the mountains, I swanned about on the back of the truck videoing Alex. She took the cue and started to speak to camera: "the weather is very good today", she said, "because normally it would be very cold"; she continued, not really knowing what she was talking about. "But here on the mountain I don't feel cold because Gary is beside me and he makes me feel so warm", said Alex sarcastically, adding "how disgusting!" before blowing me a raspberry. She then returned to television-anchor mode: "the silvergrass is pretty today, as this is the season we find it flowering. It looks nice against the mountain backdrop and stands in bunches all lined up along the road…" She went on like this for a bit. I kept quiet and waited to see what she would say next. "Tell me", she suddenly asked — "what is the prettiest journey in Taiwan? It's Sinjhu to Miaoli isn't it?" She looked at me for confirmation of this rhetorical question, at which point I almost dropped the camera as the truck swerved around a bend in the road.

Our convoy drove down a steep valley side and directly into the Wufong-village dance ground. We found ourselves surrounded by people preparing for the evening's festivities and by visitors gathering in the stands; it was immediately apparent that Wufong's Pas-taai was more developed as a tourist event than Nanchang's. Once again a festive spirit prevailed; log fires burned and children played in the dirt. The becoming red smocks of the Saisiat were in evidence everywhere around the countryside amphitheatre; Saisiat girls were indeed pretty. After getting off the truck, Alex and I walked around and found a suitable spot to camp on the steep hillside overlooking the communal dance ground. Word of the Wufong Pas-taai had got out, and the crowds milling about the village, like medieval pilgrims, reflected a cosmopolitan milieu; I was once again struck by Taiwan's human diversity. As darkness fell, we rejoined our friends from the convoy at the dance ground and waited with anticipation for the Pas-taai to begin.

The Wufong ceremony began in grand style as the tribe entered the dance ground, arms linked in a show of unity. Preceding the dancers, men holding banners swept into the centreground, and a flag of sorts was hoisted at the far end of the makeshift arena. Fires burning at the four corners of the dance site added drama to the night scene. The dancers soon settled down into the familiar two-step pattern, circling around in a steady rhythm. By now quite a large crowd had gathered to watch the proceedings, and the stalls selling food and drink next to the dance ground did a roaring trade. The event was truly crossgenerational, and it was nice to see so many teenagers enjoying themselves and taking a healthy interest in one another. Later in the night lots of visitors joined the dancing, which became something of a drunken melee. This time Alex and I did not join in the dancing.

Returning to our tent, we listened to the singing, which continued late into the night. A couple having a violent argument on the mountain near our camp disrupted the uncertain harmonies. What the couple were screaming about was anyone's guess, but could it be that a jealous man was angry at a Saisiat girl's sexual indiscretion? The dancing had fizzled out by the time we surfaced later in the morning, and for us the Pas-taai was over. Around midday we walked out of the village and hiked towards the main county highway, stopping here and there to admire blooming poinsettias and other wild flowers that thrived in Taiwan's mild winter. Some other visitors had also camped by the roadside and were busy cooking meals against the pretty backdrop of the green Miaoli foothills. We later hitched a ride down to County Route 122, and from there got another ride up to Cingcyuan.

THE IDEA of walking along a wild high-mountain river valley appealed to my adventurous side, but it was not something I had actually attempted to do before. Here at Cingcyuan was the ideal opportunity, it seemed. According to the map, the distance from the Atayal settlement to Wufong downriver was about ten kilometres — a manageable one-day hike for Alex. The idyllic beauty of the valley was deceiving though. At an elevation of 500 metres, the river fell in altitude quite rapidly, and it moved dangerously fast. There was no easy way out of the river's flood plain in the event of a sudden downpour. Getting along the valley floor would be challenging, especially at points where the river meandered sharply. It was with this foreknowledge that I proposed to Alex that we give it a go, and she agreed to accompany me. If the river between Cingcyuan and Wufong proved to be impassable, then we could always turn back.

Cingcyuan felt eerily quiet after Wufong, but many people would have been attending the Pas-taai, and others might have gone down to the plains on business. The night was really cold. Alex bravely toughed it out inside my cosy sleeping bag, ruthlessly leaving me to freeze in her thin blanket. The next day, however, was bright and sunny, leaving us feeling grateful, like shipwreck survivors. After a hearty breakfast we scrambled down the river levee and embarked on our planned walk along the river valley. I carried my full kit; Alex carried an umbrella and a shoulder bag, as though going shopping. When Alex made fun of me for carrying so much, I pointed out to her that the gear and food afforded us self-sufficiency.

At first we made reasonably good progress. The river hugged the western bank of the flood plain, leaving us to scramble over large boulders, but we always found a way through. Significantly, there was no one about and no signs of human life by the riverside. Alex started to complain about the strenuous nature of the ramble. I told her that if the going did not improve, we could always turn back, knowing full well that the valley would widen out ahead. It did widen out and we thus found ourselves ambling along a totally isolated valley, which was easy to walk down. We pushed on over mounds of alluvial sand and an endless moraine of rocks, boulders and logs. The river bounced along edgily in the middle of the valley, like a bumper car, not reaching any depth and never calm. Calmness lay in the green mountains, and in the sweep of an occasional bird of prey overhead. After a couple of kilometres, we passed a derelict fish farm, which only served to reinforce our feeling of isolation. As we hiked, I carefully checked the time and estimated the distance we had travelled. The weather, however, remained perfect and we carried on down the valley unworried by the threat of rain.

About four kilometres from Cingcyuan at a sharp turn in the river our luck ran out. We faced a meander in the river, which swept up against the side of steep rocks, effectively hemming us in on one side of the river. To proceed down the valley, we had either to cross the river or to climb around the vertical rock curtain. My primary consideration was safety, and no way would we be taking any unnecessary risks, which ruled out trying to cross the river. After a brief reconnaissance, we decided to attempt climbing up and around the rock face. There was some kind of path leading up onto the hillside, and we followed it into what was basically a subtropical secondary forest. During a stressful 30 minute hike through this dense forest, Alex showed a lot of mental fortitude, and it was really me who found it all to be a bit too much. Falling on a bamboo stump, I injured my leg, and being unable to find a way forward, I decided to give up on the cross-country hike. Brave but inexperienced Alex suggested we climb up to the valley road directly above us further up the slope, but I ruled this out on safety grounds too, which meant we were obliged to return to Cingcyuan, back the way we had come.

No wonder we did not meet anyone on the way back: the valley was a dangerous trap and not a place to explore blithely. Satisfied to have spent some time alone together in nature, we counted ourselves lucky to get back to our starting point in one piece. Giving the hot springs a miss, we then travelled back down to the plains, catching the last bus out of Cingcyuan that day.

AFTER ESCORTING Alex back to Taibei, I returned to Wufong to resume my journey through north-western Taiwan. I had identified a back road between Wufong and Mianping that would take me north-eastwards deep into the mountains. After loading up with provisions at Wufong, I sought out this road. On the main highway, I passed a bunch of finger signs glossed "Wufong Tribe", "Old Shinbaer Tribe", "Shang Dai-ai Tribe" and "Bailian Tribe" in both Chinese and romanized script. But to get on to the small county road, I needed to get across the Wufong Great Bridge. After finding the bridge, I hiked across it, getting to the far side of the Dagan River. The Atayal village on the far side of the bridge was rather poor and depressed, but not completely depopulated; I even saw a couple of pretty teenage girls there. At a small shop I stopped to buy a soda and chatted with the shop owner, an Atayal man. He told me Huayuan, the next major settlement, was four kilometres distant. I resolved to walk to the mountain village before nightfall. The back road was quiet, surrounded by thick forest, and damp. Water gushed from streams by the roadside, making redundant the need to carry lots of water. Eager to get to Huayuan before dark, I marched quickly along the obscure highway, but only made it as far as the next Atayal village.

Tucked away in an isolated, wet and flora-rich valley, Shang-Bilai did have a fairy story-like quality to it. A small bridge led into the quiet village, which consisted of one large dormitory-style building — a police station of some kind — and a cluster of houses built on an outcrop of land above a small tributary river. After asking about, I was given permission to camp outside the courtyard of a disused house, much to the amusement of the local children. An Atayal woman, highly suspicious of me at first, soon became solicitous after I gave her a tin of beef as a courtesy gift. She did not need the food, but appreciated the gesture and reciprocated by offering me a bed in her house, an offer I declined. It felt good to be travelling again, and this was a classic travel situation: I had blazed a trail through a remote mountain area, found shelter among friendly strangers, and had an intriguing route to follow the next day. The village children came by to talk to me during the evening. To them, camping seemed like terrific fun, which it is, and they asked me many questions about it. Exhausted after a long day, I eventually had to excuse myself, and then collapsed into a deep sleep. It rained during the night, the only rain I would encounter during the entirety of Trip Six — not that I noticed it until the morning.

The kids pounced on me early the next day. Groaning, I told them to go and do their homework — that tired parental stratagem — but they were not going to be shooed away. They watched fascinated as I cooked breakfast and then broke camp. But the tent was still soaking wet from the night's downpour and this obliged me to put it out in the morning sun for a bit. Whilst I waited for the tent to dry, the children left for school. The weather could not have been fairer, and soon the nylon sheeting dried out. After saying goodbye to the spry old woman and the other villagers, I hit the road. The splashing autumn sunshine, chirping bulbuls and erupting flowers made this one of the most delightful and light-hearted mornings on my travels. The road to Huayuan, however, soon steepened.

Gaining altitude, the view over the valley broadened out and ShangBilai disappeared behind me. I arrived in Huayuan half an hour later, panting heavily, and slowly walked up and through the village, which — with its churches and blooming roadside bougainvillea — resembled some kind of alpine idyll. But baskets of black beans drying in the sun and the abstract patterning painted onto roadside crash barriers revealed the scene to be uniquely Taiwanese — Atayal, that is. The village was subdued except at the local elementary school, where pupils on break played noisily in a yard. I tried to spot the youngsters from Shang-Bilai but couldn't see them. In any case the children were far too wrapped up in their games to notice me. With a little sigh I left the early-morning peace of Huayuan and continued my journey up the road past another rural church and fantastic stands of bright red poinsettias.

I was now approaching the border between Wufong District

and Jianshe District. A pickup truck came by and gave me a ride up to the watershed. I stood on the back of the truck to get a better view of the countryside; the wind blew through my sweat-soaked shirt, cooling me nicely. It was a really gorgeous day and the surrounding mountain peaks stood out sharp against a perfectly blue sky; silvergrass shone like optic fibres in the sun in amongst tall green grasses. We bobbed on up the track, eventually reaching some kind of new village in the hills. The line of prefabricated houses in this village had a soulless feel to them, however; and indeed there were few signs of life about. The two Atayal men in the truck had business in the village, so I parted company with them and walked down the far side of the mountain into Jianshe.

On the far side of the hill, waves of mountains stretched for several kilometres into the interior. Walking through this green wonderland in the sun was a priceless moment — the grand tour was ending well. Mianping, my destination for the day, was still a few kilometres away, but I was unconcerned. I hiked on down the mountain road towards another village. The day had become really warm, and by the time I got to the settlement in the valley, it was time to take a little break and get my boots off. Later I continued walking through the quiet and beautiful rolling hills of Jianshe District, eventually arriving at Mianping mid-afternoon. Mianping sprawled over quite a large area. It lay by a river, and a road that ran parallel to this river looked inviting. Following the road upriver a little way brought me to a pleasant hotspring area. I found a patch of ground to camp on and set up the tent before enjoying the rest of the afternoon, sitting in a hot tub overlooking the river. In the evening I strolled around the small Atayal village by the resort. The village was quite poor compared to the commercialized spa area. As often proved the case, the Atayals had lost out on the benefits of economic development, not having a capitalist mentality or means to exploit their land resources.

The village of Sumakusa, an Atayal mountain settlement southeast of Mianping far into the mountainous interior, was not that far from Mianping as the crow flies. In recent years the village had become something of a tourist pull because of its proximity to a stand of ancient red-cedar trees. I had made a memorable trip to this high mountain village with friends in 1998. Given the good weather a revisit almost ten years later would, I thought, round off my grand tour nicely. Getting to Sumakusa, however, was no easy task. The mountain road to the village was long and almost impassable in places. But part of my motivation for going there again would be to get a better understanding of the geographical context of the area and to enjoy once more the adventurous journey out. So in the morning, I headed back down the riverside road to Mianping and then hitched a ride over to Jianshe, the village at the centre of the district, where I bought provisions for the trip. I then hiked back up the road towards Yufong and Sumakusa.

Another perfect sunny day made the morning's walk extremely pleasant, but with 37 kilometres to go, it was necessary to hitch a ride, and luckily one came along soon enough. An Atayal man returning to his home village of Yufong for the weekend picked me up. His fourwheel-drive vehicle whooshed us up the highway like a souped-up Mini. After about 20 minutes we arrived at yet another fork in the road, which split two ways down the sides of the deep valley; the north branch led to Yufong, the south branch to Sumakusa. The Yufong villager dropped me off at a tiny police station near the fork in the road. I walked over the lip of a hill into a fantastic green mountain landscape. Mountain ridges and peaks dominated a wide horizon illuminated by the sun, puffs of smoke from village fires visible here and there. I could just about make out Yufong on the distant side of the valley, but Sumakusa remained well out of view. Taking a deep breath, I began hiking down the road.

The small police post marked the beginning of Atayal territory proper, and relatively few Han Taiwanese lived in the hills beyond. There were one or two Atayal settlements on the way to Sumakusa, and I walked into this territory vaguely aware of its social and ethnic geography, but not really knowing it in any detail. A ride with a couple of police officers on their way to work got me halfway to my destination and then two Atayal workers gave me a ride up to a nearby checkpoint. For a nominal fee I paid to enter the Sumakusa mountain area.

Sumakusa was still 15 kilometres away along mountain roads, and it took a little while to get there. I hitched a ride with grass cutters, but also hiked many kilometres along the road. I eventually made it to the bottom of the valley, where of course the highway levelled out. Another half-kilometre walk got me to a bridge. Here I waited for a ride, as there was no way I was going to attempt to walk up the other side of the valley — my destination remained several kilometres distant, and it was uphill all the way. A two-seater four-wheel-drive vehicle came by, but there was no room in it for me. The valley went quiet after the vehicle passed, and the air started to cool as the sun dipped over the mountain rim above. I eyed the terrain for a spot to camp, but finally a couple out on a joy ride picked me up and took me the rest of the way to the village.

What had once been an isolated mountain village was now, I was surprised to see on arriving, something of a tourist Mecca. Not yet dinnertime, the village was quiet, but I noticed that all manner of new buildings had gone up since my last visit, including large dormitorystyle chalets, shower blocks and a reception building. All this development was really quite impressive and obviously the result of a carefully coordinated plan. With the tourism came modern commercial values and I was stunned to be told at reception by an Atayal girl that camping was not allowed in the vicinity of the village. Instead I was supposed to pay top dollar for a dorm room — they had got the capitalist bit down here all right. I was not going to pay, period. Instead I begged some space from a village household who were very accommodating and allowed me to camp under one of their outdoor shelters. Camping there in full view of the public marked the beginning of an all-weekend battle between me and a steady stream of tourists who seemed to delight in making as much noise as possible right next to my tent.

That evening I took a walk around the settlement to see what was going on. At the local Catholic Church — there was one in every Atayal village — youngsters were preparing for the Christmas carol service. In a creative twist on the tradition of static hymn-singing, some girls were practicing Hawaiian dancing whilst singing hymns. Meanwhile, in another part of the village, an old woman sat huddled next to an open fire, burning the hairs off a rat. She told me she was preparing the rodent to be pickled in wine, an Atayal specialty. The blackened rat did not look too appetizing to me, but then again, people typically like to eat whatever they grew up eating, and who knows maybe the old lady might baulk at the sight of cornflakes soaked in milk. There was no disputing the fact that burning the hairs off a rat was a fiddly job though. My circuit of the village eventually brought me back to the common, where a huge lodge-style restaurant had been built. Here I chatted to one of the cooks, who hailed from Vietnam. In a sign of the times and of the village's new-found wealth, she had married a local Atayal man. We conversed in Chinese and she told me that the village had been set up as a kind of collective; one of the villager's children had gone to Israel and upon returning to Taiwan led a transformation of Sumakusa, effectively turning it into a kind of kibbutz. Apparently, all the villagers got an allowance to live on and free meals in return for mucking in with the chores. Most people were happy with an arrangement that rationalized resources and provided them with a guaranteed living, the cook informed me. It all sounded terrific, but I wondered who was getting all the money coming in from the tourism. I would find out later that the church siphoned off a good part of it.

Over the next two days, I remained in the village and watched the wheels go round. Starting mid-morning the next day, hordes of visitors came up the mountain by car and chartered bus — some of them specifically to hike out to an ancient tree grove nearby, but many just for the ride and a meal at the mountain restaurant, which did a brisk trade. In a study room near where I was camped, some kind of workshop took place, the theme of which must have been "The Economic Transformation of an Atayal Village" or something similar. Various academic types and church leaders droned on to a bored audience as tourists loudly picnicked on their doorstep. Knowing that most Atayal villages were in severe decline, the transformation of Sumakusa, even if it was based on tacky tourism, had to be a good thing. If young people could be persuaded to stay and work in the village, then the more the better. As for the influx of tourists, they had as much right to be there as anyone else, and they put a lot more money into the local economy than I did; so my disdain for the quacking city dwellers was really neither here nor there. I noticed, however, that some of the local Atayals resented the vulgarity and poor communal sense of some of these visitors — transformation imperfect.

Later on this day, I escaped the hubbub of the village by walking out along the wonderfully scenic path to the tree grove. Only three kilometres long, the walk acted as an antidote to the noise of the village; the views out over the mountains were as impressive here as almost anywhere else in Taiwan's extensive mountain ranges. I walked along the track and drew another deep breath, taking it all in one last time, not knowing when I might be able to get back out this way again. At the distant grove the massive and wondrous cedars stood like statues in an ancient temple. A few tourists mingled at the base of these tremendous trees, everyone more or less relaxed. It was on such a tree that Mono Rudo, leader of the Wushe rebellion, had hanged himself; and it was difficult to look at the perpendicular branches of the trees without thinking of him. Later whilst walking back to the village, I heard a gun report; some Atayals were out hunting — no doubt a permitted and controlled hunt undertaken for the benefit of tourists.

Feeling that things had come full circle, I cut my stay in the mountains short. A tradesperson visiting the village on Sunday offered me a ride all the way to Taoyuan, the nearest major city on the plain and I accepted the offer. As I waited for my ride, a priest from Sinjhu who had come up for the workshop unnecessarily thanked me for helping out at a vegetable stall earlier that day. As we stood talking, a local Atayal man came up to the priest and palmed him a thick wad of banknotes; takings had been quite good over the weekend. The priest also offered me a ride back down the mountain in his swish car, but at that moment the tradesperson hailed me over and I left with him.

We drove down the mountain in the gathering dusk. The Taiwanese trader, who knew the area well, filled me in a little bit on developments in the area, but my mind was elsewhere. I knew this was going to be the last ride on the grand tour and the end of my travels in Taiwan. Feeling both sad and euphoric, I wound down the cabin window beside me and breathed in the aromatic smell of night flowers as we slowly made our way over the bridge, up the hairpin bends, past the mountain police post, and back towards the Yufong fork. As night fell, the bright lights of towns on the plain floated in the dark, like the lights of an ocean liner on a voyage. The specs of light seemed to represent a million untold stories, and the task of writing my own story about Taiwan suddenly loomed large. The trader dropped me off in Yingge, a major town in Taoyuan County north of Taoyuan City. Hesitating to return immediately to Taibei, I ambled about town, but the evening's damp coolness and a dismal downtown soon decided matters, and before long I found myself once more on a commuter train bound for the capital. The train ride marked the end of 4,100 kilometres of overland travel. If the end was a bit of an anticlimax, it was nonetheless final, drawing a line under a fascinating and adventurous but also exhausting series of trips that were probably unrepeatable… at least for me.

OTHER PUBLICATIONS
FROM THE CAOSHAN PRESS

Faced with the need to travel from Saudi Arabia to the UK, Gary Heath made the unusual decision to take the overland route. His three principles were to stay on the ground, avoid back-tracking, and do minimal sightseeing.

The ever-changing situation in the Middle East meant that the rules had to be bent on occasion, yet as he travelled across Eritrea, Sudan, Egypt, Libya, Tunisia and Morocco, he succeeded in beating his own path around the tourist traps, gaining unique insights into Arabic culture as he went.

Written just a few months before the Arab Spring of 2011, this book reveals many of the underlying tensions that were to explode onto the world stage just shortly afterwards, and has been updated to reflect the recent changes.

ISBN: 978-1-8381577-1-5

Lightning Source UK Ltd.
Milton Keynes UK
UKHW020620260522
403556UK00005B/187